STUDIES IN THE GOSPELS

STUDIES IN THE GOSPELS

BY

RICHARD CHENEVIX TRENCH, D.D.

THIRD EDITION, REVISED

BAKER BOOK HOUSE
Grand Rapids, Michigan

Reprinted 1979 by Baker Book House
from the edition issued in 1874 by
Macmillan and Company

ISBN: 0-8010-8848-8

PHOTOLITHOPRINTED BY CUSHING - MALLOY, INC.
ANN ARBOR, MICHIGAN, UNITED STATES OF AMERICA
1979

PREFACE

SOME *Studies on the Gospels* are here offered to the
reader. I have never been able to consent with that
which so often is asserted—namely, that the Gospels are
in the main plain and easy, and that all the chief difficulties of the New Testament are to be found in the
Epistles. There are, indeed, by the gracious provision of
God, abundance of plain things—so plain that no way-
farer, who seeks his waymarks, need err for lack of such,
—alike in these and in those. But when we begin to set
the hard things of one portion of Scripture against the
hard things of another, I cannot admit that they have
right to assume it as lifted above all doubt that those
of the Epistles infinitely surpass those of the Gospels.
How often the difficulties of the Epistles are merely difficulties of form ; not of the thought, but of the setting
forth of the thought ; of the logical sequence, which only
requires a patient disentangling, and all is comparatively
clear. But in the Gospels it is not the form of the
thought, for that for the most part presents little or
nothing perplexing, but the thought itself, the divine fact

or statement, which itself constitutes the difficulty. Nor, if I am right in affirming it to be so, is this in any way strange. For while there must be deep things everywhere in Scripture, things past man's finding out, else it were no revelation, surely it is nothing surprising that the Son of God, who moved in all worlds as in regions familiar to Him, who was not the illuminated, but the Illuminator of all others, not inspired, but the Inspirer, should utter the words of widest range and mightiest reach, those which should most task even the enlightened spirit of man to understand. Believing that it *is* thus with his words, that they must be at once the highest and the deepest of all, that in his life there must be mysteries which find only their remote resemblances in the lives of any other, I have often regretted that those who in our time and Church have brought the choicest gifts to the interpretation of the New Testament, have either restricted themselves to the elucidation of the Epistles, as if these alone would offer sufficient *resistance* to them ; or where their work has embraced both, have wrought out this latter portion of it with far more of thought and toil than the earlier. Surely there are hard questions enough suggested by the Sermon on the Mount, if only we would learn to look at it a little less superficially than now is our wont, questions which have never yet received an entirely satisfactory solution. So, too, in the great Prophecy from the Mount (Matt. xxiv.) there are knots, which, to my mind at least, have never been perfectly untied. Neither is the solemn judgment scene with which the twenty-fifth chapter of St. Matthew closes altogether so easy as it seems. The limpid clearness of St. John's style conceals from us often the profundity of the thought, as the perfect clearness of waters may altogether deceive us about their depth ; and we may thus be too lightly tempted to conclude that while St. Paul may be hard, St. John at all events is easy. I believe this to be very far from the case.

These *Studies*, written for the most part some years ago, are the fruit of this conviction ; not that in them I have gone out of my way to seek the hard passages in the Gospels, although I have not shunned such. They are the fragments of a much larger scheme, in which I had not advanced far before I saw plainly that I could never hope to complete it ; and which I thereupon laid aside. Gathering up lately a portion of what I had written, for publication, I have given it as careful a revision as my leisure would allow, have indeed in many parts rewritten it, seeking to profit by the results of the latest criticism, as far as I have been able to acquaint myself with them. For my labours I shall be abundantly repaid, if now, when so many controversies are drawing away the Christian student from the rich and quiet pastures of Scripture to other fields, not perhaps barren, but which can yield no such nourishment as these do, I shall have contributed aught to detain any among them.

PALACE, DUBLIN :
March 8, 1867.

CONTENTS

STUDIES IN THE GOSPELS

I. *THE TEMPTATION*

Matt. iv. 1-11; Mark i. 12, 13; Luke iv. 1-13.

OF the Temptation of our Lord we possess three records :
two more full, in the first and third Gospels, one more
summary, in the second. St. John has no report of it,
and indeed no allusion to it, except indeed we are to find
one in the words of Christ, ' The prince of this world
cometh, and hath nothing in Me ' (xiv. 30) ; though, of
course, even then the reference could not be exclusively
to it ; but only to it as the supreme moment in which
' the prince of this world ' wrought his worst, that so he
might have ' something ' in Him, as through sin he has
' something ' in every other child of Adam. Origen calls
attention to the fact that, with all the significance which
the Temptation possesses, occupying as it does a place
in the foreground of two Gospels and, although more
briefly, of a third, no place has been found for it, any
more than for the Transfiguration, in the fourth. He
suggests as a reason for this omission that it did not

belong to the *theology*, using this term in its strictest sense; not, that is, to the divine, but rather to the human, aspect of Christ's person and work; He being tempted not as He was God, who cannot be tempted with evil (Jam. i. 13), but as He was man. It cohered therefore intimately with the predominant purpose and aim of the three earlier Gospels that the Temptation should find a place in them, with the intention of the fourth that it should be absent there.

Assuredly Origen is right in starting with the assumption that some explanation is to be looked for; that there is nothing of haphazard in the admissions and exclusions of the several Evangelists; that a prevailing idea in each Gospel accounts for what it has, and what it has not; and why it has, or has not, this or the other incident or discourse. Indeed I am persuaded that, notwithstanding all which has been already accomplished, devout students of Scripture may for a long time to come find an ample, almost an inexhaustible, field of study in the tracing out in each the operation of this ever active law of exclusion and inclusion. At the same time we need not look so far as he has looked for an explanation of the important fact which he has thus noted; and which, indeed, almost all must have observed. The record of the Temptation in the previous Gospels does not to me make strange the omission of it in St. John's, but rather accounts for it; seeing that his Gospel was certainly intended to be supplementary to those which went before; not to go over ground which they had sufficiently gone over already; but to treasure up precious aspects of the life of Christ, of his words and works, which they had passed by. Such was the spiritual opulence of that life that

only so, only through a ' four-sided Gospel,' as Origen himself has called it, could that life be adequately presented
to the Church. This supplementary character of St.
John's Gospel, when once admitted, at once explains why
he did not relate what those who went before him had
so fully related.

This history of our Lord's Temptation in the wilderness ought never to be contemplated apart from that of
his Baptism. It is certain, at least, that we shall miss
much of its significance, if we dissociate it even in thought
from the solemn recognition of the Son by the Father,
the salutation of Him from heaven, and the full consciousness of his divine nature into which He was thus
brought; wherewith the Evangelical History in all its
three narratives has knit it so closely (Matt. iii. 16, 17 ;
Mark i. 9–11 ; Luke iii. 21, 22). The Church of old did
not shrink from calling her Lord's Baptism his second
nativity.[1] It is true, indeed, that when some of the
early sects made it his first *divine* nativity (and Ebio-
nites and Gnostics,[2] opposed in so much else, had a
common interest in this), she then fell back upon the
mightier fact, the Incarnation, in the assertion of which
alone she felt herself to possess a Son of God in any but a
deceptive and merely illusory sense. The Baptism may
thus have fallen somewhat out of sight, and not come to

---

[1] See a sermon to this effect which used to be ascribed to Augustine,
but which the Benedictine Editors have rightly adjudged to the Appendix
(*Serm.* 135), in which this is strongly set forth, pushed almost to a perilous
excess.

[2] The followers of Basilides, as Clemens of Alexandria tells us (*Strom.*
i. 21), kept a feast of the Baptism, which they ushered in with a night spent
in the reading of the Scriptures.

its full honours, or to all the prominence which, except for these disturbing causes, it would have obtained.

It is not however here my part to consider the Baptism more than under a single aspect, namely, in its connection with the Temptation. The Son in that Baptism had received his heavenly armour, and now He goes forth to prove it, and try of what temper it is. Having been baptized with water and the Holy Ghost, He shall now be baptized with the fire of temptation ; even as there is another baptism, the baptism of blood (Matt. xx. 22), in store for Him : for the gifts of God are not for the Captain of our salvation any more than for his followers the pledge of exemption from a conflict, but rather powers with which He is furnished, and, as it were, inaugurated thereunto ;[1] and thus that word with which the Temptation is introduced, ' *Then was Jesus led into the wilderness*,' is much more than a mere ' *then*,' designating succession of time. Linking as it does, and is intended to do, the Temptation with the Baptism, it denotes rather the divine order in which the events of the Saviour's life followed one another, and is meant to call our attention to this.

And as with the Baptism, so also with the Temptation. It is quite impossible to exaggerate the importance of the victory which was then gained by the second Adam, or

---

[1] As Chrysostom (*Hom.* 13 *in Matt.*) well says here : καὶ γὰρ διὰ τοῦτο λαβὲς ὅπλα, οὐχ ἵνα ἀργῇς, ἀλλ᾽ ἵνα πολεμῇς. Justin Martyr had put the two into a connection, if possible, closer still (*Tryph.* 103). Gregory the Great (*Moral.* xxiv. 11): Hostis noster quanto magis nos sibi rebellare conspicit, tanto amplius expugnare contendit. Eos enim pulsare negligit, quos quieto jure possidere se sentit. Hoc enim in seipso Dominus sub quâdam dispensatione figuravit, qui diabolum non nisi post baptisma se tentare permisit, ut signum nobis quoddam futuræ conversionis innueret, quod membra ejus postquam ad Deum proficerent, tunc acriores tentationum insidias tolerarent.

the bearing which it had, and still has, on the work of our redemption. Milton showed that he had a true feeling of this, when writing a poem which contained nothing more than a history of this victoriously surmounted Temptation, he called it *Paradise Regained*; setting it, as the story of the second Adam's victory, over against *Paradise Lost*, or the story of the first Adam's defeat.[1] It is not too much to say, as Augustine said often, that the entire history, moral and spiritual, of the world revolves around two persons, Adam and Christ.[2] To Adam was given a position to maintain; he did not maintain it, and the lot of the world for ages was decided. And now with the appearance of the second Adam the second trial of our race has arrived. All is again at issue. Again we are represented by a Champion, by *One* who is in the place of *all*,—whose standing shall be the standing of many, and whose fall, if that fall had been conceivable, would have been the fall of many, yea of all. Once already Satan had thought to nip the kingdom of heaven in the bud, and had nearly succeeded. If it had not been for a new and unlooked-for interposition of God, for the promise of the Seed of the woman, he would have done it. He will now prove if he cannot more effectually crush it, and for ever. Then, on that first occasion, there

---

[1] Bale had already written *A brefe Comedy or Enterlude concernynge the temptacyon of our Lord and Saver Jesus Christ by Sathan in the desert*, 1538; the Interlocutores being Jesus Christus, Satan tentator, Angelus Primus, Angelus alter, Baleus Prolocutor. It is sufficiently rude, and has little poetry in it, but is not without the merit of a certain earnestness. Only a single copy of it has come down to us, from which Mr. Grosart has drawn his reprint (1870).

[2] *Op. Imp. Con. Jul.* ii. 163: Unde fit ut totum genus humanum quodammodo sint homines duo, primus et secundus. *Serm.* 90: Venit unus contra unum; contra unum qui sparsit unus qui collegit . . . . Homo et homo; homo ad mortem, et homo ad vitam.

was still a reserve, the pattern according to whom Adam was formed ; who should come forth in due time to make what Adam had marred ;—but He failing, there was none behind ; the last stake would have been played, —and lost.[1]

' *Then was Jesus led up of the Spirit into the wilderness.*' If it be asked, of *what* Spirit He was thus led, undoubtedly of the Spirit of God ; in the words of Jeremy Taylor, ' He was led by the good Spirit to be tempted of the evil.' Some few have understood it otherwise, and that it was the same evil Spirit who afterwards encountered Him in the wilderness, who first led Him thither.[2] But this is certainly a mistake. We have here one, and of course the most signal and transcendant, of those stirrings from the Spirit of God to some heroic achievement whereof we have many anticipations in lower forms of the spiritual life in the Old Testament, as in Moses (Acts vii. 23), in Gideon (Judg. vi. 34), in Samson

---

[1] As Godet has said well : Il ne s'agit pas seulement ici, comme quand nous luttons, de savoir si tel individu fera partie du royaume de Dieu ; c'est l'existence de ce royaume qui est en question. Son futur souverain, celui qui a mission de le fonder, lutte en champ clos avec le souverain du royaume opposé.

[2] See Spanheim, *Dub. Evang.* 50. They have often found an argument in the αὐτὸν ἐκβάλλει of Mark i. 12, as though no such violent driving or thrusting forth as this word implies could have been ascribed to the Holy Spirit ; but, not to urge that St. Mark loves a strong expression, and often uses a stronger than in parallel passages do the other Evangelists (σχιζομένους, i. 10 ; βασανιζομένους, vi. 48), ἐκβάλλειν in Hellenistic use continually signifies not a violent thrusting out, but an orderly putting forth. Thus, ' Pray ye therefore the Lord of the harvest that He will *send forth* (ἵνα ἐκβάλῃ) labourers into his harvest' (Matt. ix. 38) ; the householder *bringeth forth* (ἐκβάλλει) out of his treasure new and old (Matt. xiii. 52 ; cf. John x. 4 ; Jam. ii. 25) ; and with this milder use of the word agree the ἀνήχθη and the ἤγετο by which St. Matthew and St. Luke severally describe the bringing of the Lord upon the scene of his temptation.

(Judg. xiii. 25 ; xiv. 19).[1] The Captain of our salvation
went into the wilderness, drawn by another, but at the
same time freely ; in the words of one of the Schoolmen,
as an athlete going of his own accord,[2] or, to cite
Jeremy Taylor once more, ' not by an unnatural violence,
but by the efficacies of inspiration, and a supernatural
inclination and activity of resolution.'

The scene of the Temptation was *the ' wilderness.'*
What wilderness we are not told ;[3] and all which it
imports us to note is that it *was* a wilderness, in which
this encounter of the good and the evil, each in its highest
representative, found place. There could have been no
fitter scene, none indeed so fit. The waste and desert
places of the earth are, so to speak, the characters which
sin has visibly impressed on the outward creation ; its signs
and its symbols there ; the echoes in the outward world of
the desolation and wasteness which sin has wrought in the
inner life of man. Out of a true feeling of this men have
ever conceived of the wilderness as the haunt of evil
spirits. In the old Persian religion Ahriman and his evil
spirits inhabit the steppes and wastes of Turan, to the
north of the happy Iran, which stands under the dominion
of Ormuzd ; exactly as with the Egyptians, the evil Typhon
is the lord of the Libyan sand-wastes, and Osiris of the
fertile Egypt.[4] This sense of the wilderness as the haunt

---

[1] Compare Virgil, *Æn.* ix. 184–187.

[2] Aquinas: Quasi athleta sponte procedens.

[3] Tradition places the scene of the Temptation in ' the wilderness that
goeth up from Jericho ' (Josh. xvi. 1 ; cf. Josephus, *Antt.* x. 8. 2), which
extended a great part of the way to Jerusalem (Josh. xviii. 12), and fixes it
more immediately on a steep and rugged mountain rising like a wall of rock
from the plain, and subsequently called Quarantana, from the quarantain, or
forty days of fasting, which the Lord had there observed.

[4] Creuzer, *Symbolik*, vol. i. p. 223.

of evil spirits, one which the Scripture more or less allows
(Isai. xiii. 21, xxxiv. 14; Matt. xii. 43; Rev. xviii. 2),
would of itself give a certain fitness to that as the place
of the Lord's encounter with Satan; but only in its antagonism to Paradise or the Garden, do we recognize a
still higher fitness in the appointment of the place. The
garden and the desert are the two most opposite poles of
natural life; in them we have the highest harmonies and
the deepest discords of nature. It was just that the first
Adam, so long as he stood in his original uprightness,
should be a dweller in the Garden; that his outward
surroundings should correspond to his inner life, that
there should be no disagreement between them; and it
was there, in the garden of Eden, that *his* temptation went
forward. Being worsted in the conflict, he was expelled
therefrom; and he and that race whose destinies were
linked with his, should henceforth inhabit an earth which
was cursed for his sake.[1] It is true, indeed, that in this as
in so much else the curse was in part mercifully lightened,
and the earth was not all desert; yet its desert places
represent to us still what the whole of it might justly
have been; the curse concentrates itself upon them.
The second Adam therefore, taking up the conflict exactly where the first had left it, and inheriting all the
consequences of his defeat, in the desert does battle with
the foe; and conquering him there, wins back the garden
for that whole race, whose champion and representative
in this conflict He had been. And this is not the less

---

[1] Ambrose (*Exp. in Luc.* iv. 7): Convenit recordari quemadmodum de
paradiso in desertum Adam primus ejectus sit; ut advertas quemadmodum
de deserto ad paradisum Adam secundus reverterit .... In deserto Adam,
in deserto Christus; sciebat enim ubi posset invenire damnatum, quem ad
paradisum, resoluto errore, revocaret.

true, however as yet that garden blooms not again; or blooms only in part; for in the higher culture and more complete subduing to the needs and delights of men, of those regions where the faith of Christ is owned, we may see already pledges and promises of that complete restoration of the earth to all its original fertility and beauty, which Christ's victory over Satan in the wilderness shall one day have brought about.

While we are upon this point, it is worthy of note that St. Mark, briefly as he records the Temptation (and two verses are all that he affords to it, i. 12, 13), yet gives us an intimation which we should look for in vain in the fuller accounts of the other Evangelists, and one which we should not slightly or carelessly pass over. His record of this event, in its summary brevity as compared with theirs, is very like his record of the Lord's appearance to the two disciples on the way to Emmaus (xvi. 12, 13) as compared with that of St. Luke (xxiv. 13–35). Not indeed that this is always his manner; for brief as his Gospel is as a whole, he can relate events with far greater breadth than either St. Matthew or St. Luke; as witness his account of the healing of the Gadarene demoniac (v. 1–20), and of the lunatic boy (ix. 14–29), compared with theirs. On the present occasion he tells us of the Lord, that, being in the wilderness, ' *He was with the wild beasts* ' (ver. 13). Now this notice is certainly not introduced, as many interpreters would have us to believe, merely to enhance the waste desolation and savage solitude of that scene, but at once throws us back, as it was intended to throw us back, on the Paradisaical state which in the second Adam had bloomed anew. ' *He was with the wild beasts* '—which owned Him for their rightful

Lord ; He was with them, as Adam had been with them
before he sinned.   In Him, the second Adam, the ideal
man of the eighth Psalm, the Adamic prerogatives, lost
and suspended so long, after the Deluge only partially recovered (Gen. ix. 2), fully reappeared (cf. Gen. i. 26, 28
with Ps. viii.).[1] The Apocryphal Gospels, whose *marvellous* is in general merely *monstrous*, and which so
seldom pourtray the divine Child with any traits which
are really divine, are not here so remote at once from
ideal and from historic truth, as is commonly their case.
One of these tells of the Child Jesus that in his flight
to Egypt the lions and the leopards played harmlessly
about Him, and accompanied Him upon his way.[2]

This resumption of dominion by the second Adam over
the revolted animal world should be more or less continued
in his saints.   They too should ' take up serpents ' (Mark
xvi. 18); should tread on serpents and scorpions (Luke x.
19), so reversing the threat of Jeremiah viii. 17 ; Paul
should shake the venomous beast from his hand and feel no
harm (Acts xxviii. 5 ; cf. Job v. 22, 23 ; Ezek. xxxiv. 25 ;
Hos. ii. 18).   And a true sense of this, as an ultimate prerogative destined for redeemed man, appears, though often in
extreme caricature, in the innumerable legends of saints,
to whose word and will the wildest creatures are obedient,
who summon the fishes to their preaching, who cross
rivers on the backs of crocodiles, and accomplish a thousand other feats of a like kind.   Nor can we say that this
dominion has wholly departed even from man in his natu-

---

[1] Giles Fletcher, in his too much neglected poem, *Christ's Triumph on
Earth* (ver. 1–40), has seized the meaning of these words better than any
that I know.

[2] Thilo, *Codex Apocryphus*, p. 394.

ral estate ; the fragments of his sceptre still remain in his hands ; 'Every kind of beasts is tamed, and hath been tamed, of mankind' (Jam. iii. 7 ; cf. Sophocles, *Antigone,* 343–351, a lyrical echo from heathendom of the same truth) ; but this sceptre which he only wields with difficulty, and with frequent uprisings of his rebellious vassals against him, Christ, as was manifest during these forty days, wielded with an absolute authority. So much we may read in those words, '*He was with the wild beasts.*'

To that wilderness He, ' the glorious Eremite,' was led, ' *to be tempted of the devil*;' or ' *of Satan,*' as it appears in St. Mark. Very remarkable is the prominence which Satan assumes in the New Testament, compared with the manner in which he and the whole doctrine concerning him is kept in the background in the Old. There, after the first appearance of the adversary in Paradise, which even itself is a veiled appearance, he is withdrawn for a long while altogether from the scene ; nay, there is but a glimpse of him, a passing indication here and there of such a spiritual head of the kingdom of evil, through the whole earlier economy—as in Job i. and ii., Zech. iii 1, 2, and 1 Chron. xxi. 1 ; he is only referred to twice in the Apocrypha (Wisd. ii. 24 ; Ecclus. xxi. 27). This greater prominence in the books of the New Testament may partly be explained by an analogy drawn from things natural, namely that where the lights are brightest, the shadows also are darkest. Height and depth are correlatives of one another. It is right which first reveals wrong ; and hate only can be read as hate in the light of love ; and unholiness in the light of purity ; and thus it needed the highest revelation of good to shew us

the deepest depth of evil. But this does not explain the
reticence of Scripture altogether. No doubt in that childhood of the human race men were not yet ripe for this
knowledge. For as many as took it in earnest, and as
it deserves to be taken, for them it would have been
too dreadful thus to know of a prince of the powers of
darkness, until they had known first of a Prince of Light.
Those, therefore, who are under a divine education, are
not allowed to understand anything very distinctly of
Satan, till with the spiritual eye it is given to them to
behold him as lightning fall from heaven ; then indeed,
but not till then, the Scripture speaks of him plainly and
without reserve. We may perhaps take a hint from this
in the teaching of children. The order which was observed of God in the teaching of our race, the reticence,
almost entire, but not perfectly so, which was observed
in the childhood of our race, may be profitably observed
also with children ; as also with those whose faculties are
as yet spiritually undeveloped. ' I write unto you, little
children,' says the apostle St. John, ' because ye have
known the Father ' (1 John ii. 13) ; this was what they
had learned from him, even a heavenly Father's love ; but
he proceeds : ' I have written unto you, young men, because ye are strong, and the word of God abideth in you,
and *ye have overcome the wicked one* ' (ver. 14). To them,
to the strong, it was given to know that they wrestled not
against flesh and blood, but against spiritual wickedness
in high places (Ephes. vi. 12).

' *And when He had fasted forty days and forty nights
He was afterward an hungred.*' How are we intended to
understand a fast of this length, manifestly impossible to

man under ordinary conditions? Not by bringing in, as some have done, Christ's divine power as the explanation of all; which would indeed rob this fact of its entire significance for us. We must seek the explanation elsewhere. We are far too much accustomed, in a stiff dualism, to conceive of the spiritual and natural as of two worlds altogether apart, with a rigid line of demarcation between them, so that the powers and influences of the higher cannot pass over effectually to operate in the sphere of the lower. Yet all the experience of our daily life contradicts this, and we note the higher continually making itself felt in the region of the lower. The wayworn regiment, which could scarcely drag itself along, but which revives at the well-known air, and forgets all its weariness, what does it but declare that the spirit is lord not merely in its own domain, but is meant to be, and even now in no inconsiderable degree is, the lord of the provinces of man's life that lie beneath it? Matter, instead of offering a stubborn resistance to spirit, proves in many and marvellous ways to be plastic to it. Sensuality debases and degrades the countenance; purity and love ennoble it, casting a beam even upon the outward shape. What is the resurrection of the body, or the ultimate glorification of nature, or the larger number of those miracles wrought by the Lord in the days of his flesh, but the workings of spirit upon matter? So too it fared with his forty days' fast. To bring in here his divine power, or to suppose that He then fasted otherwise than as a man, is, as has been urged already, to rob the whole transaction of its meaning. Upborne and upholden above the common needs of the animal life by the great tides of spiritual gladness, in the strength of that recent Baptism, in the solemn joy of that salutation and recognition from his Father, He found and felt no need for all these forty days. As a slighter incident of the same kind He forgets hunger and thirst, or rather is no longer conscious of them, by the well of Samaria, in the joy of winning a lost soul (John iv. 31– 34). In the lives of other men there are quite enough of analogies, which, however removed from this, do yet witness in their lower measure for this same predominance of the spirit, for the dominion which it is able to exercise over the workings of the natural life. All intenser passions, a mighty joy, an overwhelming sorrow, an ecstatic devotion, all these have continually been found to bring a temporary release with them from the necessities of the animal life, and though not for so long a time, still to suspend its claims for a season. Thus Paul at the crisis of his conversion was three days without eating or drinking (Acts ix. 9).

For forty days this fast of the Lord's endured. But wherefore for exactly this number, for forty, and neither more nor less? We are the more tempted to ask this question from the frequent recurrence of this same number under circumstances not altogether dissimilar. Of precisely this same length were the fasts of Moses (Deut. ix. 9) and Elijah (1 Kin. xix. 8) ; He, the Head of the New Covenant, in nothing coming short of those who stood forth as the chiefs and representatives of the Old, of the Law, and of the Prophets (Matt. xvii. 3). At the same time his fast of forty days is not determined by theirs ; but rather theirs and his are alike determined by the significance which this number, forty, in Holy Scripture everywhere obtains. On a close examination we note it to be everywhere there the number or signature of penalty, of afflic-

tion, of the confession, or the punishment, of sin.[1] Thus
it is the signature of the punishment of sin in the forty
days and forty nights during which God announces that
He will cause the waters of the deluge to prevail (Gen.
vii. 4, 12);[2] in the forty years of the Israelites' wander-
ings in the desert (Num. xiv. 33; xxxii. 13; Ps. xcv. 10);
in the forty stripes with which the offender should be
beaten (Deut. xxv. 3; 2 Cor. xi. 24); in the desolation of
Egypt which should endure forty years (Ezek. xxix. 11).
So also is it the signature of the confession of sin : Moses
intercedes forty days for his people (Deut. ix. 25); the
Ninevites proclaim a fast of forty days (Jon. iii. 4);
Ezekiel must bear for forty days the transgression of
Judah (Ezek. iv. 6); forty days, or twice forty in the case
of a maid child, are the period of a woman's purifying
after child-birth (Lev. xii. 2–5 ; cf. Ps. li. 5 : ' in sin hath
my mother conceived me '). In agreement with all this,
and resting on the forty days' fast of her Lord, is the
Quadragesimal Lent fast of the Church; and so not

---

[1] Jerome (*In Amos.* ii. 10): Ipse Dominus fecit nos exire de seculo, et
per annos quadraginta, qui numerus semper afflictionis et jejunii, luctûs est
et doloris, per tribulationes et angustias pervenire in terram sanctam. And
again (*In Jon.* iii. 4): Porro quadragenarius numerus convenit peccatoribus,
et jejunio et orationi, et sacco et lacrimis et perseverantiæ deprecandi : ob
quod et Moÿses quadraginta diebus jejunavit in monte Sina ; et Elias fugiens
Jezebel, indictâ fame terræ Israël, et Dei desuper irâ pendente, quadraginta
dies jejunâsse describitur. Ipse quoque Dominus, verus Jona missus ad præ-
dicationem mundi, jejunavit quadraginta dies. Cf. *In Ezek.* xxix. 11. Thus
too Origen (*In Deut.* xxv. 3): Semper observavimus numerum quadraginta
malis obnoxium esse. Unde Moses quadraginta diebus jejunavit, et post eum
Elias. Quin et Salvator noster a diabolo tentatus non manducavit quadraginta diebus et quadraginta noctibus; et magnum diluvium in terrâ contigit,
cum Deus imbrem fecisset quadraginta diebus et quadraginta noctibus.
Compare Augustine, *Quæst. in Gen.* qu. 169; *Serm.* 125, § 9; *De Cons.
Evang.* ii. §§ 8, 9. In both these latter places he attempts, not very suc-
cessfully as it seems to me, to give the rationale of forty as this number of
penitence.

[2] Ambrose, *De Noë et Arcâ*, xiii. § 44.

less the selection of this Scripture of the Temptation to supply the Gospel for the first Sunday in that season, as being the Scripture which, duly laid to heart, will more than any other help us rightly to observe that time.[1]

On one of these forties Tertullian dwells with peculiar emphasis; often bringing out the relation between the forty days of our Lord's Temptation and the forty years of Israel's trial in the wilderness. His fast as the true Israel, as the fulfiller of all which Israel after the flesh had left unfulfilled, as the victor in all where it had been the vanquished, was as much a witness against *their* carnal appetites (for it was in the indulgence of these that they sinned continually, Exod. xv. 23, 24 ; xvi. 2, 3 ; xvii. 2, 3 ; Num. xi. 4, 33)[2] as a witness against Adam's.[3] It was by this abstinence of his declared that man was ordained to be, and that the true man would be, lord over his lower nature. In this way Christ's forty days' fast is the great counter-fact in the work of redemption, at once to Adam's and to Israel's compliances with the suggestions of the fleshly appetite ; exactly in the same manner as the unity of tongues at Pentecost is the counter-fact to the confusion of tongues at Babel (Gen. xi. 7, 8 ; Acts ii. 6–11), to which the Church would

---

[1] Augustine, *Serm.* 210.

[2] *De Bapt.* 20: Dominus quantum existimo, de figurâ Israëlis exprobrationem in ipsum retorsit. Namque populus mare transgressus, in solitudine translatus per quadraginta annos, illic cum divinis copiis aleretur, nihilominus ventris et gulæ meminerat, quam Dei. Deinde Dominus post aquam segregatus in deserto, quadraginta dierum jejunia emensus, ostendit non pane vivere hominem Dei, sed Dei verbo ; tentationesque plenitudini et immoderantiæ ventris adpositas, abstinentiâ elidi.

[3] *De Jejun.* 6: Immo novum hominem in veteris sugillationem virtute fastidiendi cibum initiabat, ut eum, diabolo rursus per escam tentare quærenti, fortiorem fame totâ ostentaret ; and again, c. 5: Nam et primus populus primi hominis resculpserat crimen.

draw our attention in the selection of the latter as one of our Whitsuntide lessons.

For forty days that arrest of the sense of bodily need had continued ; but at the expiration of these the need, suspended so long, made itself felt in its strength ; ' *He was afterward an hungred.*' The Tempter sees, and thinks to use his opportunity ; and the Temptation proper, dividing itself into three successive acts, begins. But before we enter upon these, a few words may fitly find place on more than one subject of the deepest practical interest.

And first, the assertion of the existence of a Tempter at all, of a personal Wicked One, of the devil, this, as is well known, is a stumblingblock to many. Not urging here the extent to which the veracity of Christ Himself is pledged to the fact, I will content myself with observing that it is not by Scriptural arguments alone that it is supported. There is a dark mysterious element in man's life and history, which nothing else can explain. We can only too easily understand the too strong attractions of the objects of sense on a being who is sensuous as well as spiritual ; the allowing of that lower nature, which should have been the ruled, to reverse the true relation, and to become the ruler. We can understand only too easily man's yielding, even his losing, of himself in this region of sense. But there is a mystery far more terrible than this, a phenomenon unintelligible except upon one assumption. Those to whom the doctrine of an Evil Spirit is peculiarly unwelcome have been at infinite pains to exorcise theology ; and from that domain at least to cast Satan out, even though they should be impotent to cast him out from any other. All who shrink from looking down into the abysmal depths of man's fall, because they have no eye for the heavenly heights of his restoration, or for the mighty powers of God which are at work to bring this about, seem to count that much will have been gained thereby; although it may be very pertinently asked, as indeed one *has* asked, What is the profit of getting rid of the *devil*, so long as the *devilish* remains? of explaining away an Evil *One*, so long as the evil *ones* who remain are so many?[1] What profit indeed? Assuredly this doctrine of an Evil Spirit, tempting, seducing, deceiving, prompting to rebellion and revolt, so far from casting a deeper gloom on the mysterious destinies of humanity, is full of consolation, and lights up with a gleam and glimpse of hope regions which would seem utterly dark without it. One might well despair of oneself, having no choice but to believe that all the strange suggestions of evil which have risen up before one's own heart had been born there; one might well despair of one's kind, having no choice but to believe that all its hideous sins and as its monstrous crimes had been self-conceived and bred within its own bosom. But there is hope, if ' an enemy have done this; ' if, however, the soil *in* which all these wicked thoughts and wicked works have sprung up has been the heart of man, yet the seed *from* which they sprung had been there sown by the hand of another.

And who will venture to deny the existence of this devilish, as distinguished from the animal, in man? None certainly, who knows aught of the dread possibilities of sin lurking in his own bosom, who has studied

---

[1] Goethe, in the spirit of finest irony, puts these words into the mouth of Mephistopheles:—

Den Bösen sind sie los, die bösen sind geblieben.

with any true insight the moral history of the world. In
what way else explain that men not merely depart from
God, but that they defy Him; that, instead of the ungodly merely forgetting God and letting Him go, his
name is as often or oftener on their lips than on the lips
of them that love and serve Him ? How else explain the
casting of fierce words against Him, the actual and active
hatred of God which it is impossible not to recognize in
some wicked men ? What else will account for delight
in the contemplation or in the infliction of pain, for strange
inventions of wickedness, above all, of cruelty and lust—
' lust hard by hate' ? What else will account for evil
chosen for its own sake, and for that fierce joy which men
so often find in the violation of law, this violation being
itself the attraction; with all those other wicked joys,
' mala gaudia mentis,' as the poet in a single phrase has
characterized them so well ?

The mystery is as inexplicable as it is dreadful so long
as man will know nothing of a spiritual world beneath
him, as well as one above him; but it is only too easy
to understand, so soon as we recognize man's evil as not
altogether his own, but detect behind his transgression an
earlier transgression and an earlier transgressor—one who
fell, not as man fell, for man's fall was mercifully broken
by that very flesh which invited it ; but who fell as only
Spirits can fall, from the height of heaven to the depth of
hell ; fell never to rise again ; for *he* was not deceived,
was not tempted, as was Adam ; but himself chose the
evil with the clearest intuition that it was the evil, for-
sook the good with the clearest intuition that it was the
good ; whose sin therefore in its essence was the sin
against the Holy Ghost, and as such, not to be forgiven

in this world nor in the world to come. All is explicable when we recognize the existence of such a Spirit; who, being lost without hope of redemption himself, seeks to work the same loss in other of God's creatures, and counts it a small triumph to have made man bestial, unless he can make him devilish as well. Such a personal Tempter innumerable moral and spiritual phenomena of this fallen world at once demand and attest; and such a Tempter or devil existing, it lay in the necessity of things that he should come into direct and immediate collision with Him who had one mission in the world, and that, to destroy the works of the devil.

But freely admitting the existence of such a Tempter, the Temptation of Christ, the fact that He should have been tempted at all, or having been tempted, that such immeasurable worth should be attached to his victory over temptation, this has a difficulty of its own, which has, I suppose, more or less clearly presented itself to every one, who has sought at all to enter into the deeper significance of this mysterious transaction. The difficulty and dilemma may be stated thus: Either there was that in Christ which more or less responded to the temptation —how then was He without sin, seeing that sin moves and lives in the region of desires quite as really as in that of external acts? or there was nothing in Him that responded to the suggestions of the Tempter—where then was the reality of the temptation, or what was the significance of that victory which in the wilderness He won?

The secret of the difficulty which these alternatives present to our minds, so that sometimes it appears to us impossible that Christ's Temptation should have had anything real in it, leaving Him as it did wholly unscathed,

lies in the mournful experience which we in our own
spiritual life have made, namely, that almost all of *our*
temptations involve more or less of sin, that the serpent
leaves something of his trail and slime even there where
he is not allowed to nestle and make his home. Conquerors
though we may be, yet we seldom issue from the conflict
without a scratch,—a hurt it may be which soon heals,
but which has left its cicatrice behind it. Very seldom
indeed we come forth from these fires, as the Three Children, without even so much as the smell of fire having
passed upon us (Dan. iii. 27). The saint, if he shine as a
diamond at last, yet it is still as a diamond which has been
polished in its own dust. For we may take up arms
ainst the evil thought, we may rally the higher powers
of our souls, and call in the might of a Mightier to put
the evil and its author to flight, yet this we seldom do
till it has already found some place within us.[1] The fiery
darts may have been quenched *almost* as soon as they
alighted ; they may not therefore have set on fire in us
the whole ' course of nature ' (Jam. iii. 6) ; but they should
have been warded off and extinguished, *before* they
alighted, by that shield of faith, which the apostle bids
us to assume against them (Ephes. vi. 16).[2] Ours may
have been but a moment's acquiescence in the temptation.
But thus momentary and seemingly involuntary as it was,

---

[1] There is in respect of the sin, to adopt a fine distinction of Peter Lom-
bard and some others of the Schoolmen, the propassio or inception, even
where there is not the passio. Few have exercised a more watchful moral
oversight of their own hearts than Thomas à Kempis, and he traces thus the
genesis of evil in the heart of man (*De Imit. Christ.* i. 13. 5) : Primo occurrit
menti simplex *cogitatio*; deinde fortis *imaginatio* ; postea *delectatio* et motus
pravus *et assensio*. Itaque paulatim ingreditur hostis malignus ex toto, dum
illi non resistitur in principio.

[2] See Origen, *De Princ.* iii. 2. 4.

and graciously and surely as it will be included in the daily forgiveness, yet even this moment during which the evil was not abhorred and loathed is irreconcilable with the idea of an absolute holiness; for this is as a mirror whose perfect brightness no lightest breath has ever troubled or tarnished for an instant. Of course the reconciliation of an entire sinlessness in Christ with the reality of the temptations to which He was exposed lies in this, that there was never in Him this momentary delectation; even as there need not be in us; and would not be, if we always were, and had always in time past been, upon our highest guard. It is not of the necessity of a temptation that it should in the least defile. The fact that it does so, is only the sad accident and adjunct of too many of our temptations, even of those against which sooner or later we take up arms, and by God's grace do not suffer them to embody themselves in sinful acts, or even in sinful desires deliberately entertained :

Has patitur pœnas peccandi sola voluntas.

So naturally in the estimate which we form of the matter does sin follow on temptation, that when the apostle had affirmed of Christ that He was ' in all points tempted like as we are,' he counts it needful at once to add, ' yet without sin ' (Heb. iv. 15), without the sinful results which in men *almost* inevitably follow.[1]

It is quite true that even from these temptations themselves we may derive good; that they, even with issues

---

[1] Bengel has some good words here on the promptness of our Lord's resistance to each proffered temptation: Quomodo autem *sine peccato* tentatus, compati potest tentatis *cum peccato*? In intellectu, multo acrius anima Salvatoris percepit imagines tentantes, quam nos infirmi ; in voluntate tam celeriter incursum earum retudit, quam ignis aquæ guttulam sibi objectam.

sorrowful for the time as these, may yet be to us sources of ultimate strength ; that thus it may prove with us as with the oyster, which stops with a precious pearl the hole in its shell which was originally a disease ; as with the broken limb, which, having been set, *may* be stronger than if it never had been broken. It may fare with us as islanders of the Southern Ocean fancy that it fares with them ; counting, as they do, that the strength and valour of the warrior whom they have slain in battle passes into themselves, as their rightful inheritance ; for so it proves indeed with the Christian man and the temptations which he conquers and slays ; and this, even though the victory may have been won not without hurts to himself, gotten in the conflict. The strength which lay in the temptation has shifted its seat, and passed over into the man who has overcome the temptation.[1] The great Church writers of all times, all to whom any largeness of utterance has been granted, who have bravely looked man's true condition in the face, have not feared to speak bold words on this matter ; words indeed, like all other words on the subject of grace, capable of being wrested and abused by the licentious and falsehearted, of being therefore held up by

---

[1] Our theologians of the seventeenth century were fond of illustrating this truth by aid of the legend that the viper's flesh (θηριακή, from θηρίον, see Acts xxviii. 5), 'theriac,' 'triacle,' and last of all 'treacle,' was the most potent antidote for the viper's bite. Thus Jeremy Taylor : 'There is a ἡ περνικῶμεν in St. Paul. We are more than conquerors. Non solum viperam terimus, sed ex eâ antidotum conficimus. We kill the viper and make treacle of him ; *i.e.* not only escape from, but get advantage from temptations.' And Hales : 'Wonderful, therefore, is the power of a Christian ; who not only overcomes and conquers and kills the viper, but, like the skilful apothecary, makes antidote and treacle of him.' So too Gurnall : 'The saints' experiences help them to a sovereign treacle made of the scorpion's own flesh (which they through Christ have slain), and that hath a virtue above all others to expel the venom of Satan's temptations from the heart.'

the timid as antinomian provocations; but words which for all this ought not the less to be spoken. Such Augustine abounds in, as often as he treats of St. Paul's thorn in the flesh, or of St. Peter's fall; yet always keeping within just limits; which limits another overpasses when, treating of the last and of all the spiritual gains which in the end the apostle obtained through it, he exclaims, O *felix* culpa! A fault or sin is never 'happy,' is always unhappy; it is ever ' *infelix* culpa,' whatever good by the grace of God and by that wondrous alchemy of heaven which draws gold from dross, may be educed from it; and those who employ any other language or think any other thought about sin, are perilously near, however little they may guess it, to them whom the apostle Paul has denounced (Rom. iii. 5–8).

But this, the absolute rejection and repudiation of every suggestion in any way contrary to the perfect will of God, a repudiation in every case reaching to the earliest moment of its presentation to Him whereunto it is possible in imagination to travel back, this is not all. There is another point of difference between Christ's temptations and ours; namely, that all our Lord's temptations were addressed to Him from without, were distinct suggestions of the Evil Spirit. Those who, in their anxiety to do away with an external Tempter, or from any other motive resolve the temptation into an internal conflict with thoughts of self-indulgence, vain-glory, ambition, disturb, whether they are aware of it or no, that image of a perfect holiness which is essential to the character and office of a Redeemer; who only as He was Himself without sin could save others from their sins; but who would not, if this were admitted, have been without it. We cannot conceive of the temptation of the first Adam reaching him except from without. That he should have been his own tempter is irreconcilable even with the more negative holiness which we ascribe to him. It would have been infinitely more inconsistent with the more positive holiness of the second Adam.[1] One of Schleiermacher's most gifted pupils, who finished his brief career while as yet it was uncertain in which camp, whether in that of faith or unbelief, he would ultimately be found,[2] has on this point some admirable remarks : ' It is not difficult to draw a very attractive picture of the inner temptation of Jesus, such as shall not be unlike the Choice of Hercules, standing, as Prodicus has described him, at the point where the two

---

[1] Gregory the Great (*Hom.* 16 *in Evang.*) : Sciendum nobis est, quia tribus modis tentatio agitur, suggestione, delectatione, et consensu. Et nos cum tentamur plerumque in delectationem, aut etiam in consensum labimur, quia de carnis peccato propagati, in nobis ipsis etiam gerimus unde certamina toleremus. Deus vero, qui in utero Virginis incarnatus, in mundum sine peccato venerat, nihil contradictionis in semetipso tolerabat. Tentari ergo per suggestionem potuit, sed ejus mentem peccati delectatio non momordit. Atque ideo omnis diabolica illa tentatio foris non intus fuit. Compare F. Spanheim (*Dub. Evang.* li.) : Distinguendum inter tentationem admotam et admissam, inter suggestionem mali externam et internam, inter suggestionem insinuatam et receptam. Tentatio illa ratione tentatoris mala erat, non ratione tentati, admota quippe Christo duntaxat, non admissa, externa non interna, insinuata tantum non recepta. Camero (*Myrothec. Evang. on Heb.* iv. 13, p. 315) has a lively illustration : Tentatus fuit igitur Christus in omnibus, et quidem quod ad sensum doloris attinet, eâdem ratione quâ nos ; sine peccato tamen, quod nobis non contingit. Nam (utamur enim hoc exemplo) quantumvis aquam puram et limpidam exagites, non fit turbida ; sed si aquam puram quidem, ut videtur, sed in cujus imâ parte coenum est vel limus, agitaveris, continuo quæ visa est pura aqua, videtur lutulenta aut certe turbidula.

[2] Usteri. He has two articles on the Temptation in the *Theol. Stud. und Krit.* 1829, p. 449 ; 1832, p. 768 ; from the former of which my citation is taken. Nothing can be more masterly than the manner in which he deals, not with this only, but with all the attempts to explain away the Temptation which at different times have been proposed ; showing the inner contradictions which they involve ; though, having effectually done this, he cannot be content without adding another attempt of his own, not less impossible to accept.

ways separated before him. One may find it also comforting and elevating that Christ was in all points tempted
like as are we. Only how stands it then with what follows,
" yet without sin," if we examine that statement psycho-
logically and dogmatically? For first of all it must be
remembered that if such an inner struggle and conflict of
thoughts existed in the mind of Jesus, and if He remained
for an instant undecided and doubtful in regard of them,
then both trains of thought must be regarded as his own,
and the possibility of a decision upon one side as well as
upon the other be admitted. Hereby Jesus will be coordinated with all other men, in whom the conflict of the
good with the evil finds place ; and we must conceive of
this conflict not merely in the beginning of his public
career ; but where once a struggle has found place, it can
revive again, needs nothing more than the suitable conditions to reproduce it ; and only through patience and per-
severance can a skill in the vanquishing of temptation be
attained. This psychological consequence excludes the
hypothesis of such an inward struggle as was limited to
one certain moment time; and there would be nothing
else but to say, " Jesus had within Him besides the good
also an evil principle, against which He needed to be ever
on his guard, though it is only in the history of the Temptation that this struggle is symbolically attached to a
definite moment in his life." But were Jesus constituted
so, then were He not the Christ, but a man as others are,
submitted to the same conditions, with a flesh and spirit
contrary to one another ; consequently not a Redeemer,
but Himself needing a redemption ; and not only the
words in St. John on his oneness with the Father, but those
in the other Gospels on his dignity as Messiah, are either

not authentic; or if He actually spoke them, He either
deluded Himself or deceived mankind.'[1]

In the scholastic theology of the Middle Ages the discussion was carried on with considerable animation whether
a possibility of not sinning (a *posse non peccare*) or an
impossibility of sinning (a *non posse peccare*) should be
ascribed to the Lord.   The first had been, in the patristic

---

[1] H. de S. Victore, the Augustine of the middle ages, has an interesting
passage on this matter (*De Sacram.* 11, pars 1, c. 7): Sunt alii qui de
affectibus humanis in Christo (quos secundum veritatem naturæ cum humanitate et in humanitate suscepit) quædam non solum falsa sed horrenda etiam
affirmare non timuerunt.   Quia enim apostolus ait, Non habemus Pontificem
qui non possit compati infirmitatibus nostris, tentatum autem per omnia :
asserunt humanum affectum in Christo motus etiam vitiorum sensisse, absque
consensu tamen rationis : secundum eam concupiscendi rationem quâ nos qui
peccatores sumus ex illâ originali corruptione quam portamus, illicitos ap-
petitus et motus concupiscentiæ surgentis et vitii tentantis delectationem,
etiam inviti sentire solemus.   Hos autem motus idcirco Christum in carne
suâ voluntarie sustinuisse, ut quasi illis tentantibus resistendo victor existeret,
quatenus et sibi tentationem vitiorum superando præmium justitiæ acquireret,
et nobis in tentatione positis resistendi et vincendi in semetipso exemplum
formaret.   Sed absit a sensu Christiano ut ullam in illâ carne sacrosanctâ
Agni immaculati inordinatæ delectationis et concupiscentiæ illicitæ titilla-
tionem aliquo modo fuisse, aut dicat, aut credat ; qui si vel aliquam pravæ
delectationis radicem aut motum concupiscendi inordinatum in illâ fuisse
diceremus, profecto ab omni vitio liberam negaremus.   Quomodo autem
vitium mundaret, si vitium portaret ? motus quippe inordinatus ex infirmi-
tate concupiscendi surgens cum ipsâ tantum corruptione de quâ oritur, non
solum pœna est, sed culpa : quæ tamen in baptizatis ad damnationem non
imputatur, quia per gratiam novæ regenerationis excusatur.   Hæc tamen
corruptio per gratiam Sacramenti non quidem accipit ut culpa non sit, sed
ut damnabilis non sit . . . . Quapropter illam infirmitatem humanæ naturæ
quæ pœna est, solum cum susceptione carnis Christum assumsisse veraciter
dicimus : illam vero, quæ sic pœna est ut etiam culpa sit, nullatenus admisisse
indubitanter affirmamus.   Neque enim sic victorem vitiorum dicere volumus,
ut eum ipsa quæ vinceret vitia portâsse aliquando ac sensisse dicamus.
Propterea enim per solam pœnam infirmari consensit, ut eos qui et in culpâ
et in pœnâ ægrotabant, primum a culpâ justificaret, postea a pœnâ liberaret.
Compare the careful words of Augustine himself (*Op. Imperf. con. Jul.* iv.
48) : Non dicimus nos Christum, felicitate carnis a nostris sensibus se-
questratæ, cupiditatem vitiorum sentire non potuisse ; sed dicimus, eum
perfectione virtutis, et non per carnis concupiscentiam procreatâ carne
cupiditatem non habuisse vitiorum.

period, the position of Theodore of Mopsuestia and of as
many as, without being actually Nestorians, had yet theological tendencies which inclined them to advance as far
as might be in that direction ; while the second had been
maintained by Augustine.   It was with this, as with so
many of the earlier discussions, which were resumed and
carried out yet further in the period of the medieval
revival of theology ; Abelard, as was to be expected,
taking up the position of Theodore of Mopsuestia, Anselm
and others upholding the Augustinian teaching.[1]   This
question could never have been so much as started,
except in a Nestorian severance of the Lord into two
persons, and thus in the contemplation of a human person
in Him as at some moment existent apart from the divine.
When we acknowledge in Him two natures, but these at
no time other than united in the one person of the Son of
God, the whole question at once falls to the ground.
And such is the Church's faith.   Christ was perfect man
in the sense of having every thing belonging to the com-
pleteness of the human nature ; but there is not, and
there never at any moment has been, any other *person* but
the Son of God ; his human body and soul at the very
moment of their union with one another were also united
with the Eternal Word, so that there is not, nor ever has
been, any human person to contemplate, or in regard of
whom to put this question ; while in respect of the Christ,
and in the manhood after it was taken up into the Godhead, even Abelard himself does not ascribe to Him the
possibility of sinning.[2]

[1] Neander, *Kirch. Gesch.* vol. v. p. 968.

[2] *Ad Rom.* p. 539: Cum hominem qui Deo unitus est, possibile sit
peccare, non tamen postquam unitus est vel dum unitus est. Christum vero,
i.e. Deum simul et hominem modis omnibus impossibile est peccare, cum
videlicet ipsum Christi nomen Dei et hominis exprimat unionem.

When it is asked, as it continually has been, Where is the worth of an obedience which could not have *not* been rendered? where is the glory of not sinning on the part of One who could not sin? the question has its rise in the confusion of a moral and a physical necessity. God cannot lie, God cannot do evil; but shall we therefore cease to praise and glorify Him for his holiness and truth? He cannot, because He will not. The angels now cannot sin; they have so drunk in the glory of God, that, as we believe, they are lifted above the possibility of falling. But does it result from this that their obedience, then when they might have followed those ' who kept not their first estate, but left their own habitation ' (Jude 6), had a worth; which now that they cannot, it has ceased to possess? There is something better and higher, as Augustine and Anselm have taught, than the *liberum arbitrium*, even though that should on each separate occasion of choice choose the good; and that better is the *libertas*, the *beata necessitas boni*; which so soon as the creature has attained, it would certainly be strange to affirm of it that this attainment of the highest has reduced it to the state of the lowest, to the condition of stocks and stones, which indeed cannot do wrong, but, for the same causes that hinder them from this, can as little do right.[1] When two antagonists enter the lists, our moral certainty that one will overcome, may take away the breathless expectation and interest with which we might otherwise mark the several stages of the conflict, but cannot affect the real excellence and merit of the victor.

But all this, namely that the temptations were thus

---

[1] See on this matter a very interesting discussion by Anselm, *Cur Deus Homo?* ii. 19.

presented from without, and not born from within, and, again, that they found not even a moment's acquiescence, consent and entertainment in that holy soul, does not hinder in the least that what was offered may have presented itself as infinitely desirable. In the reality of the temptations we are bound to believe, nor will it be very hard to understand, in part at least, where that reality consisted when we a little consider them one by one, which now it is time to do. To these considerations some words of Professor Mill on this very matter may prove a fitting introduction. ' If,' he says, ' the highest virtue does not exclude that instinct inseparable from humanity, to which pain is an object of dread and pleasure of desire ; which prefers ease and quiet to tumult and vexation, the regard and esteem of others to their scorn and aversion ; to which ill-requited toil or experienced unkindness are sources of corroding anguish and depression ;—this very conjuncture which presents but one of these objects of dread as the concomitant of doing God's will, or associates one of their desirable opposites with neglect or disobedience—every such conjuncture must produce a conflict between duty and these necessary instincts of humanity, sufficient to constitute temptation in the strictest sense.' [1]

' *And when the Tempter came to Him, he said, If Thou be the Son of God, command that these stones be made bread.*' A certain external likeness which might exist between stones and bread (cf. Matt. vii. 9) explains why on those more than on anything else Christ should

---

[1] *Five Sermons on the Temptation*, 1844, p. 37.

have been challenged to display his power. It has been often asked, Putting his suggestion thus, did the Tempter indeed know Him whom he assailed to be the Son of God? or was the suggestion merely tentative, to make Him reveal Himself, and show by his reply what manner of person, and clothed with what power, He was? The question has been variously answered. The ancients probably are right, who for the most part reply, that the Evil Spirit was thus taking the measure of Him whom by a true instinct he recognized for his mortal foe; [1] fearing the worst; but at the same time still uncertain with whom he had to do. Nor ought we to leave out of sight the unmistakeable reference which there is here to the words 'This is my beloved Son,' so lately uttered from heaven. What God has declared certain, Satan will again bring into the region of the uncertain and problematical (cf. Gen. iii. 1). These same words with their covert taunt and implicit denial Christ was destined to hear again in the hour of a keener suffering even than this. He should be again taunted and provoked, and in exactly the same language (Matt. xxvii. 40), to prove his Messiahship, and in this very act of proving to render void the whole work which as Messiah He came to accomplish; but then as now He is able to leave the vindication of his Sonship in his Father's hands.

That to which Satan here challenges the Lord, to ' *command that these stones be made bread*,' was not sinful in itself, but would have been sinful for Him. To have complied, would have been a defeat of his whole mediatorial work. If

---

[1] So Hilary: Erat in diabolo de metu suspicio, non de suspicione cognitio. Augustine (*De Civ. Dei*, xi. 21): Dubitavit de illo dæmonum princeps, eumque tentavit, an Christus esset explorans, quantum se tentari ipse permisit, ut hominem quem gerebat ad nostræ imitationis temperaret exemplum.

on each sharper pressure of the world's suffering and pain
upon Himself, He had fallen back on the power which as
Son of God He possessed, and so exempted Himself from
the common lot of humanity, where would have been the
fellow-man, the overcomer of the world by his human
faith, and not by his divine power?[1]   The whole life of
faith would have disappeared.   At his Incarnation the
Lord had merged his lot with the lot of the race; the
temptation is, that He should separate Himself from them
anew : ' Son of God, put forth thy power.'   When in
some besieged and famine-stricken city, when in hard
straits during the march through some waterless desert,
a captain or commander refuses special exemptions from
the lot of his suffering fellow-soldiers, when a Cato pours
upon the sands the single draught of water which has
been procured in the African desert and brought for his
drinking,[2] such a one in his lower sphere acts out what
the Lord in the highest sphere of all was acting out now.
His miracles shall be all for the needs of others, never for
his own.[3]   He who made the water wine, could have

---

[1] Aquinas: Diabolus justitiâ Dei, non potentiâ, superandus fuit.   Compare Augustine, *De Trin.* xiii. 14.

[2] Lucan, *Pharsal.* ix. 510.

Excussit galeam, suffecitque omnibus unda.

There is no *historic* record, which I am aware of, that Cato so did; but
Plutarch (*Alex.* 42) tells the story of Alexander.   The act of David, as recorded 2 Sam. xxiii. 15-17, is not exactly parallel.

[3] All this I ventured long ago to embody in verse:

' He might have reared a palace at a word,
Who sometimes had not where to lay his head;
Time was, and He who nourished crowds with bread,
Would not one meal unto Himself afford.
Twelve legions girded with angelic sword
Were at his back, the scorned and buffeted;
He healed another's scratch; his own side bled,
Side, feet, and hands, with cruel piercings gored.

made the stones bread ; but to that He was solicited by the need of others, to this only by his own. And this abstinence of self-help was the law of his whole life, a life as wonderful in the miracles which it left undone as in those which it wrought.

The stress of this, as of each other of the subsequent temptations, consisted in the fact that what Satan proposed did most truly lie in the final purposes of the ministry of the Son of God ; and that it was only in his premature anticipations that the sin consisted. Thus it did lie in final issues of his ministry for man that the desert should blossom as a rose (Isai. xxxv. 1 ; lxv. 25), that all strait-ness, hunger, poverty, want, all painful sweat of the brow, hardly wringing from the soil the pittance of the day, and leaving little or no opportunity for higher mental or moral culture, that all these consequences of the primeval curse upon the earth (Gen. iii. 17–19) should cease and come to an end—that, so to speak, the stones should be-come bread. But the temptation was, to begin instead of ending with this, to bring about an outer world of abund-ance otherwise than as the expression and the result of an inner kingdom of righteousness. And in the Lord's refusal to do this is involved the condemnation of every plan for redressing the hard lot of humanity which does not grow out of a moral root, which thinks to make men happier without making them holier, all communist

---

Oh wonderful the wonders left undone !
And scarce less wonderful than those He wrought;
Oh self-restraint, passing all human thought,
To have all power, and be as having none !
Oh self-denying love, which felt alone
For needs of others, never for its own ! '

Sedulius has gathered up all this into a single line :
Atque aliis largus, sibi tantum constat egenus.

schemes, so far as they are an end, and not a means ; all
the profane millenarianism of an Owen or a Fourrier. It
is no heavenly root, but quite another, out of which these
grow. They are not of good, and can never come to
good. Yet who will dare measure the strength of this
temptation, as it may have presented itself to Him who
beheld with a compassion at once human and divine the
infinite toil and want of the children of men ; for I believe
we mistake altogether when we find in his own immediate
hunger that which gave the whole, or even the chief, stress
and force to this temptation. Standing as He did at the
centre of humanity, and commanding all the diverging
lines to their extreme circumference, that hunger was to
Him but as the key and interpreter to all the hunger, all
the need, all the distress which the children of Adam had
ever felt, or should ever feel, until the great and glorious
day when the primeval curse should be lightened from
off the earth, and it should again yield its foison with the
free bounty of Paradise. His own hunger was included ;
but this did not exclude, it embraced rather, that of every
one besides. And to be able to stay all this, to speak
the word and bring it all to an end, who, with a sinful
and therefore a selfish heart, is at all in a position to
estimate what this temptation was to the great Lover of
the bodies and the souls of men? But now for the
answer.

The Tempter had said, ' *If Thou be the Son of God* : '
Christ does not reply, ' I am ; ' nor find here, as He easily
might, a reason for not complying with the challenge ;
since, answering so, He would indeed have overcome the
adversary, but He would have overcome him only for Himself, and not also for us. No other, being only a man, and

not, in that peculiar sense, ' *the Son of God,*' could have
silenced him in the same way. The answer would have
stood apart, and would have fitted no other lips but his
own.[1] But the answer which He gives is one which every
other may employ as freely as He did : ' *Man shall not live
by bread alone, but by every word that proceedeth out of the
mouth of God.*' The hyperaspist of his whole Church,
He throws his shield not merely over Himself, but over
all those whom He has called his brethren, and with
whom in his Incarnation He has made common part and
lot; and saying, ' *Man shall not live,*' declares that He
will not separate Himself from his race. These words are
drawn, as indeed are both the other passages which He
uses, not merely from the Old Testament, but from the
history of Israel's forty years' temptation in the wilderness, and from that, as it is resumed in the Book of Deu-
teronomy. And this certainly is not for nothing, nor
without its significance; but finds its explanation in the
fact that Israel was the figure of the Son of man, was ' the
servant of God,' that should have fulfilled all righteousness, but did not ; in which fact we must seek the justification of St. Matthew's use of Hosea's words, ' Out of
Egypt have I called *my Son*' (Matt. ii. 15 ; cf. Hos. xi. 1).
Christ, as there has been already occasion to urge, is not
merely the second Adam, but the true Israel, and the
true servant of God ' (Isai. xlii. 1), who as such should
testify by his obedience that man truly lives only in and
by the everlasting word.

The words were originally spoken by Moses in reference

---

[1] Ambrose (*Exp. in Luc.* v. 20): Non enim quasi Deus utitur potestate
(quid enim mihi proderat ?) sed quasi homo, commune sibi arcessit auxilium.
Cf. Augustine, *Enarr.* 2ᵃ *in Ps.* cx. 10, 11.

to the manna : ' He fed thee with manna which thou knewest not, neither did thy fathers know ; that He might make thee know that man doth not live by bread only ; but by every word that proceedeth out of the mouth of the Lord doth man live ' (Deut. viii. 3). But this being so, what, it may be asked, was their special appropriateness at a moment like the present? They had this fitness. In the giving of the manna, and in the feeding of the people thereby, lay a signal proof that God was not limited to ordinary means ; but as then He created ' a new thing ' with which to sustain his people, so now He could feed one who trusted in Him, altogether without any external helps and appliances whatever. God is Himself the nourisher, and not the bread or anything else. The manna was but the help to a weak faith ; for that did not really nourish any, but only God's might which worked in and through the manna. And thus the Lord does not mean by this quotation that man wants something *besides* bread, has a soul which must be sustained by heavenly food, as his body is by earthly ; and that if that be fed, it imports little how this may fare. His words are still more to the point. The creative word, which alone imparts to the bread its sustaining power, can sustain, even as He is confident that in the present need it will sustain, apart from the bread.[1] The answer is in fact a keener way of saying, ' I have meat to eat that ye know not of (John iv. 32). I am not pressed as *thou*

---

[1] Cocceius : Potest Deus vivificare absque pane, et sine verbo Dei ne panis quidem ad vitam est. Spanheim (*Dub. Evang.* 58) : Tentator objiciebat, vel fame ipsi esse pereundum, vel lapides convertendos in panem, alioquin nullum dari medium ipsius conservandi. Immo, inquit Dominus, media innumera alia dari possunt præter panem : quamcunque enim rem placet Deo adhibere ad sustentationem hominis ea sufficere potest, vel verbum solum promissionis egrediens ex ore Domini.

suggestest, and as thou wouldst fain have *Me* to believe ;
I live upon God.'[1] ' God,' as Jeremy Taylor has said,
applying these words, ' will certainly give us bread, and
till He does we can live by the breath of his mouth, by
the word of God, by the light of his countenance, by the
refreshment of his promises. If the fleshpots be removed
He can alter the appetite ; and when our stock is spent,
He can also lessen the necessity ; or if that continues, He
can drown the sense of it in a deluge of patience and
resignation.'[2]

' *Then the devil taketh Him up into the holy city, and
setteth Him on a pinnacle of the temple.*' Characteristically
enough it is St. Matthew who thus calls Jerusalem ' *the
holy city*,' a phrase occurring in no other Evangelist. To
him, the Jew, it was eminently such (cf. Matt. xxvii. 53 ;
Isai. xlviii. 2 ; lii. 1 ; Dan. ix. 24 ; Rev. xi. 2 ; xxi. 2,
10 ; Ecclus. xxxvi. 13 ; 1 Macc. x. 31), ' the holy place '
(Matt. xxiv. 15), ' the city of the great King ' (Matt. v. 35) ;
' the throne of the Lord ' (Jer. iii. 17). In the parallel
record of St. Luke, it is simply ' *Jerusalem.*' I should
be unwilling to interpret this ' *taketh* ' with Hammond,
as though it were, ' carried Him through the air ; '
for such a rapture and flight, a yielding of Himself so far
to the will of the adversary, seems inconsistent with the
dignity which in the midst of all his humiliation the Son
evermore preserved. They who will have it so, observe

---

[1] It is a beautiful Jewish legend to which Philo (*De Somn.* i. 6) refers,
that Moses during his forty days' fast on Mount Horeb was fed by the melo-
dies of heaven, the music of the spheres—by which, he goes on to say, if
our ears were now purged to drink them in, we too might equally be sustained. Not unlike this in spirit is the saying quoted by Schoetgen (*Hor.
Heb.* vol. i. p. 87): Justi perfecti ex splendore Schechinæ comedunt.

[2] *Life of Christ*, i. 9.

that it is nothing strange if He who allowed Himself to
be buffeted, scourged, crucified by the servants of the
devil, should yield Himself thus far to the violence of
their master; and that all which concerns us is to keep in
mind that it was a violence which could not have been
exercised upon Him, unless He had willingly submitted
Himself to it.[1] But certainly the language which St.
Matthew uses does not require, hardly justifies, such a
meaning as this. The word we have translated '*taketh*'
(παραλαμβάνει) is the same which all three Evangelists
employ when they would describe the Lord's leading up
with Him his chosen apostles to the Mount of Transfiguration (Matt. xvii. 1 ; Mark ix. 2 ; Luke ix. 28 ; and often
elsewhere). That which may have in part induced this
interpretation, namely, the supposition that the '*pinnacle*[2]
of the temple' was some giddy point, unattainable except
by such aërial flight, is a mistake. Whatever it may have
been, it certainly was not this ; for in the history of the
martyrdom of James the Just, given by Hegesippus
and preserved for us by Eusebius,[3] the martyr is set on
this same '*pinnacle*,' which *he* could only have reached
by ordinary means, that from thence he may harangue
the people below, and when he disappoints the expectation of the Jews who had set him there, is by them cast
headlong down.

---

[1] Deyling: Noli in hâc re diaboli potentiam, sed potius Servatoris pati-
entiam, mirari.

[2] Πτερύγιον, which the grammarians explain by ἀκρωτήριον (cf. Num. xv.
38, LXX), the diminutive of πτέρυξ, a wing, pinna or penna in Latin; the
latter being the form which the word, literally employed, assumes; while
pinna, with its diminutive pinnaculum, is the *wing*like lappet of a building.
For the different views of what this πτερύγιον of the temple actually was,
see Deyling, *Obss. Sac.* vol. ii. p. 371.

[3] *H. E.* ii. 23.

'*And saith unto Him, If Thou be the Son of God, cast Thyself down; for it is written, He shall give his angels charge concerning Thee; and in their hands they shall bear Thee up, lest at any time Thou dash thy foot against a stone.*' The temple was plainly the fitting place for this, the peculiarly theocratic temptation, as the wilderness had been for that addressed to the fleshly appetite, and as the high mountain should be for the temptation yet in store from the world; even as it has been fancifully suggested that the Tempter assumed different shapes in succession, an eremite in the wilderness, an angel of light on this pinnacle of the temple, a king when he offered on the mountain the world-kingdoms to the Lord. Unfolding this temptation a little, we may better realize to ourselves wherein consisted its enticing power. What the Tempter suggested may have been very nearly as follows : 'Be acknowledged the Christ at once. Give of thy own free accord that which those in whose hands it will lie to accept or reject Thee will so often demand, namely, "a sign from heaven" (Matt. xii. 38 ; xvi. 1 ; Luke xi. 16). Descend with a pomp of angels upholding and upbearing Thee, in the midst of an admiring people. Thou art appointed to be the Christ. Why take the way of a long and tedious recognition? Why consent to be despised and rejected—bringing all which thus Thou wilt bring of evil on Thyself and on them that reject Thee, when by one noble venture of faith, and having moreover a Scripture warrant for this, Thou mightest at a single bound leap to that remote consummation which is indeed in the intentions and purposes of God?'

With what marvellous skill has the Tempter shifted in

an instant the whole line of his assault. In that first temptation he urged the Lord to a distrust of his Father's love, so that He must help Himself, if He is indeed to be helped at all; but now he urges not indeed to trust that love overmuch, for this is impossible, but to put it to the proof in a way of his own choosing, and not of God's appointing. If he cannot entangle Him in the sin of *diffidentia*, perhaps then in that of *præfidentia*,—if such a word may be allowed. Satan too has learned something else in that first encounter; he has learnt that the Scripture is the law of Christ's life; the sphere in which He lives and moves. On a word of that Scripture the Lord had grounded his refusal to make the stones bread. Here then is a word of that same Scripture, which should induce Him to consent to that which is now put before Him. 'Makest Thou so much of that word? Hopest Thou on its assurance for such a miracle in thy behalf? Then see in that which now I set before Thee, how Thou mayest show yet more gloriously thy confidence in the favour of God towards Thee.'

That ninety-first Psalm, which the adversary quotes, is written not concerning the Son of God in particular, but concerning the faithful generally. Yet for all this he cannot be charged with any abuse or mis-quotation of it in applying the promise which it contains to Christ; since whatever is written concerning the faithful in general, must be eminently true concerning Him who is their Head. Origen then,[1] it must be admitted, has not right here, when he accuses Satan of a fraudful transfer to Christ of what was written about others, and in this

---

[1] *Hom.* 31. *in Luc.*

respect of perverting Scripture; an accusation which
Chrysostom and Jerome repeat. That there is and must
be somewhere a lie in the application even of words of
truth on the part of him who is a liar and only a liar is
certain. He lies, as St. Bernard has very well shown,
leaving out, as he does, one little clause, which would
have altered the whole character of the quotation. ' *He
shall give his angels charge concerning Thee*,' this much
Satan cites; but the words following ' to keep Thee in
all thy ways,' these he omits altogether.[1] But that to
which he now challenged the Lord was not ' *a way* '
appointed by his heavenly Father for his treading, and
in which as such He might be sure that He would not
stumble (John xi. 9, 10), but a precipice from which He
would have wantonly chosen to fling Himself down ; and
the promise of being kept in all his ways no one has a
right to take to himself, who has exchanged his appointed
ways for any such headlong precipices as that now suggested to the Lord.[2]

' *Jesus said unto him, It is written again, Thou shalt not
tempt the Lord thy God ;* ' written, indeed, in almost every
page of Scripture, but the special reference is to Deut. vi.
16. But first, in that ' *It is written again* ' of Christ, lies

[1] Mendacium abscondens per Scripturam sicut omnes hæretici, as Irenæus
observes (v. 31); than whom none had larger experience of their devices.

[2] Bernard (*In Ps. Quis Latitat*, Serm. 15): Scriptum est, inquit, Quoniam
angelis suis mandavit de te, et in manibus tollent te. Quid scriptum est,
maligne, quid scriptum est? Angelis suis mandavit de te. Quid mandavit?
Animadvertite et videte quoniam subticuit malignus et fraudulentus quod
malignitatis suæ commenta dissolveret. Quid enim mandavit? Nempe
quod in psalmo sequitur : Ut custodiant te in omnibus viis tuis. Numquid
in præcipitiis? Qualis via hæc de pinnaculo templi mittere se deorsum?
Non est via hæc, sed ruina; et si via, tua est, non illius. Frustra in tentationem capitis intorsisti, quod scriptum est ad corporis consolationem.
Delitzsch : Es ist nicht die Rede von Gefahren, die man aussucht, sondern
von solchen, die den Gerechten ungesucht auf den Lebenswegen begegnen.

a great lesson, quite independent of that particular Scripture which on this occasion He quotes, or of the use
to which He turns it.   There lies in it the secret of our
safety and defence against all distorted use of isolated
passages in Holy Scripture.   Only as we enter into the
unity of Scripture, as it balances, completes, and explains
itself, are we armed against error and delusion, excess or
defect on this side or the other.   Thus the retort, ' *It is
written again*,' must be of continual application; for,
indeed, what very often are heresies but onesided exaggerated truths, truths rent away indeed from the body
and complex of the Truth, without the balance of the
counter-truth, which should have kept them in their due
place, coordinated with other truths, or subordinated to
them ; and so, because all such checks are wanting, not
truth any more, but error ?[1]

It is a weapon at once offensive and defensive, a sun
at once and a shield, which the Lord on this occasion
draws from the armoury of God : ' *Thou shalt not tempt
the Lord thy God.*'   The same apparent difficulty which lies
in St. James' declaration that ' God tempteth not any man '
(i. 13), when set over against so many other passages in
which a tempting of man is ascribed to Him (Gen. xxii. 1 ;
John vi. 9), lies also in St. James' statement made at the
same place that ' God cannot be tempted ' as compared
with so many other, in which men are warned against
the sin of tempting God, or charged with the sin of so
doing ; such as Exod. xvii. 2 ; Num. xiv. 22 ; Ps. lxxviii.
18, 56; Acts v. 9 ; xv. 10 ; and the present.   But in
this, as in those, the contradiction lies only on the surface,

---

[1] Tertullian (*De Pudic.* 16): Est hoc solenne perversis et idiotis et
hæreticis, alicujus capituli ancipitis occasione adversus exercitum senten-
tiarum Instrumenti totius armari.

and as soon as we descend a little below the surface, it
quite disappears. There is a sense in which men ' tempt '
God, as no doubt there is also a sense in which they
cannot ' *tempt* ' Him. They ' *tempt* ' God, when they mis-
trust the resources of his wisdom, his power, his goodness ;
when they will not believe Him on his simple word, but
challenge Him to make present and immediate experiment of these, before they will give Him credit for
possessing them. Thus when the children of Israel exclaimed, ' Can God furnish a table in the wilderness? '
(Ps. lxxviii. 19) this question of theirs was in the strictest
sense of the word a ' tempting ' of God ; as the Psalmist
expressly declares ' They *tempted* God in their heart '—
' they *tempted* God, and limited the Holy One of Israel '
(ver. 41). In like manner Ahaz refuses to ask a sign
from God, sheltering himself behind the precept of Deut.
vi. 16 ; and pretending to believe that to ask of God that
sign which God bade him ask, would be such a ' tempting '
of Him as is there forbidden ; ' Neither will I *tempt* the
Lord ' (Isai. vii. 12). Not otherwise we are told that the
adversaries of the Lord ' came, and *tempting* desired that
He would show them a sign from heaven ' (Matt. xvi. 1),
that is, putting Him to the proof, refusing to **accept**,
without this proof given, his claims to be the Messiah.
And when Satan would have the Saviour to cast Himself
down headlong from the pinnacle of the temple, this
would have been in the strictest sense, as He Himself
declares, a ' tempting ' of the Lord his God, that is, a
putting of Him to the proof, as one in doubt, until that
proof had been made, whether He would indeed help
and save.[1]

---

[1] Godet: Jésus caractérise la nature impie de cette suggestion par
l'expression *tenter Dieu* (v. 12). Ce terme signifie : mettre Dieu dans l'alter-

God may ' *tempt* ' man as often as He will ; for there is always an element of weakness in every man, justifying the temptation, which shall either reveal this weakness to him through a fall, and thus send him to the source of all true strength, or through a victorious struggle with it, leave him in fuller possession of God's strength than before. But men may never lawfully ' *tempt* ' God, in whom there are no such discoveries to be made, and whom then they honour most, when they believe the highest, noblest, greatest things about Him to which their hearts can attain. It was for Christ to believe in the loving-kindness and faithfulness of God, that He would uphold Him in all his ways, without tempting or putting Him to proof, as the adversary had suggested. Such a tempting could only have sprung from a secret unbelief; and would have been for Him an abandonment at the outset, of that life of faith which He came to live on earth, and by which to overcome the Wicked One.

In this refusal of Christ's are implicitly condemned all who run before they are sent, who thrust themselves into perils to which they are not called; all who would fain be reformers, but whom God has not raised up and furnished for the work of reformation ; and who therefore for the most part bring themselves and their cause together to shame, dishonour, and defeat; with all those who presumptuously draw drafts on the faithfulness of God, which they have no scriptural warrant to justify them in believing that He will honour.

It is well known that in the different Gospels this

native d'agir d'une manière contraire à ses plans ou à sa nature, ou de compromettre l'existence ou le salut d'une personne à lui étroitement liée. C'est la confiance dénaturée jusqu'à devenir le crime de lèse-majesté divine.

second temptation and the third follow in different order.
In St. Matthew the temptation to vainglory (' *Cast Thyself
down* ') comes first, and that to worldliness (' *All these
things will I give Thee*') follows after; while in St. Luke
first the kingdoms and their glory are offered, and only
when these are rejected, the temptation to spiritual pride
is suggested.   Which, it may be asked, was the true, or
rather the actual, succession? for both orders may in a
deeper ideal, though not in an historic sense, be true.   In
favour of St. Luke's it may be urged that spiritual wickednesses seem the latest and subtlest temptations of the
Evil One; those who have overcome all other, are exposed to, and sometimes overcome by, these ; the white
devil, as one has said, being more to be feared than the
black ; and temptations arranged to follow in such a
sequence and method as shall be most effectual ($\mu\varepsilon\theta o\delta\varepsilon\tilde{\iota}\alpha\iota$
$\pi\lambda\acute{\alpha}\nu\eta\varsigma$) are especially attributed to Satan (Ephes. iv.
14; vi. 11).   But on the other hand, in favour of St.
Matthew's succession it may be said that the words ' *Get
thee behind Me, Satan,*' would scarcely occur in the middle
of the Temptation, being rather the final and authorita-
tive dismissal of the Tempter, after which he would no
longer presume, for the present at least, to molest the Lord.
And altogether this fact seems to outweigh the arguments
which support the other succession ; not to say that St.
Matthew's ' *then* ' (ver. 5) and ' *again* ' (ver. 8) mark a closer
knitting together of the incidents in the order of time than
aught in the more loosely connected scenes in St. Luke.[1]

[1] In Greswell's *Dissertations* there is one *On the Order of the Temptations,* vol. ii. p. 192.   Von Meyer (*Blätt. für höhere Wahrheit,* vol. v. p. 262)
thinks the succession to have been differently given by the different
Evangelists, of a purpose and for our instruction, because the order of these
temptations is different in different men, and in the same man at different

' *Again, the devil taketh Him up into an exceeding high
mountain, and sheweth Him all the kingdoms of the world
and the glory of them ; and saith unto Him, All these
things will I give Thee, if Thou wilt fall down and worship
me.*' The inner connexion between this third temptation
and that which went before may be as follows : ' Well, if
Thou art not the Son of God, as is plain from thy inability to make bread, thy refusal to cast Thyself boldly
forth on the riches of his grace, worship me, and receive
what I will give Thee, *all the kingdoms of the world and
the glory of them.*' By these last words I understand all
which the kingdoms possessed of fairest, richest, best, the
flower and crown of all their splendours gathered to a
head (Isai. xxxix. 2 ; Matt. vi. 29 ; Rev. xvi. 26). But
before we proceed further it is worth while to enquire
how we are to understand the ' *shewing* ' to Him of all these.
An optical illusion is entirely inadmissible ; such is not
reconcilable with the Church's idea of her divine Head. It
is quite impossible that in anything, great or small, He can
have been played upon or deceived, least of all by the
Spirit of lies.[1] That Satan pointed out the quarters in
which the several kingdoms of the world lay, does not

times. Aquinas, who has anticipated so much, has anticipated also this
(*Summ. Theol.* pars 3ª, qu. 41, art. 4) : Videntur Evangelistæ diversum
ordinem tenuisse ; quia quandoque ex inani gloriâ venitur ad cupiditatem,
quandoque e converso. Augustine (*De Cons. Evang.* ii. 16) declines absolutely to decide in favour of one order or the other.

[1] Grotius strangely enough, while he allows this (neque oculos neque vim
imaginatricem Christi illusam puto), suggests notwithstanding a mere
phantasmagoria of this kind : Nimirum quasi in picturâ ponens [diabolus]
omnem qui unquam esset regiæ fortunæ apparatum. The suggestion of
Milton (*Par. Reg.* iv. 40) is different ; and is not attended by the same
objections :

> ' By what strange parallax or optic skill
> Of vision, multiplied through air, or glass
> Of telescope, were fruitless to enquire.'

seem to me altogether to satisfy and exhaust the force of
this ' *sheweth* ; ' least of all when we bring in St. Luke's
' *in a moment of time* ; '[1] although many interpreters have
been satisfied with such an explanation.[2] Jeremy Taylor
reaches out after something more : ' By an angelical power
he draws into one centre species and ideas from all the
kingdoms and glories of the world, and makes an admirable map of beauties, and represents it to the eye
of Jesus.' But whatever the manner of the shewing
was, a shewing rather than a relating is skilfully imagined,
as might have been expected from the great artificer
of falsehood. The eye is the inlet of desire ; there
is nothing so soon enticed and led away. ' It is,' says
Bishop Andrewes, ' the broker between the heart and all
wicked lusts that be in the world,' and has approved itself
as such from the beginning (cf. Gen. iii. 6 ; Job xxxi. 1,
7 ; Matt. v. 28 ; 2 Pet. ii. 14).

I have quoted the words in which this proffer of the
kingdoms of the world is made, as more briefly recorded
by St. Matthew. The qualifying addition which appears
in the report of St. Luke is very significant: ' *All this
power will I give Thee, and the glory of them ; for that is
delivered unto me; and to whomsoever I will I give it.*'
Liar as he is from the beginning, the Tempter does not
venture to claim the kingdoms of the world and their glory
as of absolute right his own. Manichæans enough there
are in the world who believe that the devil is really its

---

[1] Ἐν στιγμῇ χρόνου = ἐν ἀτόμῳ, ἐν ῥιπῇ ὀφθαλμοῦ (1 Cor. xv. 52).

[2] Origen : Διέγραψε τῷ λόγῳ τὴν οἰκουμένην, . . . πῶς γὰρ ἠδύνατο αὐτοὺς
τοὺς τόπους εἰς ἕνα τόπον πρὸς θεωρίαν σωματικὴν ἀγαγεῖν ; Maldonatus :
Reipsâ ostendisse, non ita ut viderit, sed ita ut cujusque regni plagam digito
designaverit. Bengel : Per enumerationem et indigitationem fortasse. So
Aquinas, *Summ. Theol.* par 3ª, qu. 41, art. 4.

lord and king; but he in whose favour the Manichæan explanation of the world's riddle has been started, does not himself venture to assert it. The world is not Satan's own; nor his at all, except in so far as it has been ' *delivered*' to him; that through it and the countless seductions which it offers he may on the one hand exercise and prove the faith of God's elect, to their greater final reward, on the other seduce those who are waiting and willing to be seduced, from their allegiance to their liege Lord and rightful king; or that in other ways he may work out the higher ends of God's providence and grace. So far indeed it had been suffered to come into his hands; he is now, in Christ's own words, ' the prince of this world' (John xii. 31), in the words of his apostle, ' the prince of the power of the air' (Ephcs. ii. 2), ' the god of this world' (2 Cor. iv. 4); able to give to those who serve him, ' his power, and his seat, and great authority' (Rev. xiii. 2). But whatever dominion he possesses in it, he possesses not of right, but by usurpation on his part, by permission upon God's, even as he himself must acknowledge here. To him it might be said, as to one of his servants it was said, ' Thou couldest have no power at all, except it were given thee from above' (John xix. 11). This was originally no *wicked* world (Gen. i. 31); a ' *mundus* ' indeed, but no ' *mundus immundus*,' as Augustine so often loves to declare.

Satan is playing for a high stake, and does not grudge therefore to make a great offer. It is not often that Bishop Andrewes allows himself in irony so fine and so effective as he does in one of his Sermons on the Temptation; contrasting this offer, the kingdoms offered to Christ and rejected by Him, with the unutterably paltry bribes, the mess of pottage (Gen. xxv. 34), the Babylonish garment (Josh. vii. 21), the two changes of raiment (2 Kin. v. 23), the thirty pieces of silver (Matt. xxvi. 15), for which we are so often contented to barter all. I cannot refuse to quote a part: 'There be some that will say, They were never tempted with kingdoms. It may well be; for it needs not, when less will serve. It was Christ only who was thus tempted; in Him lay a heroical mind that could not be allured with small matters. But with us it is nothing so, for we esteem far more basely of ourselves. We set our wares at a very easy price; he may buy us even dagger-cheap, as we say. He need never carry us so high as the mount. The pinnacle is high enough; yea, the lowest steeple in all the town would serve the turn. Or let him but carry us to the leads and gutters of our own houses, nay, let us but stand in our windows or our doors, if he will give us but so much as we can there see, he will tempt us throughly; we will accept it and thank him too. He shall not need to come to us with kingdoms. If he would come to us with thirty pieces, I am afraid many of us would play Judas. Nay, less than so much would buy a great sort, even " handfuls of barley and pieces of bread" (Ezek. xiii. 19). Yea some will not stick to buy and sell the poor for a pair of shoes, as Amos speaketh. . . . A matter of half a crown, or ten groats, a pair of shoes, or some such trifle will bring us on our knees to the devil.'

But this temptation, how mighty an attraction it must have had. It had not indeed that kind of attraction for Him on whom it was now brought to bear, which it would have possessed for mean and vulgar souls; but one which the very love and pity and yearning sympathy

for all the children of men that dwelt in Him, must have
lent it. Nothing was more righteous than that all the
kingdoms of the world should be Christ's, nothing more
certain than that He, as Messiah, should one day be heir
of all. Feeling then and knowing Himself to be the
rightful king of men, and to have the power of infinitely
blessing them as their king, with such prophecies going
before of his kingdom and what that kingdom should be,
as Isai. xxxii. 1–8, Ps. lxxii., He must have unutterably
desired, and it belonged to the perfection of his nature
that He should so desire, that the kingdoms of the world
should be his own. How many bleeding hearts were
waiting to be bound up by Him; how many who now
sat in darkness were waiting for light from Him; what
truths were waiting for Him to utter; what wrongs were
waiting for Him to redress, what strongholds of oppression for Him to cast down. The power of accomplishing
all this, of staunching all those fountains of tears, of imparting all that knowledge of his Father's love, of redressing all those wrongs, of destroying all the destroyers
of the earth, this was ' *the glory* ' which the royalties of
the world wore in his sight; here was the allective force
which this temptation possessed. We note ever, even
among the sinful children of men, that the nobler the
character of a man, the nobler also the semblance which
a temptation, that is indeed to exercise any power upon
him, must assume. Sordid sins, sins of a manifest selfishness, will have little or no seductive power, nay, will
rather repel than attract him. The temptation may be
a messenger of Satan's, but it must in some sort know
how to transform itself into an angel of light, before it
can obtain a hearing from him, or at all events before it

can mightily allure. And if this be true of men in whom
is any nobleness of nature, how much truer must it have
been in respect of Him who was the noblest of all.

And yet, when we are seeking to measure what was the
dynamic force of this third temptation, we must not leave
out of account, as an element herein, that in this offer lay
the prospect of evading and overleaping all the toil and
pain and suffering, to which otherwise a Saviour of the
world was bound in. The kingdoms of the world should
be his, as an easy gift ; instead of being, as otherwise they
must be, a painful prey wrung at the cost of his own life's
blood from the usurper. It is from this point of view,
and from vividly realizing to ourselves the mighty temptation which the prospect of thus escaping the cross, and not
drinking the cup, must have had for Him who knew all
which that cross and that cup meant, that we must explain that 'Get thee behind me, Satan' (Matt. xvi. 23),
with which at a later day Christ rebukes the chief of his
apostles, when he too must needs play the Hinderer, and
with his 'Be it far from Thee, Lord' (ver. 22), would fain
persuade his Lord that the suffering of many things was
not, and need not be, his portion ; that there was another
way besides that by the steps of his cross whereby He
might ascend to his throne. The saying has perplexed
many. Could He who spoke no random word, for whom
Satan was the personal embodiment of all evil, have called
by this name a servant of his own, visited a passing fault
of his with so terrible a rebuke ? They have recoiled
from admitting this ; and yet how escape the admission ?
In this way, I believe. Christ saw with the lightning
glance of his spirit in the words of St. Peter a suggestion
not so much of his as of Satan's ; who was using the

servant, and making him the organ and unconscious instrument by which he brought to bear his engines of temptation against the Master. Christ beheld Satan, so to speak, lurking behind Peter, suggesting by him, as he had in the wilderness suggested more directly, that there was a shorter way to the kingdom of his glory than by the cross of his shame; and to him the words are properly and primarily addressed; although in reaching him enough glances off from them to constitute a wholesome and most real rebuke for Peter. The words of rebuke which are spoken then are precisely the same as those spoken now, to mark that the Lord recognized in the remonstrance of Peter the recurrence of a temptation, whose strength He had known before, and no doubt still knew; but which He had already met and overcome.

But the price to be paid for that power of prodigally blessing others, in which after all lay the main stress of this temptation, what was that to be? It was no more than an act of homage to him from whom He should receive the investiture of the kingdom. This price before now men not altogether mean or base, men not altogether without noble aspirations for the good of their fellow-men, have consented to pay; having persuaded themselves that a righteous end justified the unrighteous means, that the power ill-gotten might yet be so well used as to cause the fraud, or violence, or other wrong by which it was obtained to be forgiven, if not forgotten altogether. Some among those who ended with being the very worst and wickedest in the French Revolution, saw, no doubt, an ideal kingdom floating before their eyes, which they were striving to realise, and which they linked with good for many, and not merely with some selfish good for themselves. But while no other way of bringing about that which they desired seemed open to them, they were willing that so they might hasten and make sure the coming of this kingdom, to fall down and worship Satan ; and what hideous service they rendered him at the last is written in such characters of blood as will leave their names a hissing and an execration for ever. And that act of homage which the Tempter now asked of Christ, what did it imply? Simply that of Christ He should become Antichrist—nothing short of this. Height and depth are but two opposite aspects of the same fact ; and just as Lucifer, ' son of the morning,' could only fall as he did fall, the height to which he was exalted being the measure of the depth to which he fell, and, fallen, could not be any other than the prince of darkness, so for Him who was tempted now there was no alternative but to be the Christ, or if not this, to be Antichrist. No wonder that such a proposal should call forth such an answer as it does.

Hitherto the suggestions of the Wicked One, however fraudful, have not been incapable of a favourable interpretation ; the first might have been called forth by sympathy, however ill-timed, with the Lord's hunger ; the second, by the desire, however premature, that He should openly assert the dignity of his person and office, and make manifest to all the world his dearness to God. But this is capable of no such favourable interpretation. The Tempter has shown himself now in his true colours, one who can no more be so much as mistaken for an angel of light, but manifestly the leader of the great apostasy from the worship and service of the true God. Therefore the

altered tone of the reply : ' *Get thee behind Me, Satan.* '[1]
The divine patience gives room now to the divine indignation. This the character of this suggestion required ; for
he who simply declines an infamous proposal inadequately
satisfies the claims which virtue and honour, outraged and
insulted in his person, make upon him. Indignation in
such a case is not merely justifiable, but is required, is of
the essence of a true righteousness. Such an indignation
speaks out in this reply of Christ.

And now He proceeds to justify the word of defiance
to the outrance with which He has replied, even as with
such only He could reply, to the last proposal of the
Tempter ; to justify too the fearful name of ' *Satan,*' adversary, hinderer of all good, which He has given him.
This he does by a word from the Scripture, to act in
direct disobedience to which that adversary would fain
have induced Him : ' *for it is written, Thou shalt worship
the Lord thy God, and Him only shalt thou serve* '—
' *written* ' at Deut. vi. 13, and again at x. 20 ; cf. Rev.
xix. 10. Out of the mouth of the Son of God there
might have proceeded a two-edged sword of his own
(Rev. i. 16) ; but ' the sword of the Spirit ' which he
prefers to wield is again the written word ; even as armed
with this He comes victoriously forth from his third and
last encounter with the foe. ' Thou hast magnified thy
word above all thy name ' (Ps. cxxxviii. 2). ' Blessed is

---

[1] Ὕπαγε ὀπίσω μου (cf. 2 Kin. ix. 18, ἐπίστρεφε πρὸς τὸ ὀπίσω μου), rendered
by Tyndale ' Avoid, Satan,' by the Rhemish, ' Avaunt, Satan,' is strangely
enough rendered in our Version in two different ways, ' *Get thee hence, Satan,*'
in Matthew ; ' *Get thee behind Me, Satan,*' in Luke. The words belong
properly only to the earlier, having been brought by transcribers to the later,
Gospel, from the text of which they are now omitted in the best critical
editions.

he,' exclaims Bishop Andrewes here, 'that has his quiver full of such arrows.'

'*Then the devil leaveth Him*,' or, in the far more noticeable words of St. Luke, marking two important points which St. Matthew had passed over, '*And when the devil had ended all the temptation, he departed from Him for a season.*' We shall scarce press too far the words, '*all the temptation,*' if we infer from them that the three temptations with which our great Forerunner was assailed in the wilderness, embrace the whole circle of human temptation, so that we have here the evidence, to use Jackson's words, of 'Christ's mastery over Satan at his three principal weapons.' These 'three principal weapons' we are wont to express under the three terms, the world, the flesh, and the devil; answering, as has often been observed, to the three enumerated by St. John, 'the lust of the flesh, the lust of the eyes, and the pride of life' (1 John ii. 16).[1] In the suggested gratification of the appetite contrary to the will of God, was the temptation of the flesh; in the proffered kingdoms with their glory, the temptation of the world; while, although all the temptations were from the devil, yet that was especially the devilish temptation which proposes to Christ that in vain-glory and spiritual pride He should cast Himself headlong from the pinnacle of the temple; another 'son of the morning' (cf. Isai. xiv. 12), but falling from a far higher height than any from which ever his Tempter fell.

---

[1] Augustine (in loc.): Tria sunt ista, et nihil invenies unde tentatur cupiditas humana nisi aut desiderio carnis, aut desiderio oculorum, aut ambitione sæculi. Per ista tria tentatus est Dominus a diabolo. Cf. *De Verâ Relig.* 38.

Nor should we fail further to observe the very note-worthy parallelism between this Temptation which Christ surmounted in the desert and that other under which our first parents succumbed in the garden. 'When the woman saw' ('through false spectacles of Satan's making,' as Jackson adds) 'that the tree was good for food' (the solicitation of the flesh), 'and that it was pleasant to the eyes' (the solicitation of the world), 'and a tree to be desired to make one wise' (the solicitation of the devil), 'she took of the fruit thereof, and did eat' (Gen. iii. 6). In that first sin of hers were the lineaments of every other sin, as in this victory over temptation the lineaments, and very much more than the lineaments, of every other victory.[1]

Having thus ' *ended all the temptation*,'[2] launched every one of his fiery darts, and seen them every one fall quenched and blunted to the ground, ' *the devil leaveth Him* ; ' for that word shall first be shewn true on the Prince of the faithful, to which each one of his people shall set afterwards his seal, ' Resist the devil, and he will flee from you ' (Jam. iv. 7). He ' *leaveth Him*,' but as St. Luke is careful to add, ' *for a season.*' Room is left here for a later assault, and it is in fact implied that such a later assault was in reserve, and should in due time arrive. Nor can we doubt to what period the sacred his-

---

[1] See on this matter Gregory the Great, *Hom.* xvi. 2, 3; Aquinas (*Sum. Theol.* 3ᵃ, qu. 41, art. 4): Non dixisset Scriptura quod consummatâ omni tentatione diabolus recessit ab illo, nisi in tribus præmissis esset cmnium materia delictorum; quia causæ tentationum causæ sunt cupiditatum, scilicet carnis oblectatio, spes gloriæ, et aviditas potentiæ. Compare Jackson, *Treatise of the Divine Essence and Attributes*, VIII. ii. 10.

[2] Completâ omni tentatione *illecebrosâ*, is Augustine's significant limita-tion of these words (*De Trin.* iv. 13). The whole passage, as it bears on the Temptation, is one of singular interest.

torian looks on ; that, as one great Temptation signalized
the opening of the Saviour's ministry, so another should
signalize its close, the Temptation in the wilderness being
followed in due time and completed by the Temptation
in the garden ; even as the Lord Himself, whether looking
backward or not, yet certainly looking forward to that
second temptation, when now it was close at hand, exclaimed, 'The prince of this world cometh, and hath
nothing in Me' (John xiv. 30); nothing, that is, on which
he could lay his finger, and challenge it for his own.

The two wrestlings with the Evil One differed indeed
from one another, and so may be contrasted with one
another. Their difference consisted mainly in this, that
whereas in the first he brought to bear against the Lord
all things pleasant and flattering, if so he might by aid of
these entice or seduce Him from his obedience, in the
second he thought with other engines to overcome his
constancy, tried Him with all painful things, hoping to
terrify, if it might be, from his allegiance to the truth,
Him whom manifestly he could not allure. In Augustine's words, having tried the door of desire, and found
that closed, he tried afterwards, and with the same unsuccessful issues, the door of fear ; the second Temptation of
the garden dividing itself, like that of the wilderness, into
three acts following close on one another (Matt. xxvi. 44).
And the same illustrious teacher goes on to urge that as it
was with the Captain of our salvation, so also it must be
with every one of those who fight under his banner.
They too shall need to tread under foot both the lion and
the adder, to resist, that is, now a threatening, now a
flattering, world. Indeed, it was with the very purpose
of teaching them how they should do all this, that He

Himself also suffered being tempted.[1] Jeremy Taylor adds another reason why for our sakes our blessed Lord should have accomplished ' *all the temptation* ; ' namely that, keeping this in remembrance, none hereafter, because they were greatly tempted, should therefore misdoubt of the divine love. ' The holy Spirit did drive Jesus into the wilderness to be tempted by the devil. And though we are bound to pray instantly that we fall into no temptation, yet if, by divine permission, or by an inspiration of the holy Spirit, we be engaged in an action or course of life that is full of temptation and empty of comfort; let us apprehend it as an issue of divine providence, as an occasion of the rewards of diligence and patience, as an instrument of virtue, as a designation of that way in which we must glorify God ; but no argument of dis- favour, since our dearest Lord, the most holy Jesus, who could have driven the devil away by the breath of his mouth, yet was by the Spirit of his Father permitted to a trial and molestation by the spirit of darkness.' [2]

'*And behold, angels came and ministered unto Him* '— that is, to the Son of man, to the second Adam ; even as in Jewish legend they are said to have danced before the first Adam on the day of his creation.[3] It could not indeed be said that they were here fulfilling that office which in the Epistle to the Hebrews is ascribed to them, as ' ministering spirits, sent forth to minister for them who shall be heirs of salvation ' (i. 14); for here was not one

---

[1] Augustine (*Serm.* cxxii. 2) : Ad hoc enim pugnat imperator, ut milites discant.

[2] *Life of Christ*, part 1, sect. 9, § 7.

[3] Eisenmenger, *Entdeckt. Judenth.* vol. ii. p. 17. The Mahometans have borrowed this legend from the Jews.

of these ' heirs of salvation,' but the very Author of this
salvation to all others. We have in like manner an
angel appearing to Him, and strengthening Him, in another
great hour of his temptation (Luke xxii. 43). It is probable that on this occasion they brought food (cf. 1 Kin.
xix. 5, 6); the word of the original (διηκονοῦν) may imply
as much; and that word, 'Man did eat angels' food' (Ps.
lxxviii. 25), may have thus received its highest fulfilment;
nor less may they have celebrated with songs of triumph
this transcendant victory of the kingdom of light over the
kingdom of darkness. So much the Christian poet of our
age has suggested:

> 'Nor less your lay of triumph greeted fair
> Our Champion and your King,
> In that first strife whence Satan in despair
> Sank down on scathèd wing;
> Alone He fasted, and alone He fought,
> But when his toils were o'er,
> Ye to the sacred Hermit duteous brought
> Banquet and hymn, your Eden's festal store.'

A few words in conclusion. It is nothing wonderful
that the endeavours should have been many, to explain
away the Temptation, to exhaust it of its supernatural
element, and so to reduce it to the level of an occurrence
explicable by the laws habitually at work around us and
within us. Now, if our Lord's life had been itself such
an occurrence, it would be certainly perplexing to find a
fragment of wonder such as this is, intruding into the
midst of that life; nor would the instinct be unnatural,
which, as it every where desires moral harmony and
keeping, should endeavour in some way or another to get
rid of an event, out of all such harmony and keeping with
the other events of that life. But if the manifestation of

the Son of God in the flesh be itself the wonder of all
wonders, then that this should be surrounded by a group
of secondary wonders, that there should be nothing
common in his life, or, to speak more accurately, very
much altogether uncommon, this might have been expected beforehand.   What would indeed be startling and
perplexing would be the absence of every thing supernatural from such a life—the fact that He, whose name is
Wonderful (Isai. ix. 6), should have fallen at once into
the common course and order of things, and never either
by what He did, or what was done in respect of Him,
have given any token that there was any difference between Himself and the other children of men.   Those,
however, who are ill content until the light which falls
upon the earthly path of our Lord, and lights it up with
a glory not of earth, has for them faded into the light of
common day, have been very busy with this history ; and
that for a long time past ; for it is altogether a mistake
to suppose that the attempts to resolve the Temptation
into a dream, or a vision, or a parable, or an inner conflict, or an encounter with a tempter of flesh and blood,
into any thing in short but that which on its face it announces itself to be, are of very recent origin, and belong
exclusively to the neology of later years.   It is abundantly evident that the Scriptural theologians of the seventeenth and beginning of the eighteenth century had
earnestly to resist attempts which in their time also were
rife, to empty the Temptation of its supernatural element.[1]

---

[1] It needs only to refer in proof to Wolf, *Curæ Philol.* vol. i. p. 66, and
the many treatises which he enumerates there, from whose titles it is plain
that in his time, and before it, the matter was in eager debate.   For a con-
spectus of the more modern attempts in the same line see Ullmann's *Sündlosigkeit Jesu,* 7th edit. p. 113, sqq. ; and again, p. 241, sqq.

Thus for some the Temptation is a vision. The explanation is untenable. It is manifest that the sacred historians did not mean to relate this event as a vision. When they have to tell of such, they make quite clear what they intend (Acts ix. 12 ; x. 3, 10 ; xi. 5 ; xviii. 9 ; xxii. 17); and, which goes still more directly to the root of the matter, no one can accept this explanation without implicitly renouncing the Church's faith concerning her Saviour and her Head. Christ had no visions ; it lay in the necessity of his divine nature that He should have none. There was never a door opened in heaven (Rev. iv. 1) for Him, before whom the heavenly world lay always manifest and bare (John v. 19, 20). He could not be at one time or another ' in the Spirit ' (Rev. i. 10), who was always in the Spirit ; the higher spiritual world being no strange element, into which He was rapt at intervals, but his permanent abiding place. He had no special communications or revelations from his Father, inasmuch as his whole life was one of entire and unbroken intercommunion with Him. Even those which might appear such special communications directed to Himself, are carefully explained to have another motive and reason : ' This voice came not because of Me, but for your sakes ' (John xii. 30 ; cf. xi. 41, 42). Massillon speaks very grandly in a sermon *On the Divinity of our Lord*, on this absence of all rapture, of all ecstasies, or standings out of Himself, in Christ ; shows that it was a necessary consequence of his Divinity that He should never at any moment of his life be thus borne out of Himself, as were the prophets of the Old, and, though more rarely, the apostles and others of the New, Dispensation (Acts x. 10 ;

xi. 5 ; xxii. 17 ; 2 Cor. xii. 2, 4 ; Rev. i. 10).[1] The idea
alike of the vision and of the trance or ecstasy is that of
a depression or partial suspension of the actings of the
lower life, so to prepare for a better reception of impressions or communications from a higher world ; the setting
of the garish sun of this world, that the pure stars of a
heavenly firmament may appear.[2] But in Christ this
could have been never needed ; in whom existed at all
times a perfect balance and harmony of all faculties and
powers ; in whom there was no predominance of the
lower, which could at any instant obscure or stand in the
way of the perfect actings of the higher.

The same objection, only in a higher measure, forbids
an explaining of the Temptation as a dream, which, indeed, is only a subordinate kind of vision ; namely that it
is impossible to reconcile it with the idea of the Son of
God. Even servants of God who have made any considerable advances in the spiritual life, are seldom com-
municated with in this manner. Rather the dream is the
channel of communication with the heathen, with an
Abimelech (Gen. xx. 3), a Laban (Gen. xxxi. 24), a Nebu-

---

[1] Nos prophètes eux-mêmes annonçant les choses futures, sans perdre
l'usage de la raison, ni sortir de la gravité et de la décence de leur ministère,
entraient dans un enthousiasme divin ; il fallait souvent que le son d'une
lyre réveillât en eux l'esprit prophétique : on sentait bien qu'une impulsion
étrangère les animait, et que ce n'était pas de leur propre fonds qu'ils tiraient
la science de l'avenir, et les mystères cachés qu'ils annonçaient aux hommes.
Jésus-Christ prophétise comme il parle ; la science de l'avenir n'a rien qui
le frappe, qui le trouble, qui le surprenne, parcequ'il renferme tous les temps
dans son esprit ; les mystères futurs qu'il annonce, ne sont point dans son
âme des lumières soudaines et infuses qui l'éblouissent ; ce sont des objets
familiers qu'il ne perd jamais de vue, et dont il trouve les images au-dedans
de lui ; et tous les siècles à venir sont sous l'immensité de ses regards comme
le jour présent qui nous éclaire.

[2] Augustine (*De Div. Quæst.* ii. qu. 1) defines an ecstasy, Mentis alienatio
a sensibus corporis, ut spiritus hominis divino Spiritu assumptus capiendis
atque intuendis imaginibus vacet.

chadnezzar (Dan. ii. 1 ; iv. 5), a Pilate's wife (Matt. xxvii.
19), with the wise men from the East (Matt. ii. 12); or
with others who, standing higher than these, yet in the
measure of their spiritual attainments fall very far below
the more eminent saints of God, a Solomon for instance
(1 Kin. iii. 5); and it is expressly brought out as part or
the dignity of Moses, that while God spoke, and made
Himself known to other and inferior prophets by visions
or dreams, He spoke mouth to mouth with him (Num.
xii. 5–8 ; Deut. xxxiv. 10).[1] How much more then would
there belong to the Son of God at every moment the
perfect clearness of waking vision. Indeed all mental
illusions of every kind were so far from Him that I must
needs esteem it a mistake when in *Paradise Regained*
Milton makes Him to dream of feasts in his hunger in
the wilderness.

Another attempt to empty the Temptation of its mysterious element was made in the seventeenth century,
and taken up in the beginning of our own by Paulus
and by others. These saw in the Tempter here a
mortal man, an emissary from the Sanhedrim, or possibly the High Priest himself, who would fain make proof
of what metal this youthful prophet from Galilee, to whom
the Baptist had just borne such glorious witness, was
made ; and whether He might not be seduced and bribed
into the service of the old corrupt theocracy ; instead of
witnessing against it and its ministers, as the examples of
the earlier prophets and many perilous indications in the
Baptist's career, made it too probable that He would.[2]

---

[1] See J. Smith, *Select Discourses*, pp. 169, 254, for an interesting account,
bearing on this very matter, of what the Jewish Doctors called the *gradus
Mosaicus* of prophecy, and its superiority over all other.

[2] See Spanheim, *Dub. Evang.* 51.

This cannot need more than to be stated and left. Unbelief has its cast-off garments, of which even itself is now ashamed, and this is of them.

The suggestion of others that the Temptation was a conflict on our Lord's part with no outward but an inward foe, with the solicitations of appetite, of ambition, of worldliness, which, born in his own mind, sought to draw Him away from the narrow and painful path appointed for his treading, is equally untenable, and this for reasons which have been stated already ; namely that it is directly contrary to the idea of a Saviour, who as such must be a Holy One, and this absolutely and completely, that thoughts soliciting to evil should have thus spontaneously risen up within Him. Christ could be tempted only from without ; not from within.[1] Coming as He did, not in this sinful flesh of ours, to which evil is native, and in which it inevitably rises up, but coming, as the apostle expressly tells us, ' in the likeness of sinful flesh ' (Rom. viii. 3), where the ' likeness ' is plainly introduced to qualify the ' sinful,' for with the flesh itself He had not likeness, but identity (1 John iv. 2 ; John i. 14), evil could in no other way have been present to Him.[2]

All the foregoing explanations, if they are not really reconcileable with the sacred narrative, are yet presented

---

[1] There is an Essay by Gelbricht (I have never seen it), *An male de animo Jesu sentiendum sit si ὁ πειράζων ἐν τῇ ἐρήμῳ Christus ipse,* i.e. *mentis ipsius cogitata fuerint ?* Alteb. 1815. How the writer answers the question which he thus puts I do not know. How he should answer it, there can be no doubt. Ullmann (*Sündlosigkeit Jesu,* 5th edit. p. 116 sqq.) answers it in the negative, does his best to show that the absolute sinlessness of the Saviour is not brought into question by the admitting of such an explanation of the Temptation, but, in my judgment at least, fails in this altogether.

[2] Augustine (*Serm.* 183. 8) Misit Deus Filium suum non in similitudinem carnis, quasi caro non esset caro, sed in similitudinem carnis peccati, quia caro erat, sed peccati caro non erat.

by their advocates as not incapable of such reconciliation. Their authors have not, in the act of offering them, avowedly cast of allegiance to the Word of God, as that within the limits of which their explanations must move, and by the authority of which they must submit to be tried. But there are who withdraw from this narrative all real historic foundation whatever, who see only a mythus here ; who see, that is, in this victorious encounter of the Prince of Light with the prince of darkness a portion of that fabulous halo of glory with which the infant Church encircled the head of its Founder ; not thereby meaning to deceive ; but unconsciously giving an outward shape and subsistence to the hopes, yearnings, expectations, and desires, which filled its heart as to what the Messiah ought to be, and therefore what He must have actually been. Strauss[1] ingeniously gathers up the Old Testament preparations for the growth of such a mythus as this, the rudiments of it which we may there detect; as that Moses and Elijah had both fasted their forty days ; that Israel, the collective son of God, as Christ was the personal Son, had been tempted forty years in the wilderness, with much more of the same kind.[2] No one will expect that I should here undertake to refute an interpretation which, as it intimately coheres with the whole mythical scheme of the Gospel, must stand or fall, as that stands or falls. Only I will observe that the nearest real parallel to our Lord's Temptation which the Old Testament actually offers, Strauss has not referred to. It is furnished by the history of Solomon (1 Kin. iii. 5–15). The resemblance, indeed, is only a remote one ; yet assuredly it

---

[1] *Leben Jesu,* 1837, vol. i. p. 471 sqq.

[2] Compare Gfrörer, *Das Jahrhundert des Heils,* vol. ii. p. 379–387.

was a temptation, when the Lord, appearing to the youthful king, and offering to him what he would, gave him the opportunity of choosing riches or long life in place of the heavenly wisdom, if so he had been inclined. At the same time in his case, as one comparatively weak in all the actings of the spiritual life, the temptation came from God and not from Satan, and did not therefore concentrate in itself the whole power of temptation.

The mythic parallel which meets us in heathendom, although wanting an historic basis, and thus only painted as upon a cloud, is much nearer—that, I mean, of Hercules, when at the beginning of his course he beheld before him the two ways, of pleasure and of toil, and was severally solicited to walk in the one and in the other. And the parallel will be felt to be closer, if only we will keep in mind that heroic character of his life and work, which many of the later legends about him have done so much to obscure, substituting mere strength and animal good-nature in its room. It was not thus that he was conceived at the first; but rather as the man who in a noble devotedness to his fellows girded himself up to undergo all labours and to affront all dangers for their sakes. Buttmann in his interesting Essay upon Herakles[1] seeks to prove that this ' Temptation of Hercules ' is not a later addition to the legend, which we owe to the sophist Prodicus, but lay in the heart, and belonged to the original stuff, of the mythus. And since it is certain that any man who has ever wrought, or who is conceived as having wrought, anything deserving of memory for his fellowmen, could only have effected this by such a noble post-

---

[1] In the *Mythologus,* vol. i. p. 246; compare Dio Chrysostom, *Orat.* 1 ; and Pauly, *Real-Encyclopädie,* vol. iii. p. 1180.

ponement of pleasure to duty, and that this postponement, which acted itself perfectly out in the Son of God, must, though in weaker forms, act itself out no less in every champion of the truth, and can scarcely help coming to a head at some turning point of his life, there is nothing improbable in this supposition.

2. *THE CALLING OF PHILIP AND NATHANAEL*

John i. 43-51.

WE are told of Saul, that when he 'saw any strong man, or any valiant man, he took him unto him ' (1 Sam. xiv. 52); and as we read the catalogue of David's worthies (2 Sam. xxiii. 8-39), we may well believe that he too in this effectual manner filled the ranks of his host. And as these the ancient kings, as Saul and as David, so too the Son of David, the true King of Israel, wherever He saw any man ' fit for the kingdom of God,' strong or valiant, He claimed him for his own, He ' took him unto Him.' This He did not by any exercise of outward power, but by those secret attractions and affinities which draw the brave to a braver, the noble to the noblest of all. In this first burst of his ministry, his triumphs in this kind rapidly succeed one another. ' *The day following,*' following, that is, the day on which He enlisted three of the foremost among his future disciples, He makes two more his own ; these also great ones, even though they may not attain to the first three. On this day ' *He would go forth into Galilee* ; ' the words imply that He was about to undertake the journey thither, but had not actually begun it; ' *and findeth Philip.*' The fact that Philip, though born a Jew, for he should be one of the twelve apostles of the Lamb, thus bears a Greek

name, even as Andrew does the same, is a remarkable
illustration of the extent to which Galilee ('Galilee *of the
Gentiles*') had been hellenized, penetrated through and
through with the customs and language of Greece. It was,
as will be remembered, by his mediation that the Greeks
who would fain speak with Jesus at the feast sought to
obtain and obtained their desire (John xii. 20–22). It is
well worthy of note how often this *finding* recurs in this
chapter; Christ *finding* disciples as here; disciples
finding each his friend, as at ver. 41, 45; and reporting
how they have at once been *found* by, and have themselves *found*, the Messiah (cf. Gal. iv. 9). It is throughout
the chapter of the *Eurekas*.

Thus finding Philip, He '*saith unto him, Follow Me.*'
This '*Follow Me*' might seem at first sight no more than
an invitation to accompany Him on that journey from
the banks of Jordan to Galilee, on which He was just
setting forward. It meant this (thus compare Matt. iv. 19;
ix. 9; Luke v. 27); but at the same time how much
more. It was an invitation to follow the blessed steps of
his most holy life (Matt. xvi. 24; John viii. 12; xii. 26;
xxi. 19, 22; Rev. xiv. 4), to be a partaker at once of his
cross and his crown. How much of this Philip may have
understood at the moment it is impossible to say; but
whether much or little, he is not disobedient to the
heavenly calling. No doubt he had been more or less
prepared for it by some accounts which he had obtained
from his fellow-townsmen Andrew and Peter, of what
had passed between them and the Lord on the day preceding. As much is intimated by the Evangelist in his
mention exactly at this point of his narrative, that '*Philip
was of Bethsaida, the city of Andrew and Peter,*' a fact

which at once accounted for the acquaintance into which he had been brought with all which had passed between them and the Lord.

But Philip, being himself thus ‘ masterfast ’—if it be permitted to revive a word which with others of a similar termination, as ‘ rootfast,’ ‘ shamefast,’ ‘ bedfast,’ did useful service in the language once [1]—cannot be content till he has introduced his friend into the glorious liberty of the same service with himself, until he has done what in him lies to make his friend a sharer of his treasure and his joy. It could not be otherwise ; for if in one sense this treasure of the kingdom of heaven is one, ‘ which when a man had found, he hideth ’ (Matt. xiii. 44), in another sense it is one which will not let him rest till he has made others partakers of the same. ‘ *Philip findeth Nathanael*,[2] *and saith unto him, We have found Him of whom Moses in the Law and the prophets did write, Jesus of Nazareth*,[3] *the son of Joseph.*’ There is error and imperfection still cleaving to his own knowledge. In all likelihood Nazareth was at this time for him the birthplace of the Lord —not an unimportant error, though slight as compared to that which ‘ *son of Joseph* ’ would have involved, had he held fast to it after better teaching, had it belonged to any other than the rudimentary period of his faith.

Strangely enough De Wette and others have argued from these words, thus faithfully recording the first impressions of Philip, his imperfect theology, and the extent

[1] It appears in Skelton, in *The Paston Letters*, and elsewhere.

[2] The name, which corresponds to our Theodore (Gift of God), occurs in the Old Testament. A Nethaneel is prince of the tribe of Issachar (Num. i. 8) ; one too of David's elder brothers bears this name (1 Chron. ii. 14) ; and eight other Nethaneels are mentioned in all. Compare Josephus, *Antt.* vi. 8. 1.

[3] On Ναζαρέτ, Ναζαράτ, or Ναζαρά, and which is the correctest spelling of the word, see a learned note by Keim, *Jesu von Nazara*, vol. i. p. 319.

to which partial error was mingling still with the truth
which he had learned, not that *he* at this time, but that
St. John when he composed his Gospel, either knew
nothing of the birth at Bethlehem and the miraculous
Conception, or gave no credit to them. The fact is that
St. John, as a truthful narrator, records not what Philip,
if at that time he had been better instructed, ought
to have said, but what in that twilight of his knowledge he
actually did say; even as it is not in the least wonderful
that in one brief interview he had not become acquainted
with the most secret and mysterious events in the life of
his future Lord ; events of which even apostles themselves
only obtained gradual glimpses, as they were able to bear
them. The partial error which clave to Philip's faith did
not hinder him from grasping that central truth which
in good time would detach from itself whatever, not of
its own nature, was cleaving to it. He is sure that this
whom they have found is He ' *of whom Moses in the Law* '
(see Gen. iii. 15 ; xlix. 10 ; Num. xxiv. 17, 19 ; Deut.
xviii. 15–19) ' *and the prophets* ' (see 2 Sam. vii. 12–16 ;
xxiii. 1–7 ; Isai. vii. 14 ; ix. 6 ; liii. ; Jer. xxiii. 5 ; Ezek.
xxxiv. 23–31 ; Mic. v. 2 ; Zech. xiii. 7) ' *did write.*'

One weak point in Philip's statement, one apparent
flaw in the credentials of the Messiah whom he announces,
Nathanael detects at once ; for indeed his objection, ' *Can
there any good thing come out of Nazareth?* ' contains
more than a reference to the general low esteem and
disrepute in which Nazareth was held (Matt. ii. 23), the
unlikelihood therefore that aught preeminently good
would come forth from it. The difficulty which he feels,
and which in consistency with his guileless character he
at once expresses, is identical with theirs who somewhat

later objected, ' Shall Christ come out of Galilee? Hath not the Scripture said that Christ cometh out of the town of Bethlehem, where David was?' (John vii. 41, 42; cf. ver. 52); the difference between him and those other gainsayers being that he gladly dismisses his difficulty, yearning as he does to believe; while they gladly cling and hold fast to theirs, exempting them, as it seems to do, from the unwelcome necessity of believing. This ' *good thing*,' which Nathanael is persuaded that Nazareth cannot yield, must be understood as that one ' *good thing*,' that ' gift of God ' (John iv. 10), in which all other good things are included; and is a distinct reference on the part of one not probably unversed in the prophecies which went before of Christ, to the clear fore-announcing in them that Messiah's goings forth in time should not be from Galilee, therefore not from Nazareth, but from Bethlehem in Judæa (Mic. v. 2).

' *Come and see*,' which is all the reply vouchsafed by Philip to the objection of his friend, is manifestly an echo of Christ's ' Come and see ' of the day preceding (ver. 39). That immediate personal intercourse which had proved so effectual in the case of Andrew and another (Philip, as has been noted already, had no doubt heard from his fellow-townsmen how they had been won for the truth), shall not prove less effectual in the case of Nathanael. It was a wise answer then, and is often a wise one now. The highest heavenly things are in their nature incapable of being uttered in words, and ' *Come and see*, come and make proof of them,' is sometimes the only true reply to difficulties about them, an indication of the only effectual way by which those difficulties shall be removed. There are truths in the heavenly world which, like the sun in the natural world, can only be seen by their own light; which in no other way will be seen at all. Philip has a confidence which the result abundantly justified, that in that holy presence, if only he could bring his friend within the range of its influence, all preconceived objections would dissolve and disappear. Perplexities might still remain, but he would be content to adjourn the solution of them to a later day, which indeed is what faith is summoned to do evermore.

He who knoweth the proud afar off, his eyes are also on the faithful of the land that they may dwell with Him (Ps. ci. 6) ; and in Nathanael He recognizes at once one of these. Him therefore He prevents with that word of highest praise, saying, not *to* him, but yet *of* him, and intending that he should hear, ' *Behold an Israelite indeed, in whom is no guile.*' ' *An Israelite indeed,*' Nathanael pertained not only to that ' Israel after the flesh ' of which St. Paul speaks (1 Cor. x. 18), but to the ' Israel of God ' (Gal. vi. 16), which the apostle is so careful to distinguish from it ; a Jew not outwardly, but inwardly (Rom. ii. 28, 29 ; ix. 6) ; of the only ' true circumcision ' (Phil. iii. 3 ; cf. Jer. iv. 4) ; for whom therefore this title of highest honour was not a mere empty name, or worse than this, a contradiction of all which he truly was (Rev. iii. 9); fulfilling as in his innermost life he did, all whereof that name was the promise and the pledge. ' *Israelite* ' was the title which on many accounts the Jew was best pleased to bear.[1] There were others who were Abraham's seed as well as he ; the Ishmaelite and the Edomite ; but ' *Israelite* ' was a title exclusively his own. And then too

---

[1] See my *Synonyms of the New Testament,* § 39.

it was the theocratic title (Acts ii. 22; iii. 12; v. 35; xiii. 16; Rom. ix. 4; xi. 1; 2 Cor. xi. 22); a record of the glorious achievements of their forefather Jacob; a name which he had won from God Himself, when by faith and prayer he had prevailed even with Him (Gen. xxxii. 28). He who knew what was in man declares of Nathanael that he is a true descendant of this Israel; not of Jacob merely; for in Jacob, the supplanter, there *was* guile: it was indeed the most marked fault and failing of his character (Gen. xxvii.; xxx. 37–43; xxxi. 20), until that character had been ennobled and elevated by a divine discipline, till he had struggled out of Jacob into Israel (Gen. xxxii. 24–32; Hos. xii. 4).

At the same time the absence of guile, here imputed to Nathanael, must not be pressed too far. This guileless nature is as the kindly soil in which all excellent graces will flourish (Luke viii. 15; x. 6); but does not do away with the necessity of the divine seed, out of which alone they can spring. He who is ' *without guile* ' is not therefore without sin; this, at least, could only be asserted of One (1 Pet. ii. 22); but rather he is one who seeks no cloke for his sin; does not excuse, palliate, hide, diminish, or deny it (Gen. iii. 12). Being a sinner, he confesses it, and thus finds pardon for the sin which he confesses. So David had declared long ago (Ps. xxxii. 1, 2); to whose words Christ is probably here distinctly referring.[1]

---

[1] Augustine (in loc.) has excellent observations : Quid est, in quo dolus non est? Forte non habebat peccatum? forte non erat æger? forte illi medicus non erat necessarius? Absit. Nemo hic sic natus est ut illo medico non egeret. . . . Si dolus in isto non erat, sanabilem illum medicus judicavit, non sanum; . . . videt istum sanabilem quia dolus in isto non erat. Quomodo dolus in illo non erat? Si peccator est, fatetur se peccatorem esse. Si enim peccator est, et justum se dicit, dolus est in ore ipsius.

Some have enquired, How did the Lord know of Nathanael that he was this true Israelite which He here
avouches him to be? Was it from any previous familiarity? It may have been so in part. He who knew what
instruments He would need for the work which He was
meditating, may before this have seen in Nathanael, or
heard concerning him, what gave Him assurance that there
were fitnesses in him for a future disciple, perhaps for a
future apostle, even for one of the twelve foundation stones
of the Heavenly Jerusalem. Yet there is not the slightest
necessity for assuming such a previous acquaintance.
Christ read, as often as He needed to read, not merely
the present thoughts, but also so much as He desired of
the past histories, of those who came in contact with Him ;
and this He did, not merely by that natural divination,
that art of looking through countenances into souls, interpreting the inner life from the outward bearing, which
all men in a greater or less degree possess, and He doubtless in the largest measure of all (Isai. xi. 3); but ' in his
spirit ' (Mark ii. 8), by the exercise of that divine power,
which was always *in* Him, though not always active in
Him. It was thus, for example, that He read the life-
story of that Samaritan woman (John iv. 17, 18, 29 ; cf.
v. 14) ; where it is impossible to presume a previous acquaintance ; it was thus most probably in the instance
before us.

This simplicity or absence of folds, this guilelessness or
absence of deceit, which the Lord imputes to Nathanael,
reveals itself in his reply, ' *Whence knowest Thou me?* '
There is no affectation here of declining the praise ; no
seeming to consider it as a compliment which he does not
rightly deserve ; but only a question of admiration how

the Lord should have known him so exactly, and declared
him so truly.   And then in proof that this was no happy
guess, no random arrow which, shot at a venture, had yet
hit the mark, the Lord refers him to some circumstance
which we do not exactly know, but which Nathanael
entirely understood : ' *Before that Philip called thee, when
thou wast under the figtree I saw thee.*'   The mere sitting
of an Israelite under his figtree was of itself too common
an occurrence (1 Kin. iv. 25 ; Isai. xxxvi. 16 ; Mic. iv. 4 ;
Zech. iii. 10) to yield such a sign.   It is plain that our
Lord must here refer to some passage, outward or inward,
in Nathanael's life, most probably inward and spiritual,
some earnest prayer, some great mental struggle, the
overcoming, it may be, of some strong temptation, which
under that figtree had lately found place ; immediately,
as it would seem, before Philip had found him, and invited him to Jesus ; for that call too the Lord declares to
be known to Him ; known therefore as well, though not
imputed, the slighting words with which Nathanael at
first received the invitation.   But now he makes good
that hasty speech which he uttered then.   This word of
Christ is enough ; he feels as the Psalmist, ' O Lord, Thou
hast searched me and known me ; Thou compassest my
path and my lying down, and art acquainted with all my
ways ' (Ps. cxxxix. 1, 3); feels that He before whom he
stands is a searcher of hearts (Heb. iv. 12, 13) ; and at
once that full and free confession of faith, which only the
confessions of Peter (Matt. xvi. 16), of Martha (John xi.
27), and of Thomas (John xx. 28), all those too at much
later periods of Christ's ministry, matched or surpassed,
' *Rabbi, Thou art the Son of God, Thou art the King of
Israel*,' breaks forth from his lips.

A word or two upon each of these ascriptions, being as
they are, the first an acknowledgment of the dignity of
Christ's person, the second of the greatness of his office.[1]
And first, ' *Thou art the Son of God.*' We do not here
suppose for an instant that Nathanael, giving this title to
the Lord, intended by it all which the Nicene Fathers
intended, and which we intend, by the same ; and yet
nothing less was wrapped up in that title, to be unfolded
from it in due time. And it meant much, even on
Nathanael's lips, and was no mere language of honour
uttered at random. How much it implied we may clearly
perceive from the active opposition, the earnest hostility,
which this title awoke on the part of the Scribes and
Pharisees, as often as the Lord implicitly or explicitly
claimed it as his own (John v.18 ; x. 30–39 ; xix. 7).
But however these may have denied the superhuman
character of Messiah, there were enough glimpses of this
in the Old Testament to explain how as many as had
searched more deeply into it, or whose vision was less
obscured and distorted by preconceived prejudices, should
have recognized in Him a partaker of the divine nature,
and therefore ' *the Son of God.*' It is sufficient to refer
to Ps. ii. 7, 12 ; Isai. ix. 6. We are then justified in
ascribing nothing short of such a recognition to Nathanael.

And the words which follow, ' *Thou art the King of
Israel,*' words in which the ' *Israelite*' accepts, owns, and
does homage to Israel's king, avouching himself a subject
of his,[2] amount very nearly to the same thing. He who

---

[1] Bengel: Confessio de personâ et officio Christi.
[2] Lampe : Et quia testimonium quod Jesus ei tanquam vero Israëlitæ
exhibuerat, conscientiâ bonâ fretus admiserat, hinc sigillatim suum nomen

said in that second Psalm, ' Kiss *the Son*, lest He be angry '
(ver. 12), said also of the same, ' Yet have I set *my King*
upon my holy hill of Zion ' (ver. 6 ; cf. Zeph. iii. 15 ; Isai.
ix. 7 ; Jer. xxiii. 5, 6). In all these passages the identity
of Israel's King and Israel's God is plainly involved ; and
the same looks plainly out from many other prophecies
concerning the Messiah, as eminently from the seventy-
second Psalm.

But to him that hath shall be given. He who hears
and believes may walk now by faith, but hereafter by
sight. ' *Jesus answered and said unto him, Because I
said unto thee, I saw thee under the figtree, believest thou?
Thou shalt see greater things than these. And He saith
unto him, Verily, verily, I say unto you, Hereafter shall
ye see heaven open, and the angels of God ascending and
descending upon the Son of man.*' [1] This ' *Verily, verily*,'

inter subditos hujus regni profitetur, ac Jesu tanquam suo legitimo Regi in
obsequium se addicit.

[1] This is the first occasion in the recorded Evangelical history upon
which our Lord used and applied to Himself the name of ' Son of man.'
Bengel's note on this phrase is a wonderful specimen of the close packing of
matter the most interesting and the most important in his *Gnomon*. There
are materials in this note which it would not be very difficult to expand into
a volume. I quote a part: Frequens apud Evangelistas et diligentissime
observanda est hæc nomenclatura, quâ nemo nisi solus Christus, a nemine,
dum Ipse in terris ambularet, nisi a semetipso appellitatus est *Filius hominis*.
Primum Joh. i. 52, ut primum reperti fuere qui Eum Messiam et Filium
Dei (ibid. ver. 50) agnoscerent; et deinceps sæpissime, ante prædictionem
passionis et post. Nam ab iis, qui fidem in Ipsum suscipiebant, dictus est
Filius David. Recte suspicati sunt Judæi, eâ designari Messiam (Joh.
xii. 34). Nam ut Adamus primus cum totâ progenie dicitur *Homo*, sic
Adamus secundus (1 Cor. xv. 45) dicitur Filius hominis ; non eâ notione
quâ *filii hominis*, id est tenues, opponuntur *filiis viri*, id est potentibus
(Ps. xlix. 2), quâve homines communiter dicuntur filii hominum (Marc.
iii. 28; Ephes. iii. 5 ; Ezek. ii. 1, et passim), sed cum articulo, ὁ υἱὸς τοῦ
ἀνθρώπου. Videtur articulus respicere prophetiam Dan. vii. 13. Unus hic
nempe homo est, quem Adamus post lapsum, ex promissione exspectavit pro
totâ suâ progenie ; ὁ δεύτερος, secundus (1 Cor. xv. 47), quem omnis prophetia
Veteris Testamenti indigitavit, qui totius generis humani jura et primogeni-

this double amen which here occurs for the first time (but compare Num. v. 22; Neh. viii. 6), is peculiar to St. John; he alone records our Lord's use of it, but he on no less than twenty-five occasions. It becomes the lips of Him, who is Himself ' the Amen ' (Rev. iii. 14), ' the God of truth ' (Isai. lxv. 16), in whom all the promises of God are Yea and in whom Amen (2 Cor. i. 20). How different too the majestic, ' *I say unto you*,' of Christ from that, ' *Thus saith the Lord*,' of all the prophets preceding—they bearers of the word of another, He the utterer of his own (Heb. iii. 1–6). In the promise itself with which the Lord rewards the commencing faith of Nathanael (cf. Ezek. i. 1; Matt. iii. 16; Acts vii. 55; x. 11) we are at once, as by almost all expositors ancient and modern is admitted, thrown back upon that wondrous ladder which Jacob saw, reaching from earth to heaven, with the Lord at the summit, and with angels of God ascending and descending upon it (Gen. xxviii. 12).[1]

turam sustinet (Luc. iii. 23, 38) et cui uni, quod humani nominis nos non pœniteat (Ps. xlix. 20), debemus (Rom. v. 15). Porro hâc appellatione Christus, inter homines ambulans, et expressit, et pro œconomiâ illius temporis occultavit (cf. Matt. xxii. 45) inter homines, et Satanam celavit, se esse τὸν Υἱὸν, *Filium* absolute dictum, id est Filium Dei, promissum datumque homini (Gen. iii. 15; Esai. ix. 6, ortumque ex homine (Heb. ii. 11), perinde uti uno *exaltationis* vocabulo et crucem et glorificationem suam insignivit (Joh. xii. 32). Compare the article, *Son of Man*, in *The Dictionary of the Bible*, and for all the more recent literature on the subject of this title, Keim, *Jesu von Nazara*, vol. ii. p. 65.

[1] Witsius indeed (*Melet. Leiden*, p. 296) suggests that the reference here may after all not be to this passage, as we all take for granted, but to another: Non diffiteor interim fieri potuisse ut et alio respexerit Dominus. Magnam affinitatem cum hoc dicto habet Dan. vii. 13, 14, ubi Messias vocatur *Filius hominis*, et repræsentatur ut *Filius Dei*, veniens in nubibus cœli ad Antiquum Dierum, additurque *datum ei esse dominatum et regnum*. Quum itaque professus esset Nathanaël Jesum esse Filium Dei et Regem Israëlis, utrumque admittit Jesus, protestaturque se revera esse filium hominis, de quo prophetaverit Daniel, quod manifestum futurum ipse præ-nunciat ex insigni illo ministerio sibi ab angelis exhibendo. Nam sicut ad majestatis divinæ gloriam facit quod thronus Antiqui Dierum myriadibus angelorum cinctus sit, ita et argumentum cælestis regni in filio hominis est,

What Israel saw, the '*Israelite indeed*' shall behold the same ;[1] yea, what the one saw but in dream, the other shall behold in waking reality ; and more and better even than this ; for in that earlier vision God was a God afar off ; the Lord stood above the ladder and spake from heaven ; but now standing at its foot, He speaks as the Son of man from earth, for now the Word has been made flesh ; and the tabernacle of God is with men (Rev. xxi. 3).

At the same time there is that in this promise of Christ which has at all times perplexed interpreters not a little. This is plain from the omission of '*hereafter*,' or '*from henceforth*,'[2] in many Greek copies ; the absence of which, however, while it might lighten, would not remove the difficulty ; as again from various gratuitous suppositions, as of some special, though unrecorded, 'vision of angels' vouchsafed to Philip and Nathanael. It appears not less in the fact that several expositors, Augustine for instance uniformly,[3] explain away these '*angels* into *messengers* of the New Covenant, apostles and others, who should find in Christ the middle point of all their spiritual activity—going forth from Him, and returning to Him again (Luke x. 1, 17). These all can only be regarded at the best as devices for escaping such difficulties as this passage may offer, not as methods of solving them. Equally unprofitable, and leading as little to a true solution, are all those

---

quod iidem angeli ad ipsius nutum quaquaversum volent, adscendentes et descendentes prout jusserit. This is certainly ingenious; but does not shake one's conviction that the other and generally received allusion is the true one.

[1] Augustine (*Serm.* 122. 5) Quasi diceret, Cujus nomine te appellavi, ipsius somnium in te apparebit. Cf. *Con. Faust.* xii. 26. Grotius : Quod ibi in somnio vidit Israël, idem vigilans visurus dicitur verus Israëlita.

[2] Ἀπ' ἄρτι, which some suppose to have found its way here from Matt. xxvi. 64.

[3] *Con. Faust.* xii. 26 ; *Enarr. in Ps.* xliv. 8 ; *In Ev. Joh. Tract.* 7.

considerations whether this word of Christ's might not have been fulfilled at the Baptism, when, as we are told, the heavens were rent (Mark i. 10; cf. Ezek. i. 1), or at the Temptation, when angels ministered to Him (Matt. iv. 11), or in the garden of Gethsemane, when an angel strengthened Him (Luke xxii. 43), or at some other moment when we may presume angels in especially near communion with the Lord. He who enquires *when* this promise was fulfilled, declares by the fact of making such enquiry that he has failed to enter into the meaning of the promise. We can select no single moment as that in which it found its fulfilment, because it was being fulfilled evermore.

Assuredly the Lord would indicate by these wondrous words that He should henceforward be the middle point of a free intercourse, yea, of an uninterrupted communion, between God and men; that in Him should be the meeting place of heaven and of earth (Ephes. i. 10; Col. i. 20); which should be no longer two, as sin had made them, separated and estranged from one another, but henceforward one, now that righteousness had looked down from heaven, and truth had flourished out of the earth.[1] And this the glory of Christ they, his disciples,

---

[1] Calvin well: Multum autem errant meo judicio qui anxie quærunt tempus et locum, ubi et quando Nathanaël et reliqui cælum apertum viderint. Potius enim quiddam continuum designat, quod semper extare debebat in ejus regno. Fateor quidem aliquoties discipulis visos fuisse angelos, qui hodie non apparent; . . . sed si probe reputemus quod tunc factum est, perpetuo viget. Nam quum prius clausum esset regnum Dei, vere in Christo apertum fuit. Chemnitz (*Harm. Evang.* c. 25): Docet igitur Christus, officium suum esse cælum aperire, et cælestia rursus conjungere cum genere humano, quod per peccatum et a Deo et a sanctis angelis avulsum fuerat. It is very noticeable that the only occasion on which that phrase of depth and meaning inexhaustible, namely, 'the kingdom of God' (βασιλεία τοῦ Θεοῦ), occurs either in the Old Testament or the Apocrypha,

should behold, and should understand that they too, children of men, were by Him, the Son of man, made citizens of a kingdom which, not excluding earth, embraced also heaven. From earth there should go up evermore supplications, aspirations, prayers,—and these by the ministration of angels (Rev. viii. 3, 4), if some still want a certain literal fulfilment of the promise ;—from heaven there should evermore come down graces, blessings, gifts, aid to the faithful and plagues for them that would hurt them (Rev. viii. 5 ; Acts xii. 7, 23). Heaven and earth should henceforward be in continual interchange of these blessed angels,

> ' And earth be changed to heaven, and heaven to earth ;
> One kingdom, joy and union without end : '

the Son of man, Jesus of Nazareth, being the central point in which these two kingdoms met,[1] the golden clasp which bound them indissolubly together.[2] And so it is only according to the right order that these angels should be described as first *ascending,* and only then *descending* ; when we might rather have anticipated that they would have descended first, and ascended afterwards. The order of priority here can only be rightly understood, when we lift ourselves above all notions of space or room or of a local heaven. The angels needed not to come

it is with a manifest allusion to Jacob's dream, in which dream, vouchsafed to the patriarch, it is said, ' Wisdom shewed him *the kingdom of God'* (Wisd. x. 10).

[1] Calvin : Ideo super ipsum ascendere et descendere dicuntur : non quod illi soli ministrent, sed quod ejus respectu atque id ejus honorem complectantur suâ curâ totum Ecclesiæ corpus.

[2] The heathen parallel to this of Jacob's ladder, thus binding heaven and earth together,—that which is, as it were, a feeling after this glorious union which Christ here at once proclaims and constitutes,—is the golden chain by which poets feigned that this earth of ours was linked to the throne of Zeus.

down on the Son of man, before they went up from Him ;
where He was, there were they. The person of the
Son of man was, so to speak, the point of starting for
them ; and because the Lord here contemplates Himself
not as in heaven, but upon earth, they therefore ascend
first, and only afterwards descend.[1]

A few words in conclusion on the question whether
this Nathanael of St. John is one and the same with the
Bartholomew of the synoptic Gospels. The identifying
of the two, which, when once suggested, carries so much
probability with it, and which in modern times has found
favour with so many, was quite unknown to the early
Church. Indeed Augustine more than once enters at
large into the question, *why* Nathanael, to whom his Lord
bore such honourable testimony, whom He welcomed
so gladly, was *not* elected into the number of the Twelve.
The reason he gives is curious. He sees evidence in
Nathanael's question, ' *Can there any good thing come out
of Nazareth?* ' that this disciple was a Rabbi, learned in
the wisdom of the Jewish schools (that he should be
numbered among fishermen, John xxi. 2, makes this
unlikely, yet not impossible) ; but such the Lord would
in no case choose to lay the foundations of his Church
(cf. 1 Cor. i. 26) ; lest that Church might even seem to

---

[1] Plato in a beautiful passage (*Symp.* 23) describes the middle powers
which maintain the commerce between heaven and earth, gods and men, in
language that forcibly reminds us of this of our Lord. I will quote his
words, for though sufficiently familiar, I have never seen them brought into
relation with the Scripture before us : καὶ γὰρ πᾶν τὸ δαιμόνιον μεταξύ ἐστι
θεοῦ τε καὶ θνητοῦ, ἑρμηνεῦον καὶ διαπορθμεῦον ϲεοῖς τὰ παρ' ἀνθρώπων, καὶ ἀνθρώποις τὰ παρὰ θεῶν, τῶν μὲν τὰς δεήσεις καὶ θυσίας, τῶν ϲὲ τὰς ἐπιτάξεις τε
καὶ ἀμοιβὰς τῶν ϲυσιῶν· ἐν μέσῳ ϲὲ ὂν ἀμφοτέρων συμπληροῖ, ὥστε τὸ πᾶν αὐτὸ
αὑτῷ συνϲεϲέσθαι.

stand in the wisdom of man rather than in the power of God.[1] The arguments for the identity of the two, which identity was first suggested, I believe, by Rupert of Deutz in the twelfth century, are very strong; though not so absolutely decisive as those for the identity of Sheshbazzar (Ezra i. 8, 11) and Zerubbabel (Ezra ii. 2). They are mainly these; that the calling of Nathanael here is co-ordinated with that of apostles, as of equal significance; that on a later occasion we meet him in the midst of apostles, some named before him, some after (John xxi. 1, 2); that the three earlier Evangelists never mention Nathanael, the fourth never Bartholomew; that Philip and Bartholomew in the catalogue of the apostles are grouped together, as a pair of friends, but with Philip first, even as he is here the earlier in Christ (Matt. x. 3; Mark iii. 18); that the custom of double names seems to have been almost universal at that time in Judæa, so that all or well nigh all the apostles bore more than one; to all which may be added that Bartholomew, signifying son of Tolmai (2 Sam. iii. 3), is of itself no proper name. All these arguments in favour of the identity, with nothing which can be urged against it, bring it very nearly to a certainty, that he to whom the promise of the vision of an opened heaven, with angels ascending and descending on the Son of man, was vouchsafed, was no other than the apostle Bartholomew.[2]

---

[1] *Enarr. in Ps.* lxv. 2; *In Ev. Joh.* tract. vii. § 17. Cf. Gregory the Great (*Moral.* xxxiii. 16): Prædicatores infirmos adjectosque habere studuit Dominus; unde in Evangelio Nathanaëlem laudat, nec tamen in sorte prædicantium numerat; quia ad prædicandum eum tales venire debuerant, qui de laude propriâ nihil habebant.

[2] The subject is well discussed by John Henry Newman, *Sermons on the Festivals of the Church, Sermon* 27; and compare Keim, *Jesu von Nazara,* vol. 2, p. 311. I need hardly observe that in *The Christian Year* the identity is taken for granted.

3. CHRIST AND THE SAMARITAN WOMAN.

John iv. 1-42.

IT is very characteristic of the Eastern colouring of Scripture, that so many of its most interesting events should find place in the neighbourhood of wells, and in one way or other stand in some connexion with them. By a well the loveliest idyllic scene in Genesis, rich as it is in such, I refer to the first meeting of Abraham's servant with the future wife of Isaac, is laid (Gen. xxiv. 11-28); there Jacob's first greeting of Rachel (Gen. xxix. 1-10); with a well too is closely linked an important passage in the life of Moses (Exod. ii. 16, 17). But deeper, more attractive, laying a mightier hold on the Church in all after-times than any or all of these, is the interest which attaches to a meeting beside Jacob's well, of which we have the record here.

The Evangelist explains to us first the circumstances which brought that meeting about: ' *When therefore the Lord knew how the Pharisees had heard that Jesus made and baptized more disciples than John, . . . He left Judæa and departed again into Galilee.*' This quitting of Judæa, with the retreat into the safer Galilee recorded here, I identify with Matt. iv. 12, Mark i. 14, Luke iv. 14, in the synoptic Gospels. As Christ had taught his disciples that there were occasions when, without compromising the fealty which they owed to the truth, they might withdraw from the malice of their foes (Matt. x. 23 ; cf. John xi. 57), so He was Himself withdrawing now.   That malice, as He knew, would be roused to the uttermost by the manifest successes of his ministry, by the multitude of disciples whom He had baptized—more even than the Baptist himself (iii. 26–30) ; although the mere ministerial act of baptism, as St. John is careful to note, He accomplished by other hands than his own ; '*though Jesus Himself baptized not, but his disciples*' (cf. Acts x. 48 ; 1 Cor. i. 14–16), He reserving the baptism with the Holy Ghost for Himself.   He had left Judæa, the head-quarters of all the bitterest opposition to Himself and to his work ; and as, in retiring to Galilee, He did not choose to take the circuit of Peræa, which was the manner with some of the stricter sort of Jews, who would come into no contact whatever with the heretical Samaritans, '*He must needs go through Samaria.*'[1]   St. John is thus careful to note that this was no mission to the Samaritans which the Lord undertook.   On the contrary, the law which He imposed on his disciples, 'And into any city of the Samaritans enter ye not' (Matt. x. 5), this, during the days of his flesh, He observed Himself.   He was not sent ' but to the lost sheep of the house of Israel ' (Matt. xv. 24 ; Acts xiii. 46) ; and if any grace reached Samaritan or heathen, it was, so to speak, but by accident, a crumb falling from the children's table.

' *Then cometh He to a city of Samaria, which is called Sychar.*'   The unusual form in which the name of this city here appears, must not hinder us from recognizing in it the Sichem where Abraham built an altar (Gen. xii. 6) ;

[1] See Josephus, *Vita,* § 52.

under the oak in whose neighbourhood Jacob buried the idols of his household (Gen. xxxv. 4) ; the city which Simeon and Levi so cruelly and treacherously wasted, forfeiting their birthright thereby (Gen. xxxiv. ; xlix. 5–7) ; not far from which Joseph was sold (Gen. xxxvii. 12) : the last resting place of his bones (Josh. xxiv. 32) a city thus of ancient fame in Scripture, as of great political importance at some periods of Jewish history ; so much so that in all likelihood, had the tribe of Ephraim attained to the leadership of the nation instead of Judah, had this tribe not forfeited and let go the preeminence which it possessed for a time (Ps. lxxviii. 67), this Sichem, Sychem (Acts vii. 19), or Shechem, instead of Jerusalem, would have been the metropolis of the kingdom. It was in Joshua's time the centre to which the tribes were gathered (Josh. xxiv. 1) ;[1] the seat of the abortive kingdom of Abimelech (Judg. ix.) ; a city twice mentioned by the Psalmist for no other reason than its dignity and strength (Ps. lx. 6 ; cviii. 6) ; the place whither the tribes were gathered on that fatal day when the great schism of the nation actually began, and for a while the chief city of the revolted ten (1 Kin. xii. 1, 25), until, that is, the capital was transferred first by Jeroboam to Tirzah (1 Kin. xiv. 17 ; xv. 33), and finally by Omri to Samaria (1 Kin. xvi. 24). With the building by the Samaritans of the temple on Mount Gerizim, of which more presently, Shechem, standing immediately at the foot of that mountain, on the ridge or saddle which connects it with Mount Ebal, became the ecclesiastical metropolis of the Samaritans, the middle point of their worship (Ecclus. l. 26), and continues

---

[1] See Hengstenberg, *Authentie d. Pentateuch,* vol. ii. p. 13.

such to this day for the feeble remnant of them which survives.[1]

But if ' *Sychar* ' be thus identified with Sichem, and only a few, as Ewald and Meyer for example, refuse to identify them,[2] how are we to account for the form which the word has here assumed ? We must for this keep in mind the enigmatic character of St. John's Gospel, the mystical significance which he loves to trace in names, either to find in them, or himself to suggest (see ix. 7 ; xi. 16). His Gospel, apparently less thoroughly steeped in the spirit of the Old Testament, is indeed far more so, is connected with it by finer and subtler links, than any one of the other three. A change in the form of the word, if only it were significant, would be quite in the spirit of the Old Testament, and in agreement with the importance which names everywhere there assume ; being, as they are, continually modified, now for the better, as Abram into Abraham (Gen. xvii. 5), Sarai into Sarah (Gen. xvii. 15), Oshea into Jehosuah (Num. xiii. 16) ; now for the worse, thus Bethel into Bethaven (Hos. x. 5), Achan, because he *troubled* Israel (Josh. vii. 25), reappearing as Achar (1 Chron. ii. 7) ; or it may be that a new name is superadded to the old (Gen. xxxii. 28 ; xxxv. 10 ; Judg. vi. 32), sometimes puts the old quite out of use ; this new

---

[1] It is now known as Nabulus, a corruption of Neapolis, which name was given to the city by the Herodians, who in the Roman times adorned and in part rebuilt it. On all which concerns Nabulus, Gerizim, the Samaritans of the past and of the present, see Robinson's *Researches in Palestine*, vol. iii. pp. 92–139. There is much too of original information in the article *Samaria*, in Herzog's *Encyclopädie*, vol. xiii. pp. 359–391 ; and also in Heidenheim's *Deutsche Vierteljahrsschrift*, No. i. pp. 1–43 ; 78–128, who, p. 14, gives further notices of the literature on the subject.

[2] Keim, who has a learned note on the subject, does not absolutely decide in either sense. (*Jesu von Nazara*, vol. iii. p. 15.)

also being sometimes for honour (Gen. xlii. 45 ; Dan. i. 7 ; iv. 8), or more rarely for dishonour.

How deeply seated in our nature this disposition to change or modify names is, the curious ways in which it is evermore at work, springing as it does out of a sense that the name connotes, or if it does not connote, should be made to connote, the object which is named, there are examples in multitudes to prove.[1] That the kingdom of grace has not refused to avail itself of this instinct, the many instances just now cited in proof abundantly testify. St. John by this turn of the word, which has brought it into closest connexion with the Hebrew for a lie, declares at what rate he esteemed the whole Samaritan worship, by anticipation declares at what rate it was esteemed by his Lord (see ver. 22). If religion be anything higher than the outcome and utterance of man's spiritual needs and desires, if it rest not on what man has thought and felt about God, but on that which God has revealed about Himself, and only has worth as it is the true revelation by God of Himself to his creatures, then that whole Samaritan worship was a hollow cheat, a husk with no kernel within ; and, professing as it did to be much more than this, was a lie. If it sound severe on the part of the beloved apostle to say as much, and if some urge, as against this explanation of *Sychar* put here for Sichem, that he never could have said it, one can only reply that the truth *is* severe, that in the very faithfulness of love it must declare darkness to be dark, and

---

[1] For various illustrations of this determination to bring the name and the thing into a real relation with one another see my *Study of Words*, 13th edit. pp. 29–38. Vigilantius becomes Dormitantius, Epiphanes Epimanes, Tiberius Claudius Nero Biberius Caldius Mero, Athanasius Satanasius, and so on

bitterness to be bitter ; cannot affirm that the one is light, or the other sweet; or, when men have left God's truth, and are worshipping instead of this some invention of their own, that their worship is anything better than a lie.

This city was '*near to the parcel of ground that Jacob gave to his son Joseph*' (Gen. xxxiii. 19; xlviii. 22 ; Josh. xxiv. 32). '*Now Jacob's well*[1] *was there.*' Of Jacob's well there is no mention in the Old Testament; though we learn there that it was the custom of the patriarchs to dig wells (Gen. xxi. 30; xxvi. 18–22). There seems no reason whatever to call in question its identity with the well which the Samaritans of the neighbourhood designate by this name to the present day. The digging of it must have been a work of enormous labour. Maundrell, who visited it in 1697, gives this account : '❘It is dug in a firm rock, and contains about three yards in diameter, and thirty-five in depth, five of which we found full of water.' The rock has since crumbled, or in other ways the well has been in part filled in, and a recent measurement gives a depth of seventy-five feet only, the spring at the bottom

---

[1] It would certainly have been preferable to render πηγή here by 'fountain' or 'spring' than '*well*;' for we can better understand 'a springing fountain' than a 'springing well' (ver. 14). Πηγή and φρέαρ, it may be observed, are used now the one, and now the other, throughout this chapter: but there is always sufficient reason to account for the use of one or of the other: thus πηγή twice in this verse, and at verse 14, φρέαρ at verses 11, 12. Our Translators, who have rendered both by '*well*,' have failed to mark the alternation of words; which the Vulgate has noted, rendering the first by 'fons,' the second by 'puteus.' And indeed 'all the Old Versions except the Anglo-Saxon render the Greek literally, giving a different term for πηγή and for φρέαρ' (Malan, *Notes on St. John*, p. 49). The two Augustine here discriminates well (*In Joh. Evang. Tract.* 15): Omnis puteus fons, non omnis fons puteus. Ubi enim aqua de terrâ manat et usui præbetur haurientibus, fons dicitur: sed si in promtu et superficie sit, fons tantum dicitur; si autem in alto et profundo sit, ita puteus vocatur ut fontis nomen non amittat. We have φρεάτων πηγή, Prov. v. 15.

being choked. '*Jesus therefore, being wearied with his journey, sat thus*[1] *on the well; and it was about the sixth hour.*' The weariness of Christ, so soon to be the refreshment of one, should in due time be the refreshment of all. St. John perhaps may name the exact hour, in this way to bring more vividly to our consciousness the oppression and burden of the time : it was '*the sixth hour,*' exactly the heat of the middle noon. Yet we must not leave out of sight that elsewhere he notes the hour, where it is difficult to say what of emphasis the story gains thereby, as at i. 39 ; xix. 14. Perhaps here, as there, it is the significance of the event, which makes its every detail of interest to himself, and as he judges to his readers.

'*There cometh a woman of Samaria to draw water ;*' a woman,[2] not of the city of Samaria, for that was some six miles distant, but of the country (so Acts viii. 5), still called by the name of that city which had been once its capital. The office was a woman's (1 Sam. ix. 11) ; and to that same well she oftentimes may have come already ; day by day, perhaps, during many a weary year. And now she came once more, little guessing how different should be the issue of this day's coming from that of all the days which had gone before.[3] The benefit and blessing which here lay, as it were, in ambush for her, was not indeed, as she was fain at the first to imagine, that she should

---

[1] Οὕτως, which may be explained with Chrysostom, ἁπλῶς καὶ ὡς ἔτυχε. Bengel : *Sic*, uti qualiscumque loci opportunitas ferebat, sine pompâ, solus, ut qui non præ se ferret expectationem Samaritidis, sed meræ lassitudinis causâ quietem vellet capere. Admiranda popularitas vitæ Jesu ! Compare Mark iv. 36.

[2] The Roman martyrology knows her name, Photina, the names also of her children.

[3] Augustine : Venit mulier ad puteum, et fontem quem non speravit, invenit,

never need to come and draw water from that well again
(ver. 15); but, far better than this, that in the midst of
all the weary toil, outward and inward, of this earthly
life, she should have within herself a fountain of joy,
springing up unto life eternal, should draw water with joy
from unfailing wells of salvation.

She had probably already filled her pitcher, when the
stranger beside the well, whom she may have seen only
to avoid, for she recognized in him those unmistakeable
features of Jewish physiognomy with which the Samaritans
had nothing in common, to her surprise addressed her
and to her greater surprise addressed her with a request:
'*Give me to drink*' (cf. Gen. xxiv. 16, 17; 1 Kin. xvii.
10). A real thirst, witnessing against all docetic notions
concerning the person of the Lord (cf. John xix. 28;
Matt. xxi. 18), was one motive of this request; though
that which He most truly thirsted after was her faith, the
salvation of her soul;[1] for we see hunger and thirst not
so much forgotten as disappearing in the joy of winning
such a lost soul for the kingdom of his Father (ver. 31,
32). In this request of his, and in the discourse to
which it was the prelude, there was a threefold testimony
against the narrow-heartedness of his age and people—
against that of the Jew who hated the Samaritan, of the
Rabbi who would have thought scorn to hold this familiar intercourse with a woman (see ver. 27), of the
Pharisee who would have shrunk from this near contact
with a sinner (Luke vii. 39; xv. 2; xix. 7).

The notice which follows, '*for his disciples were gone
away unto the city to buy meat*,' is commonly taken to

---

[1] Augustine: Ille autem qui bibere quærebat, fidem ipsius mulieris
quærebat.

explain the constraint under which He lay of asking this
favour of the woman.   The disciples were gone, and had
left him ' *nothing to draw with* ' (ver 11), such as, had
they been present, would have been at his command.
But how very unlikely that the means of drawing water
should have been part of their travelling gear; or if it
was, that they should have carried this with them into
the town.   The notice here interposed has no such super-
ficial meaning.   The Lord, allowing the disciples all to
leave Him, had of intention made this solitude for Himself, that He might the easier win to repentance and
confession of sin the poor sinner for whom He had appointed this meeting, though she knew it not;[1] for, while
there is none who may not take to himself that beautiful
line of the *Dies Iræ*,

Quærens me sedisti lassus,

to her of first and best right it belongs.   This absence of
theirs was designed, was part of his counsel of love in her
behalf.   The freedom from interruption which it afforded
He now improves to the uttermost; for, Himself the great
' Fisher of men ' (Mark i. 17; Luke v. 10), He is as
watchful and eager to take a single soul by the angle as
a vast multitude of souls at once by the casting net or the
sean; giving here a lesson to those whom He sends into
the world to ' catch men,' which they will do well never
to forget.   Hengstenberg, indeed, thinks that *all* had not
left, that St. John was a witness of the interview which
he describes; but for this there is no shadow of ground.

He who asks a favour places himself, in the estimate

---

[1] Corn. à Lapide : Factum id est tacitâ Dei providentiâ, ut, discipulis
omnibus in urbem dimissis, solus ipse, liberius cum muliere impudicâ, ejus
pudori consulens, ageret.

of a common mind, though often it is exactly the contrary, in a position of inferiority to the person from whom the favour is asked, and with whom it lies to grant or to withhold it. And thus there was a certain satisfaction which the woman could not conceal, a gratifying of her national vanity, wounded so often by Jewish taunts, in thus having a Jew a petitioner for a favour from her, a Samaritan.[1] The humiliation, for such she esteemed it, was much greater than if she, a Samaritan, had been a suitor for an equal favour from a Jew ; inasmuch as the holding aloof and the refusing to be on terms of communion, either social or ecclesiastical, had been at the first, and still was, mainly on the side of the Jews ; who denied, rightly as regarded the fact, though wrongly in respect of the temper in which they did it, that the Samaritans had any claims to be considered as heirs with themselves of the promises made to Abraham and his seed. It was, as St. John expresses it, for the words are not the woman's, but his, the Jews that would ' *have no dealings with the Samaritans*,' no familiar intercourse, that is, and indeed none of any kind which they could avoid ; and only as a consequence necessarily involved in this, that the Samaritans have no dealings with the Jews ; and so it had been from the beginning (Ezra iv. 1–3). The woman, therefore, not certainly a daughter of Rebekah in this (see Gen. xxiv. 17–20), instead of complying with his request, asks, with a feeling that for the present the tables are turned, and with the intention that He shall feel this also, ' *How is it that Thou, being a Jew, askest drink of me, which am a woman of Samaria ?* ' An Israelite she

---

[1] See my *Notes on the Parables*, 11th edit. p. 314 sqq.

would have called herself, for such the Samaritans claimed to be, as descending from the tribe of Ephraim. A ' *Jew* ' for them was one of the tribe, or at most of the kingdom, of Judah.

If we take this as the temper out of which her question proceeds, the Lord's reply will then exactly meet the thought of her heart. He is not the receiver, but the giver. ' Thou errest in thinking that it is I who need thy help, when thou rather hast need of mine. *If thou knewest the gift of God, and who it is that saith to thee, Give me to drink; thou wouldest have asked of Him, and He would have given thee living water.*' This ' *gift of God* ' has been very variously interpreted. Augustine understands by it the Holy Ghost. Hengstenberg will not allow that there can be any question on the matter, but refers to Isai. ix. 6, ' to us a Son is *given*,' and to John iii. 16, as decisive proofs that Christ designated Himself as ' *the gift of God.*' By ' *the gift of God* ' Grotius and others understand the Lord more generally to mean that gracious and golden opportunity vouchsafed to her, and as yet to her alone among all her people;[1] 'If thou knewest this, and what it is to have met Me here, the Saviour of the world, thou wouldest have been a petitioner of mine, for a far better gift than any I have sought at thy hands.' Lampe, citing Rom. vi. 22, where ' eternal life ' is styled ' the gift of God,'[2] and strengthening his position by the aid of such passages as Isai. lv. 1 ; Rev. xxii. 17, understands generally that ' eternal life ' to be ' *the gift of God*,' whereof here the Saviour speaks. But these explanations, one and all, seem to me either too

---

[1] Occasio nempe quam tibi nunc Deus præstat, quantumvis Samaritidi.
[2] Χάρισμα there, δῶρον here.

vague and indefinite, or otherwise beside the mark ; and
the right interpretation to have been strangely overlooked
by most expositors; not indeed by all, for Stier has it.
To me this carries such conviction that, unless so many
had missed, I should have been tempted to say that it
was impossible to miss it. ' *The gift of God*' is here an
anticipation of what is immediately to follow, namely, ' *He
would have given thee living water.*' ' If thou knewest,' the
Lord would say, ' that God has given to souls thirsting in
the wilderness of this world water of life, such as will
slake the thirst, not of their bodies but of their souls, and
" *who it is that saith to thee, Give me to drink*," even He
that has that water to bestow, whom the Father has made
to be Himself a fountain and spring of this life, then,
instead of moving the embers of that wretched quarrel
between Samaritans and Jews, thou wouldest have asked
these waters at his hands.' The ' *living water*' seems
to me, beyond all doubt, to be itself ' *the gift of God*'
whereof Christ speaks.[1]

Having asked for water, He sets forth this ' *gift*' under
the image of water; as at John vi. 48–51, where men are
waiting on Him for the bread that perishes, He sets forth
the same ' gift' under that of bread. In this as in every
thing else a pattern to those who should come after, He

---

[1] There is a singular decorum in the use of words here. The woman has
said, not unnaturally, ' How is it that Thou *askest* ($\alpha i\tau \epsilon \hat{\iota} \varsigma$) of me ? ' But
$\alpha i\tau \epsilon \hat{\iota} \nu$ is a word of petition as from an inferior to a superior, in this different
from $\dot{\epsilon}\rho\omega\tau \hat{\alpha}\nu$, which has more of equality in it (see my *Synonyms of the New
Testament*, § 40). Christ therefore, when He refers to that request of hers,
does not take up and allow her word. He says not, ' who it is *that asketh
of thee*,' but ' who it is *that saith to thee*' ($\dot{o}$ $\lambda\dot{\epsilon}\gamma\omega\nu$ $\sigma o\iota$) ; while the *asking*
He goes on to describe as the proper attitude for her: ' thou wouldest *have
asked* ($\dot{\eta}\tau\eta\sigma\alpha\varsigma$) of Him.' There lies often in such little details as this an
implicit assertion of the unique dignity of his person, which it is very
interesting and not unimportant to trace.

links on the heavenly to the earthly, uses the earthly as a ladder by which He mounts up to the heavenly. At the same time He must have been quite prepared for a temporary misunderstanding of his words. ' *Living water* ' is not necessarily equivalent with ' water of life ' (Rev. xxi. 6; xxii. 1, 17) in the highest spiritual sense of the words. On the contrary there are natural waters which have, and in their lower sphere deserve, this name; that is, fresh springing waters, as contrasted either with rain-water gathered into cisterns, or indeed with any other, the water of reservoirs; and in this natural sense the phrase often occurs in the Old Testament; as at Gen. xxvi. 19; Lev. xiv. 5; Cant. iv. 15.[1] Here, however, the words are used in their highest sense,—waters, which coming from Him in whom is the absolute life, who is the αὐτοζωή (John i. 4; x. 40), impart life to as many as they reach. In one of the ' visions of God,' seen by the prophet Ezekiel, we have a magnificent symbolism of this, the life-giving power of these waters: ' And it shall come to pass that every thing shall live whither the river cometh;' that is, the river issuing from under the threshold of the House of God (xlvii. 1–9; cf. Joel iii. 18; Zech. xiv. 8).

Yet although she misses the deeper meaning of his speech, taking the figurative literally, and the spiritual naturally (cf. John iii. 4; vi. 52), there is that in the words and bearing of this stranger, which has already so far inspired her with respect, that the ' *Sir*,' or ' *Lord*,' which was absent from her first answer, finds place in her second; however she may hardly maintain herself

---

[1] In all these places the LXX have ὕδωρ ζῶν, = vivum flumen, vivus fons, in Latin.

throughout it at the level of respect which this opening word would imply.   Indeed she proceeds with the evident intention of showing Him that these pretensions of his involved an absurdity : ' *Thou hast nothing to draw with,*[1] *and the well is deep ; from whence then hast Thou this living water ?*   From this well it cannot be that Thou wilt draw that living water of which Thou speakest, for the well is deep ' (as we have seen, more than a hundred feet deep, with only a few feet of water at the bottom), ' and Thou hast no means with which to draw it up.   And even if Thou hadst discovered another well ' (for this is the connexion of ver. 11 and 12), ' *art Thou greater than our father Jacob* ' (cf. viii. 53), for such ' *father* ' she calls him, though with no shadow of right [2] (Matt. x. 5) ; ' *who gave us the well, and· drank thereof himself, and his children,*[3] *and his cattle ?* ' [4]   That Jacob himself and his sons should have drunk of that well might be taken as an evidence of its sweetness, that his servants and flocks and herds should have drunk of it, an evidence of its abund-ance,[5] the waters of it thus satisfying the needs of him and

---

[1] The ἄντλημα here, ' *bucket* ' in most of our early Versions, ' *hauritorium* ' in Augustine (the word has not found its way into our Dictionaries of later Latinity), must not be confounded with the ὑδρία or ' *water-pot* ' which the woman presently leaves behind in her haste to communicate her good tidings to her people (ver. 28).   It is the 'situla, generally made of skin, with three cross sticks tied round the mouth to keep it open.   It is let down by a rope of goats' hair, and may be seen lying on the curb stones of almost every well in the Holy Land ' (Malan).   We may suppose the woman to have held this in her hand, while she talked with the Lord, and reminded Him that He had nothing of the kind.

[2] Theophylact : πατέρα ἑαυτῆς ποιεῖται τὸν Ἰακώβ, εἰς τὴν Ἰουδαϊκὴν εὐγένειαν αὐτὴν συνωθοῦσα.

[3] Or ' *his sons* ' rather, ' since one daughter to twelve sons would not make them τέκνα τοῦ Ἰακώβ in a narrative written in Greek ' (Malan).

[4] Θρέμματα probably includes household servants as well.

[5] Theophylact : τὸ δὲ καὶ αὐτὸς ἐξ αὐτοῦ ἔπιεν, ἐπαινός ἐστι τῆς τοῦ ὕδατος ἡδύτητος· τὸ δὲ καὶ τὰ θρέμματα αὐτοῦ, ἐνδεικτικόν ἐστι τῆς ἀφθονίας.

of all that were his. ' Art Thou greater,' she would imply,
' that so Thou couldst give to those waters, even if Thou
hadst discovered such, a higher consecration, or constitute
them waters of greater price to us than these with which
the patriarch Jacob has endowed us?' There speaks out
in this question of hers a certain slight resentment at
what seems to her an intentional depreciation of this
holy well, for such no doubt it was esteemed by these
Samaritans. The well was one of the venerable memorials
of the past (it is possibly alluded to Gen. xlix. 22 ; Deut.
xxxiii. 28), by aid of which they sought to put themselves
in connexion with the early patriarchal history. It lay,
as we have seen, in the parcel of ground given by Jacob
to his son Joseph (ver. 5, 6), and it was from Joseph that
the Samaritans boasted their descent. This we should
conclude from the fact of their claiming to be the representatives of the ten tribes, of which Ephraim, descended
from Joseph, was chief; even if Josephus did not twice
expressly mention the fact.[1] Here is the key to the
voluble eloquence, not unmixed with a certain tartness,
of her reply. The woman suspects, though she cannot
quite understand his words, that He, a Jew, means to
cast a slight upon the venerable traditions and memorials
which her people claimed as especially, if not peculiarly,
their own.

The Lord does not entangle Himself in a direct reply
to the question, ' *Art Thou greater than our father Jacob?*'
which could lead to no result ; and yet implicitly He does
reply. For as, in magnifying the bread which He would
give, as compared with the manna which Moses gave,
He reminds his hearers that those who ate the manna died

---

[1] *Antt.* IX. 14. 3; XI. 8. 6.

notwithstanding, leaving them to draw the conclusion
that He, who gives bread which if a man eat thereof he
shall not die, must be greater than Moses, who could give
no such ' salve of immortality ' (John vi. 49, 50); even
so the same follows here : ' I *am* greater than your father
Jacob ; for this water which you boast to have received
from him does not slake thirst for ever. *Whosoever
drinketh of this water shall thirst again.* But it is otherwise with the water of which I am the dispenser. *Whosoever drinketh of the water that I shall give him shall
never thirst.'* It is needless to observe of how much wider
application the words, ' *shall thirst again,*' are than to the
matter immediately in hand. All human suppliances for
the satisfying of the cravings of the body or of the soul
have in them this defect, that they do not satisfy for ever.
They only serve to dull and deaden the present sense of
the want, but do not remove it. That want after a while
revives again in its strength ; for man is full of hunger
and thirst; a fact which may, indeed, be his heaven,
yet may also be his hell. But the water which Christ
gives, slakes the spirit's thirst, and slakes it for ever—not,
of course, as though one draught of it would do this ; it
is he who drinks, and who continues to drink, that shall
not thirst any more.

It is worth our while here to note how Christ gathers
to a head innumerable promises and invitations of the Old
Testament, and claims them as fulfilled in Himself; thus
eminently Isai. lv. 1 ; cf. xli. 18 ; xlviii. 21 ; xlix. 10 ;
even as this is by no means the only place in the New
Testament where He sets forth the blessings which He
imparts to the children of men by aid of the same figurative
language, at once so beautiful, so familiar, and so intelli-

gible to all; thus see John vi. 35; vii. 37; Rev. vii. 16; xxi. 6. He is Himself the true ' fountain of Jacob ' (Deut. xxxiii. 28); this name He implicitly challenges as his own. There is only One, who can be what Christ here declares that He is, namely, ' a fountain of living waters ' (see Jer. ii. 13; xvii. 13), and that is God. On the strength of this saying Augustine rightly claims Ps. xxxvi. 9, ' With Thee is the fountain of life,' as fulfilled in Christ, and brings that passage into closest connexion with this.[1]

But what, it may be fitly asked, is the exact force of the promise which follows, ' *But the water that I shall give him shall be in him*[2] *a well of water springing up into everlasting life*'? Is it not this? ' He who receives this living water of Me shall become himself in some sort, although of course only in a secondary sense, a springing well; no cistern merely to contain,[3] but a springing fountain, out of which shall flow, these same waters;[4] shall minister to others the same salvation which has been

---

[1] De quâ ergo aquâ daturus est, nisi de illâ, de quâ dictum est, Apud Te est fons vitæ? Nam quomodo sitient, qui inebriabuntur ab ubertate domûs tuæ?

[2] Origen here asks, τίς δὲ ἐν ἑαυτῷ ἔχων πηγὴν, διψῆσαι υἱός τε ἔσται;

[3] H. de S. Victore (*In Eccles. Hom.* 2): Scimus namque quia cisterna idcirco foditur, ut aqua extrinsecus collecta in eam defluat, et ex eâ rursum in usus hominum transitura hauriatur. Sed hæc quia venam vivam non habet, quantumlibet magna et aquarum collectione redundans videatur, aliquando exhauriri potest et exsiccari; quia cum sublatum fuerit et consumptum quod aliunde infunditur, nihil ei de suo superest unde reparetur. Sed fons qui vivam habet venam, etiamsi modicus est, deficere tamen omnino non potest, neque effusionis suæ defectum aliquando sentit, cui sine defectu semper de proprio incrementum accedit.

[4] The imperial philosopher of Rome uttered a great truth, but an imperfect one; he saw much, but did not see all, did not see that this well of springing water must be fed, and fed evermore, from the ' upper springs,' if it is not presently to fail, and which without this all the digging in the world would profit nothing, when he wrote, ἔνδον βλέπε · ἔνδον ἡ πηγῆ τοῦ ἀγαθοῦ, καὶ ἀεὶ ἀναβλύειν δυναμένη, ἐὰν ἀεὶ σκάπτῃς. Cf. Plutarch, *De Virt. et Vit.* 1.

already ministered to himself; '[1] even as the Lord expresses the same truth elsewhere : ' He that believeth on Me, out of his belly shall flow rivers of living water ' (John vii. 38).[2] There are other images as of the spark, which, fastening where it lights, kindles into a flame and spreads, or of the seed which, taking root, shoots up again into the air ;[3] either of which would lend itself more perfectly to the setting forth of the truth which Christ here proclaims. He does not however think good to travel out of the circle of images which the well and the water supply. And not only shall these waters spring up, but they shall spring up ' *into everlasting life.*' They shall find their own level : they shall return whither they came : coming from God, they shall go to God again.[4] There is a tacit comparison here with the waters of this world, and another superiority claimed over these. Whatever upward impulse they may receive, it is presently spent, and they fall back to the earth again ; but the water of life

---

[1] Origen quotes with approbation Heracleon's interpretation of these words, the same which I have given above : οὐκ ἀπιθάνως δὲ τὸ, ἀλλομένον, διηγήσατο, καὶ τοὺς μεταλαμβάνοντας τοῦ ἄνωθεν ἐπιχορηγουμένου πλουσίως καὶ αὐτοὺς ἐκβλύσαι εἰς τὴν ἑτέρων αἰώνιον ζωὴν τὰ ἐπικεχορηγημένα αὐτοῖς. Gregory of Nyssa, in his *Homilies* on *The Song of Solomon,* has some beautiful remarks in the same sense on Cant. iv. 15, where *the Bride* is compared to ' a well of living waters.' I quote a few words : τοῦτο δὴ τὸ πάντων παραδοξότατον· πάντων γὰρ τῶν φρεάτων ἐν συστήματι τὸ ὕδωρ ἐχόντων, μόνη ἡ Νύμφη διεξοδικὸν ἐν ἑαυτῇ ἔχει τὸ ὕδωρ, ὥστε τὸ μὲν βάθος ἔχειν τοῦ φρέατος, τοῦ δὲ ποταμοῦ τὸ ἀεικίνητον.

[2] Godet (*Comm. sur l'Évangile de S. Jean*): Jésus définit lui-même la nature de l'eau vive ; c'est celle qui, se reproduisant par sa virtualité propre, étanche la soif à mesure qu'elle s'éveille, de sorte que le cœur qui la possède ne peut plus jamais ressentir le tourment du besoin. L'homme dans le cœur duquel jaillit cette source intarissable, possède par conséquent un bonheur indépendant de tous les objets extérieurs.

[3] Maldonatus : Loquitur de aquâ tanquam de plantâ aut semine aliquo quod jactum in terrâ nascatur.

[4] Grotius : Emphasis est in voce *saliet.* Solent enim aquæ salire ad altitudinem usque suæ originis.

is borne upward by a supernatural impulse, till it reaches again that heaven from which it came.[1]

Olshausen and others have invited us to notice, upon these words, the contrast between this promise of Christ and another of the Son of Sirach. In a glorious passage, one of the noblest in the books not directly inspired of the Bible, Wisdom praising herself exclaims, ' They that eat me shall yet be hungry, and they that drink me shall yet be thirsty' (Ecclus. xxiv. 21). We are invited to note here the deep insight into the different blessings of the Old and of the New Covenant, which a comparison between the promises of the two passages affords—the blessing of the Old Covenant, the awakening of the desire, that of the New, the satisfying of this same desire; there the blessing, so to speak, on its more negative, here on its more positive, side. Now whatever truth there may be in the fact thus stated, and a relative truth there is, yet I scarcely think that we can fairly trace it here. When Christ says that whoever drinks of the water which He gives ' *shall never thirst*,' it is surely meant that he shall never thirst for any other water save this living water which He Himself imparts.[2] He too, no less than Wisdom in the elder Covenant, would say that for this water he shall thirst and thirst again. This, that he does so thirst again, that draughts of the waters of life breed no satiety, such as the draughts from the fountains of this

---

[1] Lampe: Elegans hic latet oppositio inter has aquas et illas quæ ex scaturigine terrestri proliciuntur. Quantocunque enim impetu prorumpant, vix tamen ultra aliquot pedes in aërem elevantur. Hic vero sistuntur aquæ quæ vi plane supernaturali in cælum ipsum et vitam æternam saliunt.

[2] Cocceius: Cum eâ satietate non pugnat sitis et fames justitiæ, et spes atque ὑπόστασις et expectatio bonorum Dei in hâc vitâ et translationis in alteram.

world's joy so quickly bring about, that these waters kindle the thirst which they assuage, is not the infelicity of him who drinks, but his blessedness rather. No one counts that it was faring ill with David, then, when he exclaimed, ' As the hart panteth after the waterbrooks, so panteth my soul after Thee, O God; my soul thirsteth for God, for the living God' (Ps. xlii. 1). How many, as they read, have rather yearned that they might be athirst with him, have only mourned that their own thirst was so languid, while they knew that there is a river of God at which this thirst may be at once stilled and quickened, stilled in all which implies a want and a discomfort, quickened in all which shall drive it to seek for ever new supplies from Him, who is the indeficient fountain of all good.[1] Only so could it have been said, ' Blessed are they which do hunger and thirst after righteousness ' (Matt. v. 6 ; cf. Isai. xii. 3 ; xliv. 3 ; Ps. lxxxvii. 7).

There is a certain blind longing after this springing water awakened in the soul of this poor sinner, who had thirsted so long, and who now at this time was seeking to slake her thirst at muddiest pools of sensual gratification ; and out of this she exclaims, ' *Sir, give me this water, that I thirst not* '[2] (cf. John vi. 34), though still there is confusion and contradiction in her mind about it, for she imagines that it will exempt her from the toil of coming

---

[1] Thus Drusius excellently well, reconciling the earlier words of Wisdom with the later : Qui aquam sapientiæ bibit sitit et non sitit. Sitit, id est, magis magisque appetit id quod bibit.   Non sitit, quia ita expletur ut alium potum non desideret.

[2] Sedulius (*Carm. Pasch.* 229) :

> Orat inexhausti tribui sibi dona fluenti,
> Æternam positura sitim, quâ nemo carere
> Dignus erit, Domini nisi mersus gurgite Christi.

to draw from that well any more—'*neither come hither to draw.*'

How are we to explain the check and abrupt turn which the conversation here receives, this '*Go, call thy husband, and come hither,*' with which our Lord seems to interrupt it, just at its most interesting point? Is it, as some say, that being about to confer on her a benefit, He would not confer it on her alone; but on her and her husband together? This can hardly be; it is indeed contradicted by the fact that Christ knew perfectly well about her, that her relations to him with whom she was living were not those of a wife to her husband. The words can only be regarded as spoken for the calling out of that very answer which they did call out; of bringing her in this way to a wholesome shame. They attain the object with which they were uttered. The confession, indeed, which they elicit, '*I have no husband,*' is only a half confession; not all the truth, it is yet true as far as it goes; and for the truth's sake which it contains He accepts and allows it: '*Thou hast well said, I have no husband;*' with an emphasis on '*husband,*' which is marked in the Greek by its position in the sentence, and which might have been so marked in our Version— '*Husband I have not.*' This she has '*said well*' (cf. Matt. xv. 7; Luke xx. 39), inasmuch as she had spoken the truth; for a true confession is always '*well*' made, however ill it may be that such a confession should need to be made. He proceeds, with how firm and at the same time how gentle a hand, to draw her from the hiding places in which she may still have hoped to lie hid, to complete the story of her life, supplying the circumstances which she has omitted, to unroll before her the blurred and blotted scroll of her past existence : '*for thou hast had five husbands, and he whom thou now hast is not thy husband. In that saidst thou truly.*' Many words, He would imply, which she had spoken had not been true, but this mournful testimony which she had thus borne against herself was true. Meyer, including in these '*five husbands*' him whom she now had, and making him the last of the five, and not a sixth added to them, proceeds to argue that ' *husbands* ' must not be taken strictly ; but must probably include paramours, since certainly the last was such. But the argument rests on a misunderstanding. He with whom she is now living is not one of the five ; but she, falling ever deeper and deeper in degradation, is now content to go without that legal sanction to her condition which in other times she may have required. Hitherto, we may well suppose, her life had been full of manifold disorders; the five husbands had scarcely made room for one another by death ; and even in that case there must have been un- seemliest hastening of nuptials, most inordinate desires, which no dealings of God could chasten or restrain. But, doubtless, there had been worse than this ; husbands whom she had forsaken ; or whom she had compelled by breach of wedlock to put her away (Deut. xxiv. 1, 2 ; Matt. xix. 9).[1]

[1] Augustine has called this with which we are dealing, a history plena mysteriis et gravida sacramentis. Fully admitting it to be this, I yet find it impossible to accept the allegorical interpretation of these '*five hus- bands,*' which Hengstenberg, in his Commentary on St. John, traces here. For him this woman is, so to speak, the representative of that Samaria out of which she comes, of its past idolatry, its present will-worship, its future conversion—her relations with her five husbands, and with him who was not her husband, having by divine Providence been so overruled as exactly

Whether the Lord told her more which is not recorded (ver. 29 may imply as much), or so told her this as to make her understand that He knew much more, the woman, conscious that she has to do with One who knows all the wretched secrets of her disordered life, exclaims, '*Sir, I perceive that Thou art a prophet;*' for such intuitive knowledge as this could only be God's, or theirs to whom God should give it (1 Sam. ix. 19 ; 2 Kin. v. 26 ; vi. 12 ; Luke vii. 39). She did not suppose, as some in modern times have supposed, that Christ had obtained the information about her from some of her neighbours ; but she saw in Him a prophet, and one who by the exercise of his prophetic gift had thus been able to tell her '*all things that ever she did*' (ver. 29). There is no necessity of assuming that, in the case of every one with whom the Lord came in contact during the course of his earthly ministry, He knew every detail of his anterior history ; but wherever this was needed for the setting forward of the kingdom of God, for the work of that ministry which He had come to fulfil, for the best interests of that soul which He was seeking to win, there through

to set forth the history up to that moment of her people. He refers us to 2 Kin. xvii. 24, where we find the five nations, the colluvies gentium out of which the Samaritan people was formed, bringing with them into their new seats each its own god, see ver. 29-31 ; and he further cites Josephus (*Antt.* ix. 14. 3) : οἱ δὲ μετοικισθέντες εἰς τὴν Σαμάρειαν Χουθαῖοι, ἕκαστοι κατὰ ἔθνος ἴδιον θεὸν εἰς τὴν Σαμάρειαν κομίσαντες, πέντε δ' ἦσαν, καὶ τούτους, καθὼς ἦν πάτριον αὐτοῖς, σεβόμενοι. With these her idol gods Samaria lived in a real communion, but one as lightly broken off as it had been knit : while He whom now she had was no legitimate husband of hers, for those words, ' thy Maker is thy husband,' true concerning the Jewish Church, were utterly false in respect of the Samaritan. It is certainly an ingenious suggestion, resting upon a very remarkable coincidence, but is scarcely more. When it is attempted to carry it through the allegory, it breaks down, and that in parts essential. Her sin had not been polyandry ; for her five husbands had one succeeded the other ; but the five false gods of the original Samaritan worship were contemporaneous.

an act of his will He could by his divine Spirit unlock the
past, read not merely what was now passing, but all
which had ever passed in the hearts, or which had been
externally wrought in the lives, of those with whom He
had to do (Matt. ix. 4 ; John i. 47, 48 ; ii. 25 ; v. 14).
It concerned the counsels of his love that He should thus
know concerning this poor sinner, and therefore He
knew.

Her whole tone is now changed. It had been *half*
earnest before, in that request, ' *Sir, give me this water* '
(ver. 15) ; but it is *whole* earnest now ; and it is quite a
missing of the real earnestness which she now feels to take
her words which follow : ' *Our fathers worshipped in this
mountain ; and ye say, that in Jerusalem is the place where
men ought to worship,*' as though they were intended to
draw off Him with whom she was speaking from pressing
home upon her those unwelcome truths about her own
life,[1] by suggesting some general question, in which her
people indeed might possibly have the worst ; but which
would bring home no peculiar personal shame to herself.
The suggestion is ingenious, but it is much more in character with the effectual work which is being wrought,
as the issue proves, in her soul, to ascribe these words to
quite another motive. Hitherto she had never been really
enough in earnest about the worship and service of God,
to feel any misgiving or anxiety in respect of that great
controversy which was so eagerly debated between her
people and the Jews. And yet, if the Jews were right,
what was the whole Samaritan worship but a lie ; not

---

[1] So Massillon in a striking Lent Sermon on this history : Nouvelle artifice
dont elle s'avise pour détourner la question de ses mœurs, qui lui déplaît,
et qui l'embarrasse, elle se jette habilement sur une question de doctrine, les
contestations entre Jérusalem et Gérizim,

merely a service which God had not commanded, but which was contrary to his command, with unsoundness and rottenness at its very core ? She had hitherto troubled herself nothing about this ; she had taken things as she found them. But the time of such indifference was past ; it became all-important for her to know in which of the two channels the blessing indeed ran, whether salvation was of the Samaritans or of the Jews; and hence her question, or rather her statement of the point at issue, which though not clothed in the form of a direct question, is evidently presented to the Lord that He may, if possible, satisfy her mind about it.

But whom does she mean by ' *our fathers*,' on whom she would fain rely and lean, as having ' *worshipped in this mountain*,' on Mount Gerizim, which rose up immediately before them ; and given to it that consecration which her people claimed as peculiarly its own ? There are two answers, and there is certainly something to be pleaded for each. Some understand by ' *our fathers*' the founders of the Samaritan worship, the builders of the temple on ' *this mountain*,' and they argue that, ' *Our fathers worshipped*,' set over against ' *Ye worship*,' will admit no other interpretation. They would find the complete example here of one, who walking in a vain conversation defends it as having been received by tradition from her fathers (1 Pet. i. 18). So Meyer, Alford, and others. I cannot so understand the words. The woman is declaring her position to a Jew, and doing what she can to maintain it as against him. But what force would it have with him to declare that from the beginning of that schism which he condemned throughout, her people had worshipped at Gerizim ? Take on the other hand ' *our fathers*' as the common fathers of Jew and Samaritan alike, at least as those whom the Samaritans claimed for '*fathers*,' some, as Adam, Seth, Noah with right, others, as the later patriarchs, Abraham, Isaac, and Jacob, with no right at all; and then there is some cogency in what she urges, if only it had been true. They whom we and you reverence alike, and alike claim for our own, our great religious progenitors, worshipped here; in manifold ways they did honour to this mountain; and '*ye say that in Jerusalem*,' a place barely heard of till a late period of the nation's history (Josh. xv. 63; xviii. 28), occupied by the Canaanite to the time of David (2 Sam. v. 6, 7), '*is the place where men ought to worship.*' She knew that there was one such place, and one only, where the Lord would manifest his presence and put his name there, and that to this place it was the duty of all to resort (Deut. xii. 5). They could not then both be right, Jerusalem and Gerizim; nay one must be utterly wrong; but which was it? Would He, this prophet, resolve this question for her, and if she and her people were wrong, convince her that they were so?

But first, a word or two more on this assertion of hers, '*Our fathers worshipped on this mountain*,' in further confirmation of the interpretation which I have preferred. A modern writer, who has derived much of his information from personal intercourse with the Samaritan High Priest,[1] tells us what they now believe, what in all likelihood they believed in our Saviour's time, about Mount Gerizim; the honour, dignity, and preeminence which for it they challenge. It is for them the holy mountain of the world; on its summit was the seat of Paradise; from

---

[1] Petermann, in Herzog's *Encyclopädie*, vol. xiii. p. 337, art. *Samaria*.

the dust of Mount Gerizim Adam was formed; and the spot is still pointed out where he reared his first altar; the place too where Seth did the same. Gerizim is the Ararat of Scripture, on which the Ark rested (Gen. viii. 4); which the waters of the Flood had never overflowed; and which thus no dead thing borne by these waters had touched to defile. They point out further the exact spot on which Noah reared an altar to the Lord when the Flood has subsided (Gen. viii. 20); and the seven steps, on each of which he offered a burnt offering, which led up to it, are existing still. The altar too is to this day standing on which Abraham had bound his son, and the spot known where the ram was caught in a thicket by its horns (Gen. xxii. 13). At the summit of Gerizim is Bethel, where Jacob slept and saw in a dream that wondrous ladder which reached from earth to heaven (Gen. xxviii. 12, 19). There is a good deal more in the same fashion; but this is enough. That poor woman, who may have accepted all this with implicit faith, would have had warrant more than enough for her boast, ' *Our fathers worshipped in this mountain,*' if only a small part of it had been true. What is authentically recorded on this subject the following references, Gen. xxxiii. 18, 20; Deut. xi. 29; Josh. viii. 33, will exhaust.

With a deep and solemn earnestness, such as the grandeur and importance of the announcement which He was making deserved, the announcement namely of a universal religion, the Lord replies. First indeed, and as a necessary condition of this, He proclaims the passing away of every form of religion which is tied to a local centre,—by anticipation condemning Mahometanism here, as a retrograde step in the spiritual history of humanity—so to make room for that faith, which should have its centre everywhere, and its circumference nowhere. There was here, I say, a condemnation of every religion tied to a local centre ; for when Christ replied, ' *Woman, believe Me*,[1] *the hour cometh, when ye shall neither in this mountain, nor yet at Jerusalem, worship the Father*,' annulling thus such earlier precepts as that of Deut. xii. 5, 6, this ' *ye* ' must suffer no such limitation as should restrict it to the Samaritans alone, and to this question of the woman in respect of the place where *they* ought to worship. The words *may* refer, as Meyer says, to the future conversion of the Samaritans, ' who thereby set free from the service on Gerizim should not thereupon be brought to the service at Jerusalem ; ' but they have a much wider scope ; in this ' *ye* ' are included all the children of men, all the nations of the earth, as one by one they should be brought into the true fold. Christ does not indeed use the communicative ' *we*,' as another prophet would have done, as would have suited every other save Him who was the only-begotten of the Father ; but his words, while they except Himself, do not except any other.

The question which the woman had asked could not be resolved but in favour of Jerusalem ; yet very observable is the manner in which, before the Lord thus announces the pretensions of Gerizim untenable and without a warrant, He lifts up the whole matter in debate into a higher sphere, and shows how in a little while the very subject matter of it will have disappeared altogether. That there could be such a controversy as this, whether at Jerusalem or at Gerizim men ought to worship the

---

[1] Bengel has a subtle observation here : Ad Judæos et discipulos sæpe Christus dixit, *Dico vobis* (ver. 35). Uno hoc loco ad Samaritida, *Crede mihi*. Illi magis obligati erant ad credendum, quam hæc. Hanc proportionem sequuntur formulæ.

Father, the very existence of such a dispute had its rise in the fact that even true religion itself hitherto had moved among ' elements of this world ' (Gal. iv. 3), and had owned a ' worldly sanctuary ' (Heb. ix. 1), from which now it was about to disengage itself for ever ; and once disengaged from these, the controversy would be possible no more, but that great prophetic word of Malachi would be fulfilled, ' *and in every place* incense shall be offered unto my name, and a pure offering ' (Mal. i. 11).

As concerns, indeed, the present and the past nothing can be more absolute than the decision which Christ pronounces in favour of Jerusalem and its worship, and against Gerizim and the will-worship conducted there : ' *Ye worship ye know not what ; we know what we worship ; for salvation is of the Jews.*' This neuter ' *what* ' has often made a difficulty ; we should certainly have expected, ' Ye worship ye know not *whom* ; ' and again, ' We know *whom* we worship.' Some therefore have made this ' *what*' to express rather the *manner* than the *object* of worship. But it was more probably selected to express the unreal character of their whole worship, the absence of any relation on their part to a living personal God. It will then find its exact parallel in St. Paul's use of ' the Godhead ' (τὸ θεῖον) at Acts xvii. 29. God is only truly worshipped by them to whom He has shewn how to worship Him, and who worship Him in the way which He has shewn. He is only known of those to whom He makes Himself known. The Samaritan was eminently an *invented* religion ; more so in many respects than the traditional heathenism, which at all events was not manufactured, and may have still kept traces, not wholly effaced, of the original revelation ; it was a name without a power, a temple without a temple's God.   The altar they reared was, in the saddest sense of the words, ' To an Unknown God,' and one whom by means of that worship they could never know.   The other ' *what* ' in the second clause of the sentence will then be there only for the sake of concinnity.   Had the assertion stood alone, it would have been, ' *We know whom we worship.*'   ' *We* '—for Christ here makes common part with his people, and speaks at once in his *human* character, therefore as a worshipper, and in his Jewish character, therefore as a worshipper at Jerusalem and in and through the service of the temple,—' *we know what we worship,* no dream and imagination of man's own heart, but One who has appointed ways by which He may be approached, and who, sitting between the Cherubim, meets them who approach Him by these.'   A Jew might be full of darkness, many were so, in respect of the God whose name he bore, whose worshipper he professed to be; but that was his separate individual guilt, and sprang from a refusing to use, or from a not using aright, that knowledge of God to which he had been called; meanwhile every Jew, who was such in truth and not in name only, knew what and whom he worshipped.   It was otherwise with the Samaritan.   He did not fail in the right application of what his religion taught him of God; but that religion itself was a device of man, a vanity and a lie, no help to him in the finding of God, but a hindrance rather.

A rapid oversight of the circumstances under which the Samaritan worship came into being, and the conditions of its existence at this time, will enable us best to understand the uncompromising severity of the verdict which the lips of truth have just pronounced against it.   It is true that the upgrowth of this worship, with the building of the temple on Mount Gerizim, which for two hundred years, according to Josephus, but probably for more nearly three hundred, was an offence and a provocation to those who worshipped on Mount Moriah (the rivalry of the religions has survived the destruction of both temples), is clothed in much obscurity ; yet not an obscurity so deep as to hide from us the unreal character which clung to it from the first. To regard Samaritanism as in any sense a continuation of the schism, political and religious, of the Ten Tribes [1] is altogether misleading. It is true, as mentioned already, that the Samaritans at a later day claimed their descent from the tribe of Ephraim ; in which, as they affirmed, the true line of God's promises ran, appealing in proof to Gen. xlix. 22–26 ; Deut. xxxiii. 13–17 ; and ignoring, as some tell us, Eli and Samuel and the house of David altogether. But this was an after-thought. The only real thread of connection between the two is the well-known fact recorded in the Second Book of Kings (xvii. 24–28), namely, that when the heathen colonists planted by the king of Assyria in the land left desolate by the deportation of its Israelitish inhabitants, were annoyed in their new seats by lions, these 'proselytes of the lions,' as the Jews were pleased insultingly to call them, sought and obtained that a priest from among those who had been thus carried away might be sent back to teach them ' the manner of the God of the land,' hoping so to avert his displeasure. But one of Jeroboam's priests, himself entangled in the idolatries of Dan and Bethel, was not likely to accomplish much, and from the sacred narrative we gather that he accomplished nothing at all, in

---

[1] As Witsius does in his *Decaphylon*, ch. 3, and many more.

the way of extirpating the various idolatries which the Persian and Median colonists had brought with them (ver. 29–41) ; some of these idolatries surviving in forms the most hideous (see ver. 31); however he may have managed to combine with these certain outward ceremonies, and to impart a knowledge of certain outward facts, of the true religion.

When the children of the Captivity, restored to their own land, were engaged in the rebuilding of their temple, the Samaritans, as is familiar to all, requested, not on the ground of a common nationality, for that they do not venture to plead, but as seeking the same God with them, to be allowed to share in the work ; with, of course, the condition understood, that the temple, reared by both, should be common to both (Ezra iv. 1, 2). The Jews refused ; and they could not do otherwise. The Jewish Church might even then receive proselytes one by one into its bosom ; but the time of any freer larger adoption of the nations was yet far off; and it was God, not man, who must determine when the hour for this had arrived. For the present their strength lay in their isolation. That alone could preserve them from the infinite spiritual dangers which surrounded them. Mingling with the heathen, or suffering these to mingle with them, they would soon have learned their works. The Samaritans resent the refusal; put many spiteful hindrances in the way of the work ; and the seeds of an enmity which has lasted to this day, seeds hereafter to spring up in ten thousand bitternesses of hate and scorn and wrong on the one side and on the other, were sown.

There are no means of tracing the steps by which the Samaritan worship in the course of time eliminated from itself the grosser heathen elements which it contained (its kernel was heathenish to the last, see ver. 22), or the modifications which it underwent, until at last it became so plausible a counterfeit of the truth, that it did not hesitate to enter the lists even of theological argument; disputing,—it does so here by the mouth of this woman —as to which was the truth, and which the lie. But though the several steps of this transformation may be beyond our power to trace, there was one event, or series of events, which must have exercised an enormous influence in bringing such a result about, which perhaps alone made it possible. This was the secession from Jerusalem of one or more members of the high-priestly family; accompanied or followed by that of other distinguished refugees; who for one cause or another driven from Jerusalem, or malcontents quitting it of their own accord, found refuge and welcome in Samaria, and brought a knowledge with them of the Jewish ritual and theology to those whose faith and worship must till their arrival have been a very poor, maimed, and ignorant thing.

Josephus[1] has a story exactly of the kind, which cannot indeed pass muster as he tells it; but which yet is generally recognized as possessing a foundation of historic truth, as the more or less inaccurate version of an event recorded thus by Nehemiah : ' And one of the sons of Joiada, the son of Eliashib the High Priest, was son-in-law to Sanballat the Horonite ; therefore I chased him from me' (Neh. xiii. 28) ; or, if not this, to be another event of a like character, which in the telling has been more or less confused with this. If indeed Josephus refers to the same event as Nehemiah, then, besides other

[1] *Antt.* XI. 7. 2, and 8. 2.

mistakes, he has placed it some eighty years later than
he ought. His story is of one Manasses, brother of
Joiada the High Priest, who about the year B.C. 332 was
chased from Jerusalem on account of a marriage con-
tracted by him with the daughter of Sanballat, the Persian governor of Samaria ; which marriage, when required,
he refused to dissolve. He was received with open arms
by his father-in-law, who undertook to rear for him on
Mount Gerizim, the highest mountain in Samaria, a temple
more magnificent than that from which he had been
driven ; where he should himself exercise the office of
High Priest. The worship there was in this way set on
a far more formidable footing than it had before attained ;
not to say that the secession, once begun, was presently
reinforced by other fugitives and apostates, many of them
priests, who, now that a rallying point and a refuge was
prepared for them, fell away as Manasses had done. Such
is the story of Josephus ; not without serious inaccuracies,
yet possessing evidently its substratum of truth. The
temple thus reared was destroyed by John Hyrcanus B.C.
129 ;[1] but the worship continued on Mount Gerizim,
which by this time the Samaritans had learned to regard
as the holiest mountain in the world,[2] some sort of
edifice no doubt occupying the place of the temple which
had disappeared. Nor could the imitation have been a
contemptible one ; else it could never have excited the
intense jealousy which evidently among the Jews it did
excite.[3] Everything in fact may have been there,—

---

[1] *Antt.* XIII. 9. 1 ; *B. J.* I. 2. 6.

[2] Josephus (*Antt.* XVIII. 4. 1): Γαριζεὶν, ὁ ἁγιότατον αὐτοῖς ὁρῶν ὑπείληπται.

[3] A story recorded by Josephus (*Antt.* XIII. 3. 4) is singularly illustra-
tive of the fierceness with which the rival claims of Jerusalem and Gerizim
were debated, not on these spots merely, but wherever Jew and Samaritan

except the presence of God. There was but one flaw, but that was a fatal one : ' *Ye worship ye know not what.*'

But if thus with them, it was very different with the Jews ; ' *We know what we worship*' (Rom. iii. 2 ; Luke xvi. 29), '*for salvation is of the Jews*' (Isai. ii. 3 ; Gen. xii. 2, 3 ; Zech. viii. 23 ; Mic. iv. 2). This '*salvation*,' where we should beforehand have expected Him to be named who was the author of that salvation, the Saviour (cf. Rom. ix. 5), this abstract for the concrete, may remind us of exactly the same language on the lips of the aged Simeon, ' for mine eyes have seen thy *salvation*' (τὸ σωτήριον there), uttered at a moment when he held the infant Saviour in his arms (Luke ii. 30), and of the words of the dying Jacob, 'I have waited for thy *salvation*, O Lord' (Gen. xlix. 18). Because salvation was thus of the Jews, therefore they knew what they worshipped,[1] and not *vice versâ*, because they knew what they worshipped, therefore salvation was of them. He who set them to minister salvation to the world, as a necessary condition of this gave them to know Himself, whom they must first know before they could declare to others.

But this declaration of our Lord's, quite irrespective of its bearing on the controversy between the rival Churches, is very important as setting the seal of his absolute authority on the Jewish institutions as divine, directly appointed of God for the bringing of mankind to

encountered. Certain of the one religion and of the other at Alexandria besought Ptolemy Philometor to decide which were in the right, pledging him beforehand to put to death those against whom his decision should be given. He solemnly heard their several pleadings and proofs alleged; which done, he decided, as he could not do otherwise, in favour of the Jews, slaying, according to the request and agreement made, the advocates of Gerizim.

[1] So rightly Lampe : In expectatione enim hujus salutis totus cultus Mosaicus fundatus erat.

the knowledge of his Name.   Wherever Christ's words
are accepted as rule and law, these words of his, spoken by
the well of Jacob, will vindicate for Israel in that period
which preceded the Incarnation a position altogether
different from that of every other nation of the earth,
Israel was the channel through which the salvation of
God should be conveyed to the world.   It was the aloe
tree, in many aspects unsightly enough, but which yet
after long waiting should blossom at last in one ' bright
consummate flower,' and having so fulfilled its mission
should then wither and die.[1]   Doubtless there were, as
the illustrious Alexandrian teachers loved to trace, preparations for Christ going forward in the Gentile world,
as well as within the limits of the Jewish Church.   That
Gentile world had its ' Evangelical Preparation ; ' but in
many respects this was negative rather than positive ;
and even where positive, it was very far from being that
direct immediate discipline, nurture, and training which
was their exclusive privilege, ' of whom as concerning
the flesh Christ should come, who is over all, God blessed
for ever ' (Rom. ix. 5).[2]

Christ has spoken already of the *where* men shall worship the Father, that it shall be ' *neither in this mountain,
nor yet at Jerusalem,*' but everywhere (cf. 1 Tim. ii. 8 ;
Zeph. iii. 11) ; He proceeds to speak (having disposed by
way of parenthesis of the question moved by the woman),
of the *how :* ' *But the hour cometh, and now is, when the
true worshippers shall worship the Father*[3] *in spirit and in*

---

[1] Augustine (*De Civ. Dei,* xvii. 11): Ipse Jesus substantia populi ejus,
ex quo natura est carnis ejus.

[2] See Dean Blakesley's *Dispensation of Paganism,* and my *Unconscious
Prophecies of Heathendom.*

[3] Grotius : Tacite Novi Fœderis suavitatem innuit, cum Deum Patrem
vocat, Rom. viii. 15 ; Gal. iv. 16.

truth ; for the Father seeketh such to worship Him.' The
'*now is*' declares that this is a future which has already
commenced (cf. John v. 25). The dispensation of the
Spirit, in which God the Spirit shall be spiritually worshipped is not merely something which is to be hereafter ;
the woman stands already upon its threshold. Prophesied
of long since (Hagg. ii. 6–9 ; Zeph. ii. 11 ; iii. 9 ; Isai.
xlv. 23), it has now actually begun. As an immediate
consequence of this, a very slight one, compared with the
far more momentous which the fact involves, she shall
not need to mend her present erroneous faith by betaking
her to Jerusalem, instead of to Gerizim. The time for
this is over.

We shall best understand what this worshipping ' in
spirit and in truth ' means, if we deal with these statements
one by one, only afterwards considering the relation in
which they stand to one another. And first, ' *in spirit.*'
St. Paul speaks of himself and those of ' the true circumcision,' corresponding to the ' *true worshippers* ' of this
passage, as worshipping ' in the Spirit of God ' (Phil. iii. 3);
of the Spirit helping our infirmities (Rom. viii. 26);
St. Jude of ' praying in the Holy Ghost ' (ver. 20) ; this
being the divine element and sphere out of which prayer
has its rise, and in which it moves. It will follow that
only there, where the mystery of the New Birth has found
place, will this condition of a true worship be fulfilled.
In his fallen nature man is not spirit, but flesh (Gen. vi. 3).
Latent and suppressed, overlayed by the flesh, utterly
unable to extricate *itself* from the superincumbent load,
there is a spirit in him, an organ, that is, for the reception of the divine Spirit, and one which by that Spirit
may be quickened into the activities of prayer and

worship. Little as this neophyte in the school of Christ may have understood of all this, she will yet have gathered from that utterance of his, still more plainly from a word which is presently to follow (ver. 24), that a living God must be worshipped in a living manner, by that which is highest and best in man, and by that informed and quickened by a breath or spirit of his own.

He adds, ' *and in truth.*' Where the Spirit is, there is the truth ; He, as the Spirit of truth, excluding not merely all the grosser falsehoods of the heathen religions, but all subtle self-delusions in which worshippers who are *not* ' *true*' may be so easily entangled ; as the service of the lips offered instead of the service of the heart (Ps. l. 16 ; Isai. xxix. 13 ; Matt. xv. 8) ; with all substitutions of the outward for the inward, as of bullocks and goats in place of thanksgivings and paying of vows (Ps. l. 8–11) ; ' thousands of rams ' and ' ten thousands of rivers of oil ' in lieu of justice and mercy and a humble walking with God (Mic. vi. 7, 8). Nor does the worshipping ' *in* truth' exclude only what is false. It excludes also what as worship is partial, rudimentary, imperfect. Those whom God enables so to worship must have passed through the lower and more imperfect stages of a religious training, have left behind them types and shadows, elements of this world, have been by the Spirit introduced into the world of spiritual realities, and must now be moving and acting in it.[1] ' The law came by Moses, but grace and *truth* by Jesus Christ ' (John i. 17). In these words, upon which the whole Epistle to the Hebrews may be said to be an

---

[1] Augustine : Foras ieramus, intro missi sumus. Intus age totum. Et si forte quæris aliquem locum altum, aliquem locum sanctum, intus exhibe te templum Dei. In templo vis orare, in te ora. Sed prius esto templum Dei, quia ille in templo suo exaudiet orantem.

extended commentary, there is a clear antithesis between the Mosaic law, with all Levitical institutions, and the 'truth.' Not antagonistic, which God forbid, they are yet distinct from one another. One has 'a shadow of good things to come,' the other 'the very image' ($\varepsilon i x \omega v$) 'of the things' (Heb. x. 1 ; cf. viii. 5). The earlier may have, and has, prophetic outlines, typical preformations ; 'but *the body*' ($\sigma \tilde{\omega} \mu \alpha = \dot{\alpha} \lambda \eta \theta \varepsilon i \alpha$ here) 'is of Christ' (Col. ii. 17). What to '*worship in truth*' is, this the author of the Epistle to the Hebrews has exactly declared : 'Having therefore, brethren, boldness to enter into the holiest by the blood of Jesus, by a new and living way, which He hath consecrated for us, through the veil, that is to say, his flesh ; and having a High Priest over the house of God ; let us draw near with a true heart in full assurance of faith, having our hearts sprinkled from an evil conscience, and our bodies washed with pure water' (x. 19–22).[1]

'*God is a Spirit*.'[2] Expositors have sometimes sought to go very deep into the meaning of these words, to find in them metaphysical announcements concerning the nature of God. Doubtless they are of an infinite depth ; but that exquisite saying of Gregory the Great,[3] that

---

[1] Keeping in mind that Christ has said elsewhere 'I am the Truth' (John xiv. 6), we shall scarcely err if to what has been said we further add —and many of the Fathers engaged in controversy with the Arians have here shown us the way,—that we have the whole mystery of the Trinity in these words declared to us, the Father to be worshipped, as He only can be worshipped, in the Spirit and the Truth. So Athanasius ; Basil the Great, in a passage full of the deepest theology, *De Spir. Sancto*, 26 ; and Ambrose, *De Spir. Sancto*, iii. 11. 81.

[2] On these words see a remarkably able article by Ackermann in the *Theol. Stud. und Krit.* 1839, pp. 873-944, *Ueber* $\pi v \varepsilon \tilde{v} \mu a$, $v o \tilde{v} \varsigma$, *und Geist*. It deals at pp. 940-944 with this verse.

[3] At least I have never traced it higher than the prefatory Epistle to his *Commentary on Job* : Divinus etenim sermo sicut mysteriis prudentes exercet,

Scripture has depths for an elephant to swim in and shallows which a lamb can wade, is capable of being pushed a little further. Oftentimes the same Scripture is at once a depth for one, and a shallow for another, and thus is it here. We should do little honour to the Lord's skill in teaching, his adaptation of his words to the needs of his hearers, if, seeking after high things, we failed to find in these words some simple truth, such as that poor ignorant woman with whom He talked was capable of grasping, and such as at that moment she needed. ' *God is a Spirit,*' or ' God is Spirit ; '—we must not miss, assuredly she did not miss, the significant image on which this word reposes ; [1] like the wind therefore, to which He is likened, breathing and blowing where He will, penetrating everywhere, owning no circumscriptions, tied to no place, neither to Mount Zion nor to Mount Gerizim ; but rather filling all space with his presence (Ps. cxxxix. 7–10 ; 1 Kin. viii. 27 ; Isai. lxvi. 1), in his essence and, as involved in this very title, free.[2] On this it follows that ' *they who worship Him, must worship Him in spirit and in truth* '—on which ever memorable words there has been already occasion to speak.

How far, we may fitly pause for a moment to enquire,

---

sic plerumque superficie simplices refovet. Quasi quidam quippe est fluvius, ut ita dixerim, planus et altus, in quo et agnus ambulet et elephas natet.

[1] Πνεῦμα from πνέω, as spiritus from spirare. It need hardly be remarked that in the Hebrew or Aramaic, which the Lord in all likelihood spoke with this woman, the identity of spirit, breath, and wind is quite as strongly marked. So too ' Geist ' appears in English in two forms, as ' ghost ' and ' gust.'

[2] So Hilary (*De Trin.* 2. 31) : Ergo quia Deus invisibilis, incomprehensibilis, immensus est ; ait Dominus venisse tempus, ut non in monte vel templo Deus sit adorandus, *quia Spiritus Deus est* ; et Spiritus nec circumscribitur, nec tenetur, qui per naturæ suæ virtutem ubique est, neque usquam abest ; in omnibus omnis exuberans ; hos igitur veros esse adoratores, qui in Spiritu et veritate sunt adoraturi.

does a declaration like this of the spiritual character of all true worship exclude forms, how far does it allow them? That it has not been counted to exclude them, the practice of the Church in all ages sufficiently declares. At the same time it must be accepted as, in the first place, stamping on them a subordinate and secondary character. They may be henceforth the vehicles of devotion; they can never in the New Covenant themselves constitute devotion. Then too, secondly, it is plain that there is allowance here for only so much of these as there is a reasonable expectation can be taken up and quickened by the Spirit which is in the worshippers. So soon as ever they are in excess of this, directly they overlay the inner life, instead of setting it forth, are present for their own sakes, and not for the sake of something of which they are the bearers, directly they tempt men to stop short with them, instead of passing and pressing through them to Him who is behind them all, they are of the things which Christ intended here to exclude. The idiosyncrasies of men, of nations, of the same people at different epochs of its spiritual growth, are so various that it can never be easy to fix the exact point where what should have been a help is in danger of becoming a hindrance. So long as man even at his best estate is at once weak and sinful, it will be always an alternative of dangers. On the one side, though worshipping One who is Spirit, he is not himself all spirit; but body and spirit; and as such craves a certain body for his devotions (a 'spiritual body' it should be), cannot afford for long not to find one; the wine of devotion, having no vessels to hold it, will inevitably be spilt and lost. On the other hand, entirely lawful concessions to this just craving of the human heart may be turned into occasions of mischief. Over and over again God had need to cast a slight on his own temple-worship, its gifts and its sacrifices, when these had become not means any longer, but ends, to his people; not helps to bring them into his presence, but substitutes for that presence (Ps. l. 8–15; li. 16; Isai. i. 10–15; Jer. vii. 22; Mic. vi. 6–8). And if that which was of divine appointment was itself thus liable to abuse, how much more that which is of man's devising. But it is impossible in a matter like this to do more than lay down the principle which should guide in rejecting or allowing. Nowhere will prudence, charity, mutual forbearance, be more needed than in the application of this principle; for wherever the line is drawn, it is certain that some will have to tolerate more of forms than they think desirable, and others to put up with less.

Something this poor sinner understands, but not much, of what has just been said to her. He with whom she speaks has brought her into deep waters, deeper than any in which she can find a footing, transported her into a sphere of truths far larger than she can grasp. This setting aside at once and for ever of the controversy between her people and his people, as something of no future interest whatever, this setting forth to her of another Father beside that '*father Jacob*,' in whom she trusted, this worship in spirit and in truth, there is that in her which dimly and obscurely responds to it all. We may take her words which follow, '*I know that Messias cometh, which is called Christ; when He is come, He will tell us all things*'[1]—as a cry of helplessness, a reaching

---

[1] There are two curious examples of this same adjourning of perplexed and difficult questions to the decision of a prophet that should come hereafter in the Maccabæan times (1 Macc. iv. 46; xiv. 41).

out after help. ' I see not my way in this new world
into which Thou hast brought me ; but one is coming,
the Messias, the Prophet promised to our fathers ; I can
only wait in confidence that He will lead us into all truth,
tell us all which it most concerns us to know.' At the
same time there pierces through her words, as it seems to
me, a timid presage and presentiment, such as she hardly
dares own, much less ventures to utter, ' Thou perhaps art
He whom we look for.'

The word ' *Messias* ' occurs only twice in the New
Testament ; here, and in Andrew's announcement to his
brother Peter, of the Saviour whom he has found (John
i. 41). It is there explained by the Evangelist as ' being
interpreted, The Christ,' or The Anointed ; the title being
drawn first from Ps. ii. 2 ; xx. 6 ; and then from Dan.
ix. 25, 26. It is exceedingly difficult to say whether
' *which is called Christ*' is here also an intercalation of
the Evangelist, or a part of her designation of the Saviour
whom she looks for. That St. John has explained
' Messias ' once does not make it the least unlikely that
he should explain it again ; for compare xi. 16 ; xx. 24 ;
xxi. 2 ; indeed the fact that he has done so before leads
me on the whole to conclude that he is doing so again,
and that these words are not the woman's, though they
would have fitted in very well to her speech, but the
Evangelist's. Since neither Psalms nor Prophets were
accepted by the Samaritans, the name ' Messias ' must
have made its way to them from the theological schools
of the Jews; as indeed in all matters of higher theology
they lived on the crumbs which fell from the Jewish
table. At the same time, with the exception of the
name, there is nothing in her expectation of the Messiah

here which she might not have derived from that Pentateuch, which and which only, as is familiar to all, the
Samaritans received. To this day they mainly ground
their expectations of a Messiah on Deut. xviii. 15–19—
which is indeed a true foreshewing of Him; but at the
same time, if taken alone, a most meagre and inadequate
one, as giving no hint either of his kingly or priestly
office, but of his prophetic only; even, as it will be
observed, it is only prophetic functions which she ascribes
to Him here.[1]

It is not a little remarkable that our Lord, who so
carefully concealed from the multitude of his Jewish
followers the fact of his Messiahship, beyond the circle
of his own disciples revealing it but to one (John ix. 37),
who so strictly charged the disciples themselves that they
should not make Him known (Matt. xvi. 20), sealing with
the seal of absolute silence the lips of the three who had
been witnesses of his Transfiguration (Matt. xvii. 9; Mark
ix. 9), does yet here announce Himself without reserve to
this Samaritan woman; and not to her only, but to the
Samaritans in general during his brief sojourn among
them, so that before He quits them they confess, ' *This is
indeed the Christ, the Saviour of the world* ' (ver. 42). And
yet the different dealing in the different circumstances is
intelligible enough. There was one chief difficulty which
our Lord found during the whole course of his ministry
among his own people, namely how to keep that ministry
clear of political excitements, to avoid rousing those tur-
bulent expectations of a change in their outer condition,

---

[1] The rise of at least one false Christ about this same time, or a little
later, among the Samaritans—I refer in particular to Dositheus,—is evidence
that Messias-hopes and expectations were stirring among them no less than
among the Jews.

which the Jewish multitude associated so closely with the coming of Messiah. Thus so soon as ever these supposed that they beheld such in Him, they sought, we are told, ' to take Him by force, and to make Him a king ' (John vi. 15), to carry Him away with them, and instal Him at once as King Messiah at Jerusalem—He to avoid this being obliged to conceal Himself from them ; even as nothing would have so effectually marred and brought to ruin his whole work as any attempt of the kind, and this whether it were defeated at once, or crowned with a temporary success (John xi. 48). There were other reasons, no doubt, which will help to explain why Luther's work continued, and Savonarola's came to nothing ; yet this, no doubt, was a chief reason, namely, that Luther's was a Church Reformation, and that he absolutely refused to make it anything else, leaving other changes to follow, as follow in their own good time they must ; while that of the Italian friar would fain have been a Reformation of the Church and State in one. But the Samaritan ex- pectation of a Messiah, if in some respects weaker and feebler than the Jewish, was yet mingled with far fewer disturbing elements ; not to say that the acceptance by the Samaritans of a Jewish Messiah could arouse no worldly hopes or expectations in their hearts ; nay rather must sound the death-knell of any proud hopes for their nation which they hitherto may have cherished, and compelled them to bid a lasting farewell to these.[1] To them, to this

---

[1] Godet (*Comm. sur l'Évangile de S. Jean*) : Quelle contraste entre la notion du Messie telle que l'exprime cette femme [ver. 25], et les notions charnelles et de nature toute politique que Jésus rencontrait sans cesse en Israël sur ce sujet ! Sans doute l'élément royal manque à la notion samari- taine du Messie. Mais combien l'absence de cet élément n'est-elle pas préférable à l'altération profonde qu'il avait subie chez les Juifs ! L'idée est incomplète, mais non pas fausse ; et voilà pourquoi Jésus peut se l'appliquer,

woman, and afterwards to her fellow-countrymen, He could declare Himself without fear of the consequences, and He did so : ' *I that speak unto thee am He.*'[1]   What a glorious fulfilment this of Isai. lxv. 1 : ' I said, Behold Me, behold Me, unto a nation that was not called by my name.'

' *And upon this came his disciples, and marvelled that He talked with the woman.*'[2]   The Oriental contempt of woman speaks out very strongly in the sayings of the Jewish Rabbis, and at this time the disciples had not themselves unlearned it.   Yet while they marvelled, they were at the same time hindered by respect and awe from expressing their surprise : ' *Yet no man said, What seekest Thou? or, Why talkest Thou with her?*'   None ventured to ask the reason of this unusual conversation (John xxi. 12).   Evidently it never entered into their thoughts that what He was seeking from her was *her* faith ; that what He was talking about with her was the worship of the Father in spirit and in truth.   Meanwhile the woman, availing herself of their arrival, which naturally caused a pause and break in the conversation, quits the spot—but quits it in the hope that she may presently return again, and not return alone.

As a sort of pledge of this her return, or perhaps rather in the forgetfulness of a great joy, ' *she left her water-pot,*'

et se dire ici le Christ, ce qu'il n'a fait en Israël qu'au dernier moment (xvii. 3 ; Matt. xxvi. 64).

[1] Let it be permitted to apply to this poor bondwoman of sin, at this blessed crisis of her life, words written long before concerning another bondwoman, when grace, though far lower grace than this, was vouchsafed also to her: καὶ ἀνέῳξεν ὁ Θεὸς τοὺς ὀφθαλμοὺς αὐτῆς, καὶ εἶδε φρέαρ ὕδατος ζῶντος (Gen. xxi. 19).

[2] There are some beautiful remarks on Christ's relations to women, and the influence He exerted on them, in Guizot's *Meditations on the Essence of Christianity, Eighth Meditation,* p. 281, English translation.

as apostles before her had left their nets (Matt. iv. 20), as
a poor blind man after her cast away his garment (Mark
x. 50); so soon has she learned to prefer the water which
Christ gives to the fountain which Jacob gave ; ' *and went
her way into the city, and saith to the men, Come, see a
man, which told me all things that ever I did.*' Little as
she could have desired at other times to direct attention
to the events of a life which could ill bear any very close
inspection, all shame of this kind is for the present over-
borne and swallowed up in feelings of wonder and of joy.
This ' *all things that ever I did* ' must, of course, be taken
as the exaggeration of one still lost in amazement at that
marvellous revelation of the leading outlines and so many
of the mournful secrets of her past history. It is with
her now as with him whom St. Paul contemplates as
coming into the Christian assembly, who is there ' convinced of all, and judged of all ; and thus are the secrets
of his heart made manifest, and so falling down on his
face, he will worship God, and report that God is in you
of a truth ' (1 Cor. xiv. 24, 25). Such a judgment, and
one still higher, she has formed of Him who had thus
made manifest the secrets of her heart and life : ' *Is not
this the Christ?* ' A more accurate rendering of her
question, ' *Whether is this the Christ?* ' or ' *Can this be the
Christ?* ' (cf. Matt. xii. 23, where a similar emendation
should find place), would not really alter the meaning ;
only, instead of seeking to force her own conviction on
those whom she addresses, she will be rather putting it to
them to judge, and to draw conclusions of their own.
The character of this woman, the scandals of whose life
must have been sufficiently notorious, can have added no
particular weight to the announcement which she now

made, or to the invitations to her fellow-townsmen which
she gave; yet her evident earnestness, with the strength
of her own convictions lending force to her words,
overbears all other considerations. They do not hesitate,
but at her invitation ' *they went out of the city, and came
unto Him.*'

In the interval between her departure and their arrival
a short but deeply interesting discourse between the Lord
and his disciples has found place. We know from ver. 8
that ' *his disciples were gone away unto the city to buy
meat.*' They have prepared the food which they had
bought, and now they '*prayed Him, saying, Master, eat.*'
But since that time a higher spiritual joy has suspended for
Him all sense of a lower bodily necessity : ' *I have meat to
eat that ye know not of.*' Let them eat ; but for Himself
He needs not this earthly sustenance.[1] As his thirst had
been not so much after the water of Jacob's well as after
her conversion who had come to draw water thence, so now
his hunger is not for the food which they have prepared,
but for those whom He beholds already hastening from the
neighbouring city, that they may hear and receive his
word. The disciples, perplexed at this answer of his, can
only suppose that supplies have been brought Him from
some quarter of which they are ignorant : ' *Therefore said
the disciples one to another, Hath any man brought Him
aught to eat?*' St. John notes various other misunderstand-
ings of Christ's words, that which He spoke spiritually being
taken literally, sometimes by his disciples, sometimes by
the Jews ; thus compare ii. 20 ; iii. 4 ; vi. 34, 52 ; xiv. 5.
He explains his meaning, and of what meat He is

---

[1] This is no doubt the force of that ἐγὼ βρῶσιν ἔχω, in which He tacitly
distinguishes Himself who needed not, from them who needed, this food.

speaking : '*My meat is to do the will of Him that sent Me*'[1] (cf. Ps. xl. 8 ; Job xxiii. 12) ; this was the 'hidden manna' that He spake of, 'sweeter,' as the Psalmist long before had said, 'than honey and the honeycomb' (Ps. xix. 10; cxix. 103) ; '*and to finish*[2] *his work.*' With such zeal did He set Himself to the carrying through of this, which his Father had set Him to accomplish, that a little later He could say, 'I *have* finished the work which Thou gavest Me to do' (John xvii. 4). In these words there is involved an answer to that question of theirs, which they longed, but did not venture, to put to Him, namely, why '*He talked with the woman.*' They could not now fail to understand that his conversation with her had no trivial motive, that it was for the winning of her into that kingdom of grace which his Father had sent Him into this world, and anointed Him with the Spirit, at once to declare and to found (Isai. lxi. 1–3). If any doubt existed on this point, the words which follow (ver. 35–38), difficult though in some details they are, would remove it.

The passage, I have just said, is difficult—more so, as it seems to me, than is generally recognized, and almost every explanation of it is encumbered with its own embarrassments. However satisfactory an explanation may prove in one part, it is almost sure to be forced and

---

[1] One of the Apocryphal gospels, the *Protevangelium Jacobi Minoris*, c. i. supplies an interesting parallel. Joachim, the father of the Blessed Virgin, retiring to the wilderness, declares his resolve to fast there till God shall grant him his heart's desire; καὶ ἔσται μοι ἡ εὐχὴ βρῶμα καὶ πόμα.

[2] Lampe : Vox τελειόω, a τέλος, designat non solum opus ad finem ducere, sed etiam ita, ut actu omnes illas partes et qualitates habeat, quæ ad opus illud requirebantur, atque adeo ut respondeat secundum omnes partes suæ delineationi, suoque scopo, cui est destinatum (Act. xx. 24; Jac. ii. 22 ; 1 Joh. ii. 5 ; iv. 12, 17, 18).

artificial in another. There is always something unreal
in the going off into general observations on the relations
between the spiritual sower and the spiritual reaper.
What we almost always seem to want is some explanation
which shall more closely attach these verses to the events
which at the moment are actually going forward, and on
which these words are a commentary. The interpretation which follows appears to me to possess this recom-
mendation. And first, the Lord reminds his disciples of
some words which, no doubt, had lately fallen from their
lips, as they looked out on that broad expanse of corn-
land, which, as modern travellers assure us, stretches out
before the eyes of one who stands, as they stood, beside
Jacob's well : '*Say not ye, There are yet four months,
and then cometh harvest?*' So it may be in the harvest
of nature : but in the harvest of grace there is a quicker
ripening than this : '*Behold, I say unto you, Lift up your
eyes, and look on the fields, for they are white already to
harvest*' (cf. Gen. xiii. 14, 15 ; Isai. xlix. 18 ; lx. 4).
That they may understand of what harvest He is speaking,
He directs their attention to the multitude already covering the space that lay between the city and the place
where they stood, and who were only waiting, so to speak,
to be gathered into the heavenly garners.

He proceeds to encourage his disciples to a work thus
made ready to their hands, addresses to them an exhorta-
tion, the same which the prophet Joel had addressed to
others long before : 'Put ye in the sickle, for the harvest
is ripe' (iii. 13) ; but he bidding to a harvest of death,
Christ to a harvest of life : '*and he that reapeth receiveth
wages*'—or better, '*receiveth a reward*' (1 Cor. ix. 17)[1]

---

[1] Μισθός, a word not seldom used for that 'reward' which of free grace
God reserves for his servants here and hereafter (Matt. v. 12; x. 41, 42;
1 Cor. iii. 8, 14 ; 2 John viii).

—' *and gathereth fruit unto life eternal.*' Here is a two-fold magnifying of the spiritual reaper's office ; he has his own reward, by anticipation and in part upon earth ; he has it in full fruition in heaven ; and, in addition to this, he ministers salvation to others ; for this '*gathereth fruit unto life eternal,*' I cannot understand, with Hengstenberg and others, 'layeth up a further and heavenly reward *for himself* :' for the '*fruit*' (καρπός) is identical with the '*harvest*' (θερισμός), and any interpretation which separates them brings confusion into the whole passage ; cf. Matt. xiii. 30 ; iii. 12.   His work, then, having these two promises, is neither an ill-requited nor a mean one ; not ill-requited, for he receives a reward ; nor mean, for his harvest is of souls, which shall be saved through Christ for ever.[1]   But why has the Lord of the harvest thus graciously brought to this early ripeness that harvest now spread forth before their eyes? The answer follows : ' *that both he that soweth, and he that reapeth, may rejoice together*' (cf. Amos ix. 13).   Here the emphasis must lie on the concluding word, '*together.*' Seldom indeed can this be the case.   There is too often an interval, not seldom a long and dreary one, between a sowing and a reaping time.   Often before the reaping time has arrived, the sower is in his grave ; such being one of the ever recurring sadnesses of this mortal life (Job xxxi. 8), this defeat

---

[1] Juvencus, in lines which are a favourable specimen of his poetry, gives, as it seems to me, the right explanation (*Evang. List.* ii. 313) :

> Quatuor hinc menses lætæ ad primordia messis
> Frugiferæ æstatis certe superesse putatis.
> Erigite ergo oculos, albentes cernite campos,
> Cunctaque maturam jam rura exposcere messem.
> Nunc quicunque metet, pulchri mercede laboris,
> Vitalique dehinc gaudebit fruge redundans,
> Et sator accipiet messorum gaudia lætus.

of men's hopes one of the constant punishments of their sins (Lev. xxvi. 16 ; Deut. xxviii. 33 ; Judg. vi. 3, 4). If both of them rejoice, yet seldom is it one and the same jubilee which they celebrate together, such as that which Christ announced that He is now about to celebrate in common with his disciples.

' *And herein,*'—in that which has just happened and is happening,—' *is that saying true,*' the proverb approves itself to be a genuine one, finding its fulfilment, as a proverb worthy of the name will do, in the actual events of life, ' *One soweth, and another reapeth.*' [1] There is no exception in the present instance to the general law, that men enter on the labours of their predecessors. ' You,' the Lord would say, 'are about to enter upon mine.' The monition shall keep them humble, whatever successes may await them. ' You desired just now to know why I talked with the woman, what I could have been seeking from her. I was a sower then, you shall be reapers in the harvest which from that sowing has so quickly sprung up. *I sent you to reap that whereon ye bestowed no labour.*' We best understand this past, ' *I sent you* ' (ἀπέστειλα), by supposing our Lord to travel back in thought, and to plant Himself, as He speaks, at the moment when He first gave them their commission, sent them forth as ambassadors of his grace, labourers in

---

[1] The words in the *Ajax* of Sophocles, 645,

ἀλλ' ἐστ' ἀληθὴς ἡ βροτῶν παροιμία,
ἐχθρῶν ἀδωρα δῶρα, κοὐκ ὀνήσιμα,

are not exactly parallel. Ajax there affirms the proverb which he cites to contain a maxim, not false, but *true*, therefore ἀληθής : our Lord affirms this saying which He has cited to be a *genuine* one, to be ἀληθινός, such as deserves to pass muster, and to take its place among the recognized sayings of men.

his harvest field.[1] '*Other men laboured, and ye are entered into their labours.*' This plural, '*other men*,' or '*others*,' as it would be better rendered, must not lead us astray, as it has led so many, and induce us to refer this to the prophets and other principal labourers in the older Covenant, who underwent their hard apprenticeship under the Law (Gal. iv. 3 ; Acts xv. 10); as though the anti-thesis were between them and the apostles of the New. It is rather between Christ Himself and his apostles; between the Master and the servants, not between two different companies of the servants. He is the sower, they are the reapers ; and as compared with his labours, theirs might be counted as none at all. What a glimpse have we here of the travail of his soul in the redemption of mankind—when He, who certainly would not under-rate what his servants wrought for Him, nor forget any labour of their love (Rev. ii. 2, 3), could yet speak in such a language as this ; all that labour and all that toil of theirs quite disappearing from his sight, when set side by side with his own.[2] Truly He trod the winepress alone, and his own arm brought salvation to Him ; and of this He counts it good to remind *them* at the present moment, who were about to share with Him in the spiritual triumphs of the time.

'*So when the Samaritans were come unto Him, they besought Him that He would tarry with them.*' While orthodox Jews besought Him that He would depart out

---

[1] Lampe : Utitur tempore præterito, Ego misi vos, quia missio eorum a vocatione Christi incipiebat, licet deinceps complementum suum acceperit.

[2] We may profitably bring together, we were probably meant to bring together, the κεκοπιάκασιν of this ver. 38, and the ὁ οὖν Ἰησοῦς κεκοπιακώς of ver. 6.

of their coasts (Matt. viii. 34), thrust Him with violence (Luke iv. 29), or plotted to scare Him by fraud (Luke xiii. 31, 32), from among them, poor heretical Samaritans make it their petition that He would tarry with them ; so have the first become last, and the last first. Nor did they make this petition in vain. Although during his earthly ministry sent only to the lost sheep of the house of Israel (xv. 24), so that his personal contact with any other was exceptional, and in one way or other was noted as such, ' *He abode there two days.*' Assuredly these days were infinitely precious to many—He during them preparing their hearts for that glad and free acceptance of the message of the Gospel, which after his resurrection it is recorded that Philip found in ' a city of Samaria ' (Acts vii. 5), it is difficult not to think in this city, the head-quarters of the Samaritan worship—and, as it would seem, ' in many villages of the Samaritans ' as well (ver. 25). Nor were these days of preparation only. This, as He has intimated already, was a sowing time and a reaping time all in one—the two drawn into marvellous nearness with one another. The Evangelist gives us assurance of this, informing us as He does, that ' *many more believed because of his word* ; ' and these, having believed, ' *said unto the woman, Now we believe, not because of thy saying ; for we have heard Him ourselves, and know that this is indeed the Christ, the Saviour of the world.*' St. John loves to mark the advancing steps of faith, and how those who believe come to believe more strongly, pass on from faith to faith, from a weaker to a firmer, from a lower to a higher ; thus see ii. 11 ; xvi. 30 ; xx. 8. This speech of her fellow-townsmen to the woman has nothing rude or offensive[1] about it; it has rather, indeed, the contrary : 'We set our own seals to the truth of thy report. *We have heard Him ourselves*, the gracious words which He speaks, the authority with which He speaks them; He has so commended Himself to us, with such demonstration of the truth, that we bow to his claims, and, qute irrespective of any witness of thine, take Him for what He avouches Himself to be, *the Christ, the Saviour of the world.*'

The fact that the Scripture allows and accepts this confession of theirs, sees in it an act not of credulity but of faith, and this, notwithstanding the very slight external proofs which to them He could have produced, attesting and making good his pretensions to be the Messiah, is very well worthy of note. It is an evidence that the Scripture ascribes to man a spiritual organ for the recognition of the highest truth when this is presented to him; that it regards the truth,—and Christ is the Truth (John xiv. 6),—as αὐτόπιστος, visible by its own light, and carrying its own conviction with it. In all this matter the woman may be said to have fulfilled for her fellow-countrymen the office which the Church fulfils for her children. She too witnesses of Christ; and then those who are brought to Him through this witness find in Him such fulness of grace and truth, that they set to their own seals that He is the Christ, and have another and a better witness of this in themselves.[2]

---

[1] Some indeed have urged that λαλιά, by which the Samaritans describe the report of the woman, is properly *garrulous* talk; thus Calvin: Videntur jactare Samaritani sibi solidius jam esse fulcrum quam in linguâ mulieris, quæ ut plurimum futilis esse solet. But λαλιά has no such slighting usage in Scripture; at John viii. 43 it is ascribed to Christ.

[2] Grotius : Notârunt veteres in hâc Samaritidi Ecclesiæ esse figuram,

This is the only occasion on which the phrase, '*Saviour of the world*,' appears in the Gospels, as only once elsewhere in the New Testament (1 John iv. 14; cf. 1 Tim. iv. 10; Luke ii. 11). Remarkably enough, though when we look a little closer most naturally, it occurs first on the lips of these Samaritan converts. Such language, with the mighty truth which was bound up with it, was still a long way off from Jewish thought, had not as yet risen above the horizon in the minds of apostles themselves; for these, even after the Resurrection itself, demanded, ' Wilt Thou at this time restore again the kingdom to Israel' (Acts i. 6; cf. Luke i. 68–79; xxiv. 21)? by their question testifying that their horizon reached no further than this, that this restoration was the ultimate limit of their hopes; even as the first half of the Book of Acts gives evidence how slowly, with how many reluctancies on the part of some, it broke upon their minds that theirs was a commission as wide as the world, that their risen Lord was not the King of Israel only, but the ' *Saviour of the world*' as well.

Many circumstances made the reception of this truth easier to Samaritans. Having once accepted Jesus as the Messiah, every motive must have led them to contemplate Him not so much this King of Israel, as '*the Saviour of the world.*' From his lips they no doubt had learned, as the woman who first brought them to Him had learned, that their pretensions as the seed of Abraham, as the one elect family of the earth, were utterly baseless, that only as the Christ was this Saviour of all men could they possess any part or lot in Him.[1] The Jew might cling to

quæ nos adducit ad verbum divinum; nos verbo, maxime propter ipsius majestatem et sanctitatem, credimus. Confer 1 Reg. x. 6, 7.

[1] Calvin: Colligimus Evangelii summam intra biduum familiarius illis

his exclusive prerogatives, and passionately refuse to
forego them. These Samaritans were under no such
temptation. Such exclusive prerogatives were not, and
in fact had been never, theirs. In their acknowledgment
of a Jewish Messiah they have passed a judgment on the
whole past religious history of their nation, have con-
fessed as the very truth of God that which, up to this
moment, they had so obstinately denied, namely, that
' *salvation is of the Jews*,' and not of the Samaritans,
of Jerusalem, and not of Gerizim ; and it only remained
for them to accept that place which in the economy of
this ' *salvation* ' was assigned to them, to rejoice that,
although ' *of the Jews*,' it was not *for* the Jews alone ; to
welcome Him who, being first King of Israel, was also
' *Saviour of the world*.'[1]

fuisse a Christo traditum, quam hactenus Hierosolymæ fuisset. Et Christus
salutem quam attulerat, toti mundo communem esse testatus est, quo melius
intelligerent ad se quoque pertinere. Neque enim tanquam legitimos
hæredes ad participandam salutis gratiam eos vocavit, sed docuit se venisse,
ut in Dei familiam extraneos admitteret, ac pacem afferret iis qui procul
erant.

[1] Some preparations they may have found for this in the prophecy of the
Shiloh, ' Unto Him shall the gathering *of the people* be ' (Gen. xlix. 10).
It is true that the Samaritans of the present day refer this to Solomon ;
but of old they referred it, and rightly, to the Messiah (Hengstenberg,
Christologie, vol. i. p. 76). Compare three instructive sermons by Bishop
Horsley (*Sermons*, 1829, vol. i. pp. 364–415).

4. *THE SONS OF THUNDER*

THE mention of the new name given by the Lord to the two sons of Zebedee is one of the many precious notices which we owe exclusively to St. Mark. From him alone we learn that the three foremost apostles, equal in so much else, were also equal in this, that they all obtained a new name, and that name imposed on them by the Lord Himself. Yet this new and magnificent title of '*Boanerges*,' or '*sons of thunder*,' with which the two sons of Zebedee were adorned, is not without its difficulties and obscurities. For, leaving out of sight those of the formation of the word, which are not inconsiderable, it must strike every thoughtful reader as remarkable, that while the name Peter, or its Aramaic equivalent Cephas, just before recorded as added by the Lord to Simon, recurs continually in the sacred narrative, is so stamped upon him as in the end almost entirely to displace the name which he bore while yet a fisher not of men but of fishes, this name, the imposition of which is related in exactly the same language and with the same emphasis, never once reappears in Scripture; ' you never find James called Boanerges, or John so called, either by themselves or by others ' (Lightfoot).

Various explanations of this fact have been offered. Thus it has been ingeniously suggested that the name was, so to speak, a dual name, and belonged to the two apostles, not severally and independently one of the other, but only as a brother-pair, and in their connexion one with the other, in the same way that Dioscuri belonged to Castor and Pollux, or to Zethus and Amphion; which being so, the occasions of its use must have been of rarest occurrence, and with the early death of James (Acts xii. 2) must have ceased altogether, the name itself becoming, as one might say, extinct with him.[1] And yet, ingenious as this explanation must be owned to be, it is doubly at fault. Even granting that this was such a dual name, and only proper as applied to the pair, yet of such opportunities for its use quite sufficient occur in the Gospel history to prove the inadequacy of this explanation. The two make together their petition that they may have the first and foremost places in Christ's kingdom (Mark x. 35). Together they propose to call down fire on the village of the Samaritans (Luke ix. 54). They are named together as accompanying Peter on that night made memorable by the second miraculous draught of fishes (John xxi. 2). But besides all this, the assumption on which the explanation rests is erroneous. There may be some ambiguity in our Version, ' *He surnamed them Boanerges*; ' but there is none in the original. Anyone turning to it will at once perceive that St. Mark distinctly implies that each of the twain, by himself and apart from the other, was by the Lord called a ' son of thunder; ' that, while the Evangelist records the

---

[1] So Theodoret: υἱοὺς βροντῆς τὴν ξυνωρίδα τῶν ἀποστόλων ἐκάλεσε.

' *name* ' Peter as given to Simon, when he tells of James and John it is no longer the ' *name* ' (ὄνομα) but the ' *names* ' (ὀνόματα), ' *sons of thunder*,' which they receive ; and thus no room is left for such a solution of the difficulty. But may not this difficulty be of a much simpler solution? Of no other than this, that the surname Boanerges, being common to both apostles, would not have sufficiently designated which of them was intended ; and that this inconvenience may have hindered it from ever growing into an appellation ; which, indeed, there was no need that it should do, having been given with quite another object and intention.

A more important question lies behind this—What was the meaning and purpose of this name? That it was intended as a name of honour was never for an instant doubted by Christian antiquity ; and indeed, since all acknowledge the title given to Simon, which immediately precedes it, to have been such an honourable superaddition, it seems wholly inconceivable that there should have been another name imposed on two other of the elect Twelve in quite a different intention and spirit. Indeed there are few interpretations of Holy Scripture more monstrous in their kind than that other supposition, namely, that the two sons of Zebedee acquired this addition, ' *sons of thunder*,' from the untimely and passionate request of theirs, that they might be allowed to call down fire from heaven on the inhabitants of that churlish Samaritan village (Luke ix. 54). Calmet was, I believe, the first who started this explanation,[1] at least I have not seen it traced to an earlier source, but it has found much acceptance since. Thus Tholuck, as quoted

---

[1] In his *Dictionnaire*, 1730.

below,[1] assumes it as certain, and affirms that the name
was imposed upon them ' to remind them evermore of
that inner foe with whom they needed to contend.'

But not to urge that there is no mention of thunder, or
allusion to it, in that passage, nor yet at 2 Kin. i. 9–12,
to the precedent of which the two apostles avowedly
refer (' as Elias did '), the deriving of their name from
this fault of theirs goes counter to the whole tenour and
analogy of Scripture. The new name there is evermore
the expressing and fixing of the new nature; it is the
record of some notable achievement, some glorious confession by word or deed, through which the servant of
God, who thus wins this name, has been permanently
lifted up into a higher region of being than that which he
moved in before (Gen. xxxii. 28; Judg. vi. 32; Acts iv.
36, 37; Matt. xvi. 18; Rev. ii. 17). It marks some
signal epoch or crisis of his spiritual life, which with its
results by aid of this new title is stamped upon him for
ever (Num. xiii. 16; Gen. xvii. 5, 15). The essence
then of the new name being everywhere else in Scripture
the expressing at once and the fixing of the new nature,
it is quite impossible that here it should be exactly the
reverse; namely, the seizing of a transient and momentary outcoming of the old nature, and the imparting
of a fixity and permanence to that. Simon's habitual
firmness, not his momentary weakness, his confession, not
his denial, of his Lord, was incorporated in his name,
Cephas, or Peter, or the Rock; nor can we doubt that in

---

[1] Wir finden ein blindes natürliches Feuer bei ihm [Johannes] in jenem
Zuge, der Luc. ix. 54 erzählt wird. Die hierbei bewiesene Gesinnung scheint
tief aus seinem Character hervorgegangen zu sein, denn Christus legte wegen
dieses Unfalls ihm und seinem Bruder denn Namen βοανεργές, υἱοὶ βροντῆς
bei, um sie immer an ihren innern Feind zu erinnern.

like manner the Lord expressed at once the noblest and most characteristic features of these two apostles in this designation which He gave them. Even in the kingdoms of this world a king does not fasten on one of his noblest and most honourable captains a title which shall remind of his single defeat, but rather one which shall be the abiding record of the most glorious victories which he has won. Not Teneriffe, but the Nile, is bound up with Nelson's title. And if thus in this lower world of ours, how much more certainly in the kingdom of grace.

It is not easy to see what the motive was for abandoning the earlier exposition. It is true that we cannot link the giving of this name with any particular incident in the lives of these two, as we can the new name which Abram (Gen. xvii. 5), which Jacob (Gen. xxxii. 28), which Gideon (Jud. vi. 32), which Simon (Matt. xvi. 16–18), which Joses (Acts iv. 36, 37), and perhaps also which Saul (Acts xiii. 7–9) acquired, with incidents and epochs in *their* lives. It must be allowed also that the usual conception of St. John, and of the character of his ministry, is somewhat different from that of a '*son of thunder.*' And yet a little deeper insight into the matter will, I am persuaded, afford us much which will help to explain and justify the bearing of this name by his brother and by himself.[1]

There can, of course, be no difficulty in regard to St. James. We have not, indeed, very much in his history

---

[1] Tillemont : Jésus-Christ en les appellant à l'apostolat, leur donna le surnom de Boanerges pour marquer la fermeté et la grandeur de leur foy, et parcequ'ils étoient destinés à faire éclater la majesté de Dieu dans tout l'univers, à ne pas aimer la terre, mais à la faire trembler pour la soumettre à Jésus-Christ, à ne point craindre toute la puissance des hommes, mais à se tenir toujours élevés au-dessus d'eux.

accounting for and illustrating this name ; but then we have not much in any shape about him ; and in what we have there is nothing which does not perfectly agree with, or even confirm, we may say, its fitness. And here, indeed, when we are gathering notices which should account for their being so called, that fiery zeal of his and of his brother, who would have burnt up the village that refused the shelter of a night to their Lord, may be fitly adduced as illustrating this title, though utterly misleading when cited as explaining and justifying it. It illustrates this title, because it shews us what in these two apostles was the natural groundwork of their character ; a groundwork which Christ certainly did not dissolve ; but rather, calling them these '*sons of thunder*,' recognized ; even while by the same act He pledged Himself to purify it from whatever of earthly and carnal mingled with it, and threatened to spoil it. The very failings which on that memorable occasion the brother apostles displayed were failings of no common souls ; were as luxuriant weeds, which, weeds as they were, testified for the richness of the soil out of which they sprang and its capacity for bearing the very noblest fruits. In their sense of righteousness and judgment, in their indignation against sin,—all this, indeed, displaying itself in an impatient and untimely severity, which would have consumed the sinners and the sin together, rather than the sin alone, with a saving alive of the sinners,—we see the '*sons of thunder*' on their natural side, and as they would have been but for that grace, which, retaining and exalting all the good of the natural character, did at the same time transform it from human to divine, separate all the drossy elements of earth, and retain only the pure gold of heaven.

And the early martyrdom of James, the fact that he, first of the apostles, stained with his blood the persecutor's sword (Acts xii. 2), we may accept this as a further attestation that he indeed *was* all that his name implied. A ' *son of thunder*,' and, as such, arousing, startling, terrifying, he may have caused the thunders of the divine displeasure against sin to be heard with a clearness and an energy which drew on him the peculiar and early hatred of the ungodly world [1]—the holiness of his life lending additional weight and terror to his words —for in him, no doubt, that saying will have found its fullest application, ' Cujus vita fulgor, ejus verba tonitrua.'

Then too much of the embarrassment which some feel, when they would make an estimate of what in St. John there is to justify this title, arises from their leaving the Apocalypse out of consideration (it is singular how often this is done), and regarding the beloved apostle as though he were the author of the Gospel and Epistles alone. Certainly those who forget the Apocalypse, or adjudge its authorship to some other than the ' beloved disciple,' must find this word of the Lord's inadequately fulfilled in the writings which will then remain to him. For, without denying that much in his Gospel also is like thunder out of a clear heaven,—the Fathers were especially fond of quoting in proof the very opening words of the Gospel,[2]— it is yet in the Apocalypse that those which eminently

---

[1] So Chrysostom (*Hom.* 56 *in Matt.*): οὕτω γὰρ ἦν σφοδρὸς καὶ βαρὺς Ἰουδαίοις, ὡς καὶ τὸν Ἡρώδην ταύτην δωρεὰν μεγίστην νομίσαι χαρίσασθαι τοῖς Ἰουδαίοις, εἰ ἐκεῖνον ἀνέλοι.

[2] See Suicer, *Thes.* s. v. βροντή.

may be called the thunder-voices make themselves heard. This they do there with a greater loudness and distinctness than in any other book of the New Testament.[1]   It needs hardly be observed that the thunder in Scripture is no mere natural phenomenon.   We do not read there that *it* thunders, but that *God* thunders ;[2] the thunder being contemplated there as his voice (Ps. xviii. 13 ; xxix. 3 ; lxviii. 33 ; lxxvii. 18 ; civ. 7 ; cxliv. 6 ; Job xxvi. 14 ; xxxvii. 4, 5 ; xl. 9 ; 1 Sam. vii. 10), as the voice above all of his displeasure against the sins of men (1 Sam. xii. 17, 18).   The terror which the thunder inspires springs from the interpretation of it which everyone unconsciously makes, from the sense which everyone has, that it is this voice in nature, with which God is speaking, and speaking in anger, to a sinful world.[3]   And what book is there in Scripture so full of these voices of God as that with which the Canon is sealed?   Nor certainly can it be regarded as a mere accident that, with the exception of

---

[1] Βροντόφωνος is an epithet given in the Greek Church to St. John. The brothers received the name of ' *sons of thunder*,' in Theophylact's words, ὡς μεγαλοκήρυκες καὶ θεολογικώτατοι.   Epiphanius says of St. John : υἱὸς ὄντως βροντῆς τῇ οἰκείᾳ μεγαλοφωνίᾳ ὥσπευ ἐκ τινῶν νεφελῶν τῶν τῆς σοφίας αἰνιγμάτων τὴν εὐσεβῆ ἡμῖν ἔννοιαν τοῦ Υἱοῦ ἀνῆκε.   See the valuable collection of passages from the Greek Fathers in Suicer, *Thes.* s. v. βροντή. Bengel among moderns has well expressed the same : Magnifica appellatio. Tonitrue in Scripturâ et terribile et festivum quiddam est.   Evangelium item mundum terret, piis lætitiam et fructum affert.   That there is a natural fitness in such an application of βροντή, the parallel use of βροντᾶν in profane Greek attests.   Pericles had the name of Ὀλύμπιος, as, like Zeus himself, lightning and thundering (ἤστραπτ', ἐβρόντα, Aristophanes, *Acharn.* 531 ; cf. *Vesp.* 624) over Greece.   In the ' geminos, duo *fulmina* belli, Scipiadas,' of Virgil we have not the identical, but a closely cognate, image.

[2] J. Grimm, in an article, *Ueber die Namen des Donners*, in his *Klein. Schrift.* vol. ii. p. 421, has some interesting proofs of the many nations among whom the same language prevails.

[3] Gregory the Great (*Moral.* xxix. 24) : Quid enim per tonitruum nisi prædicatio superni terroris accipitur?

this passage *about* St. John, only in his own writings is there any mention of thunder in the New Testament at all. In his Gospel, it is but a passing notice (xii. 29); in the Apocalypse, however, the thunders constitute a prominent part of the divine machinery and symbolism (Rev. iv. 5; vi. 1; viii. 5; x. 3, 4; xi. 19; xiv. 2; xvi. 18; xix. 6). Surely he whose ear was opened, first himself to catch, and then to give back to the Church and to the world, these thunder-voices, must be allowed to have approved himself, even to our understanding, that '*son of thunder*,' which the Lord has named him.[1]

---

[1] There is an able and interesting article by Gurlitt in the *Theol. Stud. und Krit.* 1829, pp. 715–738, on the word ' Boanerges,' and the intention with which this name was given to the sons of Zebedee. It is more valuable, however, as containing a history of the past exegesis, than as itself arriving at any satisfactory results.

5. *WISDOM JUSTIFIED OF HER CHILDREN*

Matt. xi. 16-19; Luke vii. 31-35.

As nothing which was wrought among the children of men escaped the notice of the Lord, so nothing was so far beneath Him but that He was content to use it, if it would help Him to set forth the truths of his kingdom. Those truths had in themselves such inherent dignity and grandeur that they had nothing to fear from being brought into this contact. We have a striking example of this, his fearless use of the common and the familiar, in that comparison with which He closes his testimony to the character and work of the Baptist : ' *But whereunto shall I liken this generation? It is like unto children sitting in the markets, and calling unto their fellows, and saying, We have piped unto you, and ye have not danced ; we have mourned unto you, and ye have not lamented.*' Here the Lord finds in the sports and altercations of boys playing in the streets that which shall serve his turn, shall set forth and illustrate the truth which He has in hand. One group of these children, in that spirit of imitation so characteristic of their age, has been acting now a marriage, and now a funeral ; has been piping now, and mourning anon ; but in the end complains that another band, whose help they needed, and whom they would fain have drawn into their

sports, as mourners at their mock funeral, if they would
not be revellers at their mock marriage, have stood
peevishly aloof, and refused altogether to take a share in
their games : ' *We have piped unto you, and ye have not
danced; we have mourned unto you, and ye have not
lamented.*'[1]

Christ proceeds to explain *why* and wherein that generation resembled these to whom He has just compared
them : '*for John came neither eating nor drinking*' (cf.
Luke i. 80 ; Matt. iii. 4; ix. 14); '*and they say, He hath
a devil.*' We should not have learned except from these
words that such a taunt was addressed to the Baptist ;
that they said of the servant what we know that more
than once they said of the Master (John vii. 20 ; viii. 48) ;
at the same time it is exactly the manner of taunt which
his manner of life, exaggerated and extravagant as it
must have seemed to many, was likely to provoke. ' *The
Son of man came eating and drinking*' (cf. Matt. ix. 14 ;
Luke xiv. 1 ; John ii. 1–11 ; xii. 2), ' *and they say, Behold
a man gluttonous, and a wine-bibber, a friend of publicans and sinners*' (Matt. ix. 10, 11 ; Luke vii. 39; xv. 2 ;
xix. 7).

Few, I think, who at all reflect on the matter, will
deny that the ordinary explanation of this similitude is
encumbered with considerable difficulties. According to
this explanation the children who complain of the way-
ward humour of their fellows, and that they cannot draw
them into any games which they propose, are Jesus

---

[1] Vorstius (*De Adag. N. T.* c. xi.): Ea verba Salvator tribuit pueris
sedentibus in foro, qui ludendo imitari solent quæ a majoribus natu serio
agi viderunt, et nunc nuptias celebrant, nunc funera deducunt ; neque tamen
quosdam qui morosiores sunt, movere possunt, ut et ipsi talibus operam
navent.

and John; and the meaning will then be, This is a generation which it is impossible to please. No ways of God are right in its eyes. If He send a prophet, stern, severe, calling to repentance, holding aloof from sinners, a wilderness preacher, a man himself of fasts and austerities, as was John, they say he is melancholy mad; '*He hath a devil.*' If He send One gracious and condescending, who mingles with all the common works, and walks in all the common ways of men, eating and drinking with them, they say, '*Behold a man gluttonous and a wine-bibber,*' with no eminent sanctity about Him. John took up a sadder strain, but the men of this generation would not fall in with it: he mourned to them, but they would not lament. Jesus took up a more joyful note; He piped to them; but neither would they consent with Him; they would not dance; but found as much fault with the graciousness and condescension of the One as with the strictness and severity of the other.

All this is well put by Henry More: 'Such was the perverse and wicked ignorance of those crooked superstitionists, that true goodness in no kind of dress would please them. In John the Baptist there was that eminent severity and austerity of life accompanying an unreprovable integrity and purity of heart, that he might, one would think, have commanded them to that which was good; but he must have a melancholy devil in him. Our Saviour came in a more pleasant and careless garb, laying aside that awful and rough severity that was in the other, intermingling Himself with all companies, taking not at all upon Him, being as other men are in everything, sin only excepted; (which manner of life as it is of more perfection than the other, as supposing more benignity of nature, and more firm radication in goodness, so fewer men are capable of it, much less unsteady and unresolved youth, who are to fly from suspected company as from the devouring plague ;) yet, I say, these wretched Pharisees, as true detesters of real holiness and godliness, whatever they pretend in the shadow thereof, cannot give our Saviour a good word, but interpret his goodnature good-fellowship or debauched company-keeping; and his serviceable intermingling Himself with all sorts of men (publicans and sinners not excepted) for their good, friendship and countenance to what is evil.'[1]

Such is the common explanation ; and the sense which the passage, so interpreted, renders up is in itself a perfectly satisfactory one. The only question is, whether our Lord's words yield themselves to it, whether there be not serious difficulties in this allotment of the several portions of the dramatic action here brought before our eyes. In the first place, Christ says, ' *This generation is like unto children ;*' but, according to the received explanation as given above, it would be Jesus and John who were like the children complaining that it was impossible to chime in with the shifting moods of their fellows, and not that generation at all. Maldonatus, as is usual with him, manfully acknowledges this difficulty; but seeks to set it aside by urging that not part of a parabolic saying like this must be compared with part, but the whole with the whole; and adduces as a parallel case Matt. xiii. 24 : ' The kingdom of heaven is likened unto a man which sowed good seed in his field ; ' not being, indeed, likened to him alone, but to all which follows. But the case is not exactly in point ; for at any rate he, the sower, was

---

[1] *On Godliness,* viii. 13.

included in that whereto the kingdom was compared; while here the perverse generation has no resemblance to the children who complain, and to whom they are likened, but only to the children that are complained of. We cannot then accept this solution. And then, further, since John's ministry *preceded* the Lord's, and in the interpretation (ver. 18) is the first named, we should expect to find ' *We have mourned unto you,*' which was St. John's work, adduced the first, and not, as in both Evangelists it is, the last.

Would it not then be better to shift altogether the *dramatis personæ*, and, re-allotting the parts, to make, as Euthymius, Stier,[1] and Alford have done, the children sitting in the markets, and now mourning and now piping, to be the Jews, the generation of which the Lord just before had spoken; and the companions of whom they complain, to be Jesus and John? The fundamental thought will still be nearly the same, although expressed in a somewhat different manner, although it will not be now any more Jesus and John who are introduced finding fault with that generation, but that generation finding fault with them. The Jews, as according to this explanation the Lord will declare, wanted John to be laxer; they would fain have had him give up his strict ascetic ways, his rigid separation from sinners, his stern summonses to repentance; and complained that he would not do so, that he would not dance to their piping. Christ Himself was equally, as they accounted, at fault, though in an opposite extreme. They could as little understand a prophet such as He was. They mourned to Him, and He would not lament. The bridegroom and the bringer

---

[1] *Reden Jesu,* in loco.

of joy, He would not change for any sadder note, that
note of joy to which the Gospel that He preached was
set (Luke v. 30–35), any more than John to please them
would change and renounce the note of a sterner sadness
to which his preaching of the law was attuned.

Each messenger and prophet of God the men of that
generation desired to be something other than what he
was—their distaste and disaffection extending really far
deeper than to the particular manner and fashion of the
one or of the other, to the severity of the one, or to the
laxity, as they chose to call it, of the other—their objection being indeed to *any* messenger of God, in whatever
guise he came. As it was then, so is it at all times.
Some exclaim, ' The Gospel is too strict, too severe; it
demands too much;' these are the finders of a fault in
the Baptist; while others say, ' It is too lax, too free; it
encourages sin;' these finding matter of blame in the
Lord ; the two forms of murmuring and opposition being,
strange to say, found sometimes united in the same persons. The ambassadors of Christ, who have to call men
alternately to fasts and festivals of the spirit, must expect
from the world such a captious and hostile criticism as
this; it is part of that which they must bear. They must
look for a similar indignation, that they will not at the
world's bidding be exactly the contrary of that which
they were sent to be ; this indignation being indeed the
covert under which men escape from the summons, now
to a spiritual joy, and now to a spiritual sorrow.

' *But*,' while it was thus with that generation, ' *Wisdom
is justified of her children.*' All did not so evade the law
by pleading the Gospel, nor the Gospel by pleading the
law. Some recognized in these two, and in the harmony

of these two, the law being good no less than the Gospel,
if only used lawfully (1 Tim. i. 8), 'the manifold wisdom
of God;' out of which He sent not a John only, nor a
Christ only, but sent one *and* the other, the severe and
the mild, the stern and the gracious, the preacher of the
.law and the preacher of grace, that so He might win men
by the one or by the other, or, as most commonly He
does, by handing them over *from* the one to the other
(Rom. iii. 19–26 ; Gal. iii. 24 ; John i. 35–40).

Such seems to me the general drift and tenour of these
words; which yet may claim to be more closely examined, presenting as they do, by the acknowledgment
of all, more difficulties than one. And first, seeing that
the Lord is clearing the dealings of God with men, in
other words, clearing his own, why, it might be asked,
does He let his own personality fall into the back ground,
and affirm, not of Himself, but of Wisdom, that she '*is
justified of her children?*' He does not really do this.
'*Wisdom*' here is no abstract quality, no attribute of God,
any more than at Luke xi. 49 ; but a person ; even the
same of whom such glorious things are spoken in the
Book of Proverbs, who appears there, as crying in the
streets (i. 21 ; viii. 1–3), as building her mystical house,
sending forth her maidens, gathering to herself all those
who are willing to hear her voice (ix. 1–6); being,
indeed, no other than the Word as yet *not* made
flesh, or rather that divine Word in *all* his dealings, both
before the Incarnation and after, with the children of
men;[1] who, being this absolute Wisdom, must have

---

[1] Hilary (in loc.) : Ipsum se Sapientiam vocavit. Bengel : Non enim
jam dicitur Filius hominis, ut versu præcedente, sed Sapientia; quarum
appellationum altera convenit statui Christi conspicuo, altera omnibus
temporibus (Luc. xi. 49). Porro Sapientia hoc loco dicitur, quod Ipse

chosen wisest ways in which to deal with them, and who therefore should not have been lightly charged with waywardness and folly. This word ' *Wisdom,*' which Christ uses here, has the advantage that by aid of it He can include in a common justification both his own dealings and those of John, which last He would fain vindicate not less than his own.

But '*justified of her children*'—what may be the exact force of this phrase? ' To justify,' in the uniform language of the New Testament, is to recognize and declare as righteous—falsely, it may be; that not *being* righteous, which thus declares itself, or is declared by others, to be so (Luke x. 29; xvi. 15); or, and this is far the commoner usage, truly; the realities in the moral world corresponding with the declaration thus made about them. So of course is it here, where Wisdom is contemplated as on her trial, perversely accused by some, and needing therefore to be '*justified*' by others.[1] When it is said that she is justified '*of her children,*' these last can be no other than as many as have accepted her teaching, and now walk in her ways. It is not that we are to contemplate

---

optime sciat quid faciendum sit, et actiones Ipsius, purissimâ accommodatione ad peccatores plenæ, non debuerunt sub censuram vocari (Prov. viii. 1, 32). Grotius too much lets go that the Σοφία is herself a person, when he adduces βουλὴ τοῦ Θεοῦ (Luke vii. 30) as an absolute equivalent; though, this excepted, he has perfectly seized the intention of these words: ἡ σοφία hic nihil aliud est quam quod apud Lucam vii. 30, βουλὴ τοῦ Θεοῖ, sapientissimum nimirum Dei consilium Judæos et Johannis severitate et Christi comitate ad pœnitentiam revocantis, ne quid inexpertum relinqueret, atque etiam ne quid illi causari possent . . . Johannes, ut pœnitentiæ præco, ad severitatem compositus, Christus comis ut veniæ largitor.

[1] Bengel: *Sapientia justificata est*; hoc est, criminatores illam ream fecere, scandalizati sunt in eâ (ver. 23), eoque rem adduxere, ut demum justificari debuerit ipsa, et justa asseri ostendique, omnes ejus actiones ad absorbendam injustitiam, justitiamque implendam comparatas esse, cum tamen sine exceptione fuisset amplectenda.

these as pleading her cause before the world, and so acquitting her of these unjust imputations. She needed not their advocacy, and ' babes ' (Matt. xi. 25) as they were, they could thus have done little to serve her. But yet in another sense it was out of the mouths of these babes and sucklings that her praise was perfected. In the fact that there were these children of Wisdom, that she had gathered so many round her, who owned her for their spiritual mother, hereby and herein she was justified, acquitted of all those frivolous charges and all that unrighteous blame which had been heaped upon her.[1] As Jesus spake these words, He may have looked round at the little company of his disciples. These were his justification and John's; these did themselves constitute a vindication of Wisdom's ways in the face of a gainsaying world.[2]

---

[1] So Jerome rightly, with only the fault that he limits the ' *children* ' too exclusively to the apostles; they properly include *all* the converts whom either John or the Lord had made: Ego, qui sum Dei virtus et Sapientia Dei, justifecisse ab apostolis, filiis meis, comprobatus sum.

[2] Meyer (in loc.), as it seems to me, has seized the meaning exactly: *Und gerechtfertiget worden* (das heisst, als die *wahre* Weisheit dargestellt worden) *ist die Weisheit* (die in Johannes und mir zur Offenbarung gekommen ist) *von Seiten ihrer Kinder*, dass heisst, von Seiten ihrer Verehrer und Anhänger, welche eben dadurch, dass sie sich ihr angeschlossen haben und sich von ihr leiten lassen, jene Urtheile des profanum vulgus als unrichtig dargestellt und die Weisheit factisch gerechtfertiget haben. *Die* (factische) *Bewährung ist der Weisheit von ihren Verehrern gekommen* (ἀπό, nicht ὑπό). There is more than one other explanation of these certainly difficult words, which I have not cared to deal with in the text, as they certainly appear to me wholly untenable. That which has found most favour I will give in Gerhard's words (*Harm. Evang.* 56): Divina Sapientia a filiis suis justificatur, hoc est quasi in judicium pertrahitur, disceptatur cum eâ, de jure accusatur, taxatur, reprehenditur, ut in quâ nunc hoc nunc illud desideretur. Et qui debebant esse filii sapientiæ divinæ, hoc est obedientes discipuli, illi sumunt sibi, quasi pro tribunali sedentes, jus vocis decisivæ, ut pro libitu suo vel pro vel contra divinam sapientiam possint pronunciare. Not to speak of other objections, this explanation rests on the

ascription to the verb δικαιοῦν of a meaning which, in profane Greek common enough, indeed predominant there, in Biblical Greek it never possesses. It is never there to judge and declare *guilty*, but always, to judge and declare *righteous*. The only exception to this which I know is Ps. lxxiii. 13, where it means neither one nor the other, but is used as = ἁγνίζειν. Gerhard seeks to sustain his interpretation by aid of Isai. xliii. 9; 2 Kin. xv. 4; but neither passage helps him in the least.

6. *THE THREE ASPIRANTS*

Matt. viii. 18–23; Luke ix. 57–62.

' THE manifold wisdom' of Christ, which shewed itself in
his drawing and attaching of souls to Himself, and of
which there has just been occasion to speak, must often
fill us with devout admiration; but it never does this
more than when there are brought before us in quick
succession moral and spiritual conditions, which have
much apparent similarity, and which yet are most diversely
treated by Him.[1] Such we have here. There are two,
or adding one of whom St. Luke alone keeps record, three,
who either in their own intention, or in the Lord's, are
candidates for admission into the inner circle of disciples,
into the circle, that is, of those who should not merely
themselves receive the truth, but, as Christ's witnesses,
should be actively employed in imparting the knowledge
of that truth to others. The occasion which gave room
for such a dealing with these souls was as follows: ' *Now
when Jesus saw great multitudes about Him, He gave commandment to depart unto the other side.*' One of what we
may call the lesser crises in his ministry here arrived. There
is growing up around Him that tumult and excitement, in-

[1] Augustine (*Serm.* 100): Obtulit se unus, ut eum sequeretur, et repro-
batus est; alius non audebat, et excitatus est; tertius differebat, et culpatus
est.

cident on the gathering of enormous crowds, with expectations raised to the highest, which more than anything else
threatened to defeat his plans, to alter, against his will,
the whole character of the work which He was working ;
which, therefore, by every means He sought to avert or to
repress (Luke xiv. 25–33 ; xix. 11–27); or, where this
was beyond his power, to withdraw Himself from it
(John vi. 15). The retirement which at such seasons
served Him best He found upon the other side of the lake
of Galilee ; until, indeed, the eagerness of the multitude
had learned to follow Him even thither (John vi. 2).
Such a retreat to that other side He is about now to
undertake. Who will go with Him, and thus give more
explicit announcement than he may yet have had the
opportunity of giving, that he casts in his lot with
Christ ?

First there offers himself a Scribe—' *one Scribe*,' as St.
Matthew says, with, perhaps, an emphasis on the ' *one*,'
to mark how unfrequent offers of service from such a
quarter were. And his words sound fairly, ' *Master, I
will follow Thee whithersoever Thou goest.*' They almost
remind one of the great-hearted words of Ittai to David :
' Surely in what place my lord the king shall be, whether
in death or life, even there also will thy servant be '
(2 Sam. xv. 21). Nor is there any reason to suppose
that this aspirant to discipleship meant at the time otherwise than he spoke. Yet is there not indeed in him that
true devotedness to Christ, which shall lead him so to follow that Lord in this world, that in the world to come he
shall follow Him whithersoever He goeth (Rev. xiv. 4).[1]

---

[1] Calvin : Vult quidem hic Christum sequi, sed mollem et amœnam viam,
et hospitia bonis omnibus reperta somniat, quum per spinas ambulandum

These words have more in them of Peter's confident asseveration, 'Lord, I am ready to go with Thee both unto prison and to death' (Luke xxii. 33). At all events, they inspire Him, who knowing all things (John xxi. 17) 'knew what was in man,' with no greater confidence than those other words hereafter should do ; for with no welcome for this volunteer, but rather a repulse, He answers, ' *The foxes have holes, and the birds of the air have nests ;* [1] *but the Son of man* [2] *hath not where to lay his head.*' [3] In other words, 'Lookest thou for worldly commodities through the following of Me? In this thou must needs be disappointed. These cannot be my follower's portion, since they are not mine. Beasts have

---

sit Christi discipulis, et per continuas ærumnas ad crucem pergendum. Ergo quo magis festinat, eo minus paratus est. Perinde enim facit acsi in umbrâ et deliciis, sine sudore et pulvere, extra telorum jactum militare vellet.

[1] Κατασκηνώσεις is so rendered in the Versions preceding, as well as in the Authorised Version. The Vulgate in like manner has ' nidos ; ' but an earlier Latin version ' diversoria,' while Augustine has ' nidos ' (*Serm.* c. 1), ' diversoria ' (*Con. Faust.* xxii. 48), and ' tabernacula ' (*Quæst.* xvii. *in Matt.* qu. 5) ; these latter, with the equivalent English, 'shelters ' (Chrysostom substitutes καταγωγία), being on all accounts preferable renderings. For, in the first place, birds do not retire to their nests except at one brief period of the year ; and then, secondly, κατασκηνώσεις has so much more naturally the more general meaning of shelters, habitations, latibula, cubilia, or, more strictly, umbracula ex ramis et frondibus arborum contexta (Corn. a Lapide), Wohnungen (de Wette), that one must needs agree with Grotius : Quin vox hæc ad arborum ramos pertineat dubitaturum non puto qui loca infra, xiii. 32 ; Marc. iv. 32, et Luc. xiii. 9, inspexerit. He might have added Ps. civ. 12 ; Dan. iv. 18, LXX. See Fischer, *De Vitiis Lex. N. T.* pp. 285–290 ; and on φωλεός (=τόπος, οὗ τὰ θηρία κοιμᾶται, Hesychius) see p. 287, note.

[2] Godet : Le terme de *Fils de l'homme* est précisément employé ici pour faire ressortir ce contraste entre le Roi de la création et ses plus pauvres sujets.

[3] Very curious is the turn which Augustine (*Enarr. in Ps.* xc., *Serm.* 2) gives to these words : Vulpes *in te* foveas habent ; volucres cæli nidos *in te* habent ; vulpes dolus est, volucres cæli superbia est . . . Potest in te habitare superbia et dolus ; Christus non habet ubi in te habitet, ubi reclinet caput suum. Quia inclinatio capitis, humilitas Christi est. Cf. *Serm.* c. 1.

dens, and birds have shelters, which they may call their
own ; but the Son of man is homeless and houseless upon
earth ; He who made the world has not in the world
where to lay his head.   It fares with Him as with Jacob
at his poorest estate, when, fleeing from his brother's
wrath, he tarried all night at Haran, "and took of the
stones of that place, and put them for his pillows " (Gen.
xxviii. 11).   Nor does this answer of Christ our Lord
come out to us in all its depth of meaning, till we
realize that hour when upon his cross He bowed his
head, not having where to lay it, and having bowed it
thus gave up the ghost (John xix. 30).

Whether it fared with this Scribe as with that rich
young man of a later day (Matt. xix. 22), whether this
one also withdrew and went away, we are not informed.[1]
That he did this is certainly the impression left upon our
minds.   But whatever was the issue, this reply of Christ
was not meant any more than that other, merely and only
to repel.   It was intended rather to throw back this can-
didate for the honours of discipleship on deeper heart-
searchings ; that, having made these, he might either fall
off altogether, not beginning to build a tower which he
could not finish, or else that he might attach himself to
the Lord in quite another spirit from that in which he
made his present offer of service (Luke xiv. 25–33).

The Lord, who has checked one, incites another ; for
He knew there was more truth in the backwardness of

---

[1] Corn. a Lapide : Quod audiens siluit, ac spe suâ frustratus, ab oculis
Christi se subduxit, ut tacite hic innuit Matthæus.   Tertullian (*Adv.
Marcion.* iv. 23), besides taking this for granted, assumes further that we
are to read in these words an *absolute* rejection of him on the Lord's part,
which seems to me a mistake.

him to whom He addresses Himself now than in the for-
wardness of that other who had just addressed Him.   He
has for him that significant *'Follow Me'* which He had
for a Philip, a Matthew, an Andrew, a Peter (John i. 43 ;
Matt. ix. 9 ; Mark i. 17).   It is in answer to such a summons, as St. Luke has told us, that this one replies, ' *Lord,
suffer me first to go and bury my father.*' In the early
Church this was oftenest, if not always, understood, 'My
father now lies dead ; suffer me, before I attach myself to
Thee, to render the last offices of piety to him.'   Not a
few in later times, I know none earlier than Theophylact,[1]
but with him agree Grotius, Calvin, Bengel, and others,
have understood it otherwise—as though his father was
now in extreme old age, with one foot, as we say, in the
grave ; and that the request of this son was, that he might
be permitted to tend and cherish his few days that remained ; being ready, when these offices of filial observance
were no more required of him, to obey this bidding.
But there is every reason for adhering to the earlier interpretation.   It is little likely that a disciple, or one ripe
for being a disciple, would at such a crisis have asked re-
spite from service for a period so utterly uncertain as this
would have been.[2]   Moreover, a son would scarcely speak
in such language of attendance on a father that yet lived.
The point too of Christ's rejoinder would thus be missed :
' *Let the dead bury their dead ;* ' let the spiritually dead
bury the naturally dead—which naturally dead He, designating as ' *their dead,*' implies to belong, and to have
belonged, to the same sphere of death as those who shall

---

[1] Τὸ γὰρ θάψαι ἐνταῦθα, τοῦτο σημαίνει· τὸ ἐπιμελείας ἀξιῶσαι, ἄχρι καὶ τῆς
ταφῆς.

[2] Maldonatus: Verisimile non est eum quem Christus cognoscens vocabat,
tam longi tamque incerti temporis inducias petivisse.

now perform the last offices for them.   At the same time by the former ' *dead* ' we must rather understand those in whom the spiritual life is as yet unawaked, than urge with any emphasis their death in trespasses and sins ; that must of necessity be implied, yet rather on its negative than its positive side.   'The spiritually dead, those who are not quickened as thou art with the spirit of a new life, are yet sufficient for the fulfilling of this office which would now call thee away from Me, namely, the bury-ing of the naturally dead; they can perform it as well as thou, and, under present circumstances, thou must be contented to leave it to them.'[1]   When duties come into collision, sacred duties such as that which this man pleaded (and how sacred for a pious Jew they were we see from Tob. iv. 3 ; xiv. 10, 11 ; not to mention the frequent notice in the early history of the due performance of these offices by children to their parents, Gen. xxv. 9 ; xxxv. 29 ; l. 13), even these must give way to more sacred yet.   Christ had said to this man, ' *Follow Me ;* ' so that now that saying held good, 'Whoso loveth father or mother more than Me, is not worthy of Me.'   And then, in words which we owe to St. Luke alone, Christ justifies his withdrawal of this man from attendance on the dead.   He had fitness for a work which, if not directly with the living, was yet

---

[1] Hilary: Admonetur ut meminerit quod Pater sibi vivus in cælis est . . . . mortuos autem eos esse, qui extra Deum vivant.   Et idcirco mutua mortuis officia relinquenda, ut mortui sepeliantur a mortuis ; quia per Dei fidem vivos vivo oporteat adhærere.   Augustine (*De Civ. Dei*, xx. 6): Habent enim et animæ mortem suam in impietate et peccatis . . . ut scilicet in animâ mortui, in corpore mortuos sepelirent.   Cf. *De Trin.* iv. 3 ; *Serm.* 88. 3 : Sicut enim etiam visibiliter plerumque in domo integrâ et salvâ dominus ejusdem domûs mortuus jacet, sic in corpore integro multi habent intus animam mortuam.   Corn. a Lapide: Ludit Christus in voce *mortuos*. Prius enim *mortuos* spiritualiter, fide gratiâque Dei destitutos significat. Posterius *mortuos* corporaliter intelligit.

with those who were capable of being made alive : ' *Go thou, and preach the kingdom of God ;*' as though He had said, 'Another task is thine ; namely, to spread far and wide (διαγγέλλειν) the glad tidings of life, which as many as hear shall live.[1] One of my royal priesthood (Lev. xxi. 1–12), a Nazarite of mine (Num. vi. 7), having fellowship with Me who am the Life, thy occupation is henceforth with the living, and not with the dead.'[2]

A third, of whom only St. Luke makes report, offers *himself* for discipleship : ' *Lord, I will follow Thee ;*'—yet this with conditions, and craving time for farewells which he fain would interpose ; ' *but let me first go bid them farewell who are at home at my house*'—this rendering of our English Version being preferable to that which some would substitute, ' *but let me first set in order the things in my house.*'[3] He too must learn that there is no dallying with a heavenly vocation ; that when this has reached a man, no room is left him for conferring with flesh and blood (Gal. i. 16) ; to him too, as to the king's daughter of old, the word of that precept has come, 'Forget also thine own people, and thy father's house ' (Ps. xlv. 10) ; while, as it may only too easily prove, his worst foes,

---

[1] That the antithesis is between death and life Augustine well brings out (*Serm.* lxii.): Docuit magister quid deberet præponere. Volebat enim eum esse vivi verbi prædicatorem ad faciendos victuros.

[2] Tertullian, with allusion to these two passages, one (Lev. xxi. 12) forbidding the High Priest to go in to any dead body, or to defile himself for his father; the other (Num. vi. 7) extending the same prohibition to the Nazarite, goes on to say (*Adv. Marc.* iv. 23): Puto autem et devotioni [that is, to the Nazarite vow] et sacerdotio destinabat, quem prædicando regno Dei imbuerat.

[3] 'Αποτάξασθαι τοῖς εἰς τὸν οἶκόν μου, which the Vulgate translates, renunciare his quæ [al. qui] domi sunt; but Beza better, ut valedicam iis qui sunt domûs meæ ; so Tertullian, suis valedicere parantem. There is required of him an ἀποτάσσεσθαι (see Luke xix. 33) in quite another sense from that which he contemplates.

those who will most effectually keep him back from God, may be those of his own household (Matt. x. 36, 37). The Lord therefore will give no allowance to his request, shuts out at once all dangerous delays and interludes between the offer of service and the actual undertaking of it: '*And Jesus said unto him, No man having put his hand to the plough, and looking back, is fit for the kingdom of God.*' He who holds the plough must not look behind him; if he does, he spoils the furrow, and mars the work which he has undertaken. Remarkably enough this careless marring of the furrow has lent a word to the Latin, and through the Latin to our own language; ' delirare,' originally to deviate from the ' lira,' which is strictly the little ridge of earth thrown up by the share between the two furrows, and then the furrow itself. The discipleship of Christ is such a putting of the hand to the plough, for the breaking up of the hard soil of our own hearts, for the breaking up of the hard soil of the hearts of others. We have the same image, Luke xvii. 7; 1 Cor. ix. 10. It sets forth the *laboriousness* of the work better than the more usual image of sowing (Matt. xiii. 3), and, so to speak, carries us a step further back in the spiritual husbandry. But he who, having put his hand to the plough, and thus begun well, shall afterwards, Christ does not say *turn* back, but even so much as *look* back, in token that his heart is otherwhere than in the task before him (Gen. xix. 26; Luke xvii. 32; 2 Tim. ii. 4; Phil. iii. 13, 14), he may still have his hand on the plough; but, having fallen away in heart and affection from his work, he makes no straight furrows, he breaks not up aright any fallow ground; he ' *is not fit,*' or rather, is of no service and profit, '*for the kingdom of God.*' Indeed, unless kept to his work as an hireling, it is likely that he will presently leave his plough in the half-drawn furrow, and be found to have exchanged toil and exposure abroad for the comforts and ease of his own hearth (Acts xiii. 13 ; xv. 38).

The reference to 1 Kin. xix. 19–21, which is generally here made, is not much to the point, except as an illustration by way of contrast. This bidding farewell to them of his house *was* permitted to Elisha; being included in the feast which he makes ver. 21 ; it is refused to this disciple. The comparison of that passage with this is instructive thus far, as shewing how much more urgent is the call of the Master than of the servant ; how much less it will brook question or delay.

What if those other two, and this third whose call St. Luke has associated with theirs, were, as one has suggested, Judas Iscariot, Thomas, and Matthew ?[1] In the second and third instances the summons is so plainly to a high work in the kingdom of God (that ' *Follow Me* ' of Christ ever implying as much, Matt. iv. 19 ; ix. 9 ; xix. 21 ; John i. 43 ; xxi. 19); and there is altogether so marked an emphasis about these calls, that it is difficult to suppose them calls merely to discipleship. Far more probably these were aspirants and candidates in their own eyes or in their Lord's, to a higher grade, to the apostolate itself. Indeed one of the three was a disciple already (Matt. viii. 21), whom the Lord here draws into a closer circle of service ; and the same is true of another, who, as clearly implied, had already set his hand to the plough (Luke ix. 62). Moreover, it is very noticeable that in

---

[1] The Gnostics, as Irenæus (1. 8. 3) tells us, found in them severally the representatives of the man ὑλικός, πνευματικός, and ψυχικός.

immediate sequence to the words thus exchanged by Christ with these three, St. Luke proceeds, 'After these things the Lord appointed *other* seventy also,' seeming thereby very distinctly to mark that what had just passed had relation to the Twelve; at all events to exclude one and all of these now mentioned from the Seventy. But if not disciples, not of the Seventy, what else but apostles could they have been? nor does the fact that St. Matthew's chronological order is here preferable to St. Luke's take from the significancy of this hint. In St. Matthew also we note that it is very shortly after the incidents which have just been recorded, that the Twelve are definitively set apart, that the number of those whom the Lord had been gathering one by one, appears complete (x. 1). Some in the early Church were moved by these or like probabilities to conclude that in one at least of these instances we had to do with the calling of an apostle, with that namely of Philip. This, however, though Clement of Alexandria[1] takes it for granted, could not be; Philip was already called (John i. 43); as were Andrew and Peter (John i. 40, 42), James and John (Luke v. 1–11), and Bartholomew (=Nathanael, John i. 47, 51). Three more of the apostles, the other James, Lebbæus (=Jude), and Simon Zelotes *may have been* 'brethren of the Lord;' and in that case could not have been identical with any of these three. If we have indeed the calling of apostles here, it can be that of no other than those whom I have named. At all events the conjecture has enough of historical and psychological likelihood about it to be worth following up a little further.

[1] *Strom.* iii. 4.

Thus the first who offered himself was one whom evidently the Lord welcomed with no pleasure, whom He would willingly have put back from Him, whose large professions inspired Him with no confidence whatever. And how significant is the Lord's reply to these professions. He to whom all hearts were open, saw as with a glance in the heart of this offerer what perhaps at the moment was altogether concealed from himself. There is nothing to be gotten, He tells him, no worldly advantage to be gained, through a following of Him, who, Son of Man though He be, is yet poorer even than the poorest ; [1] —as though he already beheld in spirit the unhappy disciple, who, defeated in his hope of a kingdom of this world, and of a place there among the chief, should seek to redress a little the wrong which he had suffered by purloining from the common stock (John xii. 6), and should end with making merchandize of the Lord of Glory Himself.

But while he, proffering himself, is rather repelled than welcomed, the other two have, as we have seen, summonses and invitations more or less direct to attach themselves ever more closely to their Lord ; and if they be the two who have just been suggested, there is addressed to each the exact encouragement and reproof which he probably would have needed. ' *Suffer me first to go, and bury my father.*' How characteristic of the melancholic Thomas is the excuse and the hindrance which are pleaded here—of him, who at a later day, in the very presence of the Lord and Prince of life, could only express his affection to Him by those words, 'Let us also go, that we may die with Him' (John xi. 16); who

---

[1] Cajetan : Spem lucri tollit hæc responsio.

even after the empty tomb, and the testimony of the
women and of his fellow apostles, could not disengage
himself from thoughts of death and the grave, nor be
persuaded to believe that the Lord had risen indeed
(John xx. 24, 25). How characteristic was it of him in
whose mind death was thus uppermost, that on the present occasion also the duties to the dead should seem to
him to overbear those to the living. And Christ's answer
and reproof exactly meets the disease and infirmity of his
soul : ' Thou belongest to the new creation; not to the
old world of death, but to the new world of life. *Go thou,
and preach the kingdom of God.* Disperse to others the
words of that life with which thou thyself hast been
quickened.'

And the third, who cannot obey the calling till he has
bade a solemn farewell to all in his house, might very
well be St. Matthew; who, being refused this, did not
therefore at this time accompany the Lord ; but to whom
that Lord a little later so spake that he obeyed; and
whose farewell feast, *after* he had thrown in his lot with
Christ, so that there was no longer any indecision in his
asking to be permitted to make it, the Lord allowed, and
adorned with his own presence (Matt. ix. 9, 10 ; Luke v.
27, 29); and that, although He had disallowed it, so
long as it was made the condition of obedience.

7. THE NEW PIECE ON THE OLD GARMENT AND THE NEW WINE IN THE OLD BOTTLES

Matt. ix. 14–17; Mark ii. 18–22; Luke v. 33–39.

THE FEAST which Levi made, probably as a sort of leave-taking to the other publicans, now that he had found for himself a better service than that of the Roman emperor, was very fruitful in rich and precious instruction. There was first the Saviour's answer to those who complained, not *to* Him, but *concerning* Him, that He ate with publicans and sinners (Matt. ix. 12, 13); and there was then his answer to a second remonstrance, on the part not now of the Pharisees alone, as we might conclude from St. Luke (v. 33), nor yet of John's disciples alone, as we might gather from St. Matthew (ix. 14), but a remonstrance coming from these *and* those, as St. Mark (ii. 18), reconciling the other two narratives, informs us. That remonstrance couched itself in these words, ' *Why do we and the Pharisees fast oft, but thy disciples fast not?* ' It is with this, and the answer which this called out, that I occupy myself here.

There is something strange at first sight in finding the disciples of John associated with the disciples of the Pharisees, and making common cause with them, rather than with Him to whom their Master had borne such signal witness (John i. 29, 36; iii. 26–36); for it needs not to observe that the fault which was thus imputed to Christ's disciples, if indeed a fault, would have redounded upon Him, under whose eye and with whose encouragement they bore themselves thus. But one or two considerations will help to account for a transient coalition of this kind. In the first place, while there was no jealousy on the Baptist's part, but the noblest absence of jealousy, at the larger successes and the transcendant dignity of the Lord, there was by no means the same entire freedom from such a passion on the part of all of his disciples ; [1] and the after-history of too many of these, who degenerated, as is well known, into an heretical sect which never admitted Christ as the highest, too surely testified of this. They, it is plain, did not look with a wholly unenvious eye at Him increasing, and John decreasing (John iii. 26-31 ; iv. 1). Moreover, while each true disciple of John would have held with the Lord and found himself on his side on almost every other point of difference between Him and the Pharisees, and of course in every essential, here in this external matter would be his one point of contact with them, and of a more apparent nearness to them than to Him. And thus, without any serious forgetfulness of the instructions of their master, now probably withdrawn from them, and lying in Herod's dungeon, without any deliberate purpose of strengthening the hands of Christ's enemies,[2] they may have found themselves for this once, and on this single point, upon their side ; and incautiously,

---

[1] Chrysostom however puts this somewhat too strongly : $\zeta\eta\lambda o\tau\acute{v}\pi\omega\varsigma\ \dot{a}\epsilon\grave{i}$ $\pi\rho\grave{o}\varsigma\ a\dot{v}\tau\grave{o}\nu\ \epsilon\hat{i}\chi o\nu\ o\acute{i}\ 'I\omega\acute{a}\nu\nu o\nu\ \mu a\theta\eta\tau a\acute{i}.$

[2] Jerome (in loc.) makes a severer estimate of their fault in this question : Nec poterant discipuli Johannis non esse sub vitio, qui calumniabantur eum, quem sciebant magistri vocibus prædicatum ; et jungebantur Pharisæis, quos a Johanne noverant condemnatos [Matt. iii. 7].

though not meaning to embarrass Him in the least, they may have put this question at once in the Pharisees' name, and in their own : ' *Why do we and the Pharisees fast oft, but thy disciples fast not ?* '

He answers their question with another, and with one which could hardly help causing them to remember the latest testimony borne by their master to Himself (see John iii. 29), with one which implied his exact acquaintance with the form which that testimony had taken : ' *Can the children of the bridechamber*[1] *mourn as long as the bridegroom is with them ?* ' The disciples are of course ' *the children*—or better, " *the sons* "—*of the bridechamber ;* ' not to be confounded with ' the friend of the bridegroom '[2] (John iii. 29), who is one, while they are many (Judg. xiv. 11); just as the office of the Baptist was filled by him singly and alone, being not indeed higher than the apostolate, but distinct from it. Christ here presents Himself as ' *the Bridegroom* ; ' intending, as we may very well suppose, to remind the disciples of John that under this very aspect their own master had so re-

---

[1] The phrase has been sometimes wrongly understood, but abundant parallels in the N. T. make its meaning sufficiently clear. ' *The children*,' —or better, ' *the sons*,'—where the term is used in a figurative sense, are those who stand in a near and intimate, but at the same time in a subordinate, relation to that of which they are set forth as the children. The following are all the passages in which υἱός or υἱοί occurs in this figurative sense : βασιλείας (Matt. viii. 12 ; xiii. 38); πονηροῦ (Matt. xiii. 38); γεέννης (Matt. xxiii. 15); βροντῆς (Mark iii. 17); εἰρήνης (Luke x. 6); αἰῶνος (Luke xvi. 8; xx. 34; φωτός (Luke xvi. 8; John xii. 36); ἀναστάσεως (Luke xx. 36); ἀπωλείας (John xvii. 12 ; 2 Thess. ii. 3); παρακλήσεως (Acts iv. 36); διαβόλου (Acts xiii. 10); ἀπειθείας (Eph. ii. 2; v. 6; Col. iii. 6). The idiom is rarer in the Septuagint than one would expect, but we have there υἱὸς δυνάμεως (1 Kin. i. 52); ἀνομίας (Ps. lxxxviii. 23); θανάτου (2 Sam. xii. 5); θανατώσεως (1 Sam. xxii. 26); ἐτῶν (Gen. xi. 10); with perhaps one or two others.

[2] The paranymph or ' best man '=νυμφαγωγός (Gen. xxvi. 26 ; Judg. xiv. 20).

cently hailed Him.[1] How large an amount of the
Old Testament in this single phrase does He claim for
Himself, and as finding its fulfilment in Him ; as the whole
of the Song of Songs ; the 45th Psalm ; Hosea ii. 19, 20.
How many marriages, more or less mystical there, does He
claim as pointing to this, the crowning mystery of all ; as
of Adam with Eve, of Isaac with Rebecca, of Joseph with
the daughter of Potipherah, of Moses with the Ethiopian
woman, of Boaz with Ruth, of Solomon with the princess
of Egypt, of Hosea with Gomer. How much in the New
Testament, only hereafter to be uttered, does He already
anticipate in this significant word (Matt. xxii. 1 ; xxv. 1 ;
2 Cor. xi. 2 ; Eph. v. 23–32 ; Rev. xix. 7, 9 ; xxi. 2).
He, ' *the Bridegroom*,' was now with them ; it was not
indeed that the marriage of the Lamb was yet arrived ;
that should not be till long after ; but these were his
espousals ; for as such espousals the brief period of his
first sojourn upon earth might be fitly regarded ; during
which indeed He did but as it were salute the bride, whom
hereafter, but only after a long intervening period of
absence, He should lead home (Matt. xxv. 1–13). He
would not trouble with untimely mourning the brief
gladness, so soon to disappear, of the present hour. The
bridegroom was yet to ' *be taken from them*,'—in that
phrase ' *taken from them* ' there lies already a hint that
his absence should be no voluntary withdrawal upon his
part—a removal rather by violence,—and then they who
were so jocund now should have both reason enough and
time enough to mourn. Our Lord contemplates the
whole interval between his death and his second coming

---

[1] Chrysostom ; ἀναμιμνήσκων αὐτοὺς τῶν τοῦ Ἰωάννου ῥημάτων.

as a time suitable for mourning, being the time of his absence from his Church.

It might be objected to this interpretation, it has been objected by Olshausen, that He was given back to his Church at the Resurrection. This is so far true, that the mourning is now a mourning of hope, and not of despair; the Church mourns not for a dead, but only for an absent Lord; but still she mourns; and the measure of her love to Him will be the measure of her yearning for Him and for his return. At the same time it is true that within this period of her mourning there will be alternations of joy and sorrow. The Church will have festivals as well as fasts; she will have, that is, some periods when her sense of her Lord as taken away will be the foremost thought and most vivid feeling in her mind; she will have other periods, when she will put off for a while her garments of heaviness, and anoint herself with the oil of gladness; although only for a while, and as well knowing that she shall not put them off for ever, that everlasting joy shall not be upon her head, till her Lord has come back to her again. The note of sorrow is the key-note of the Church during all the time that her Lord is taken from her; '*then shall they fast.*'

There is something of an infinite compassion, of a pitying thoughtfulness, in this the Lord's determination not to trouble, nor yet suffer to be troubled by others, this present joy—seeing as He did into the depths of time, and all the weary and painful way which was yet to be travelled over before the final and triumphant goal should be won. And as this question was put to Him at a feast, and at one which He would not see troubled, so we may trace something festal and festive in the whole character of his reply. In festal images, these also drawn from garments and from wine, He clothes the justification of his disciples and of Himself.[1] The images are two, and this is the first : ' *No man putteth a piece of new cloth upon an old garment, for that which is put in to fill it up taketh from the garment, and the rent is made worse.*' In St. Luke's report of these words of Christ some points are more distinctly made than in St. Matthew's; and indeed the whole image, or ' *parable,*' as by him, and by him only, it is called, appears to a certain degree in a modified form. It there stands thus : ' *No man putteth a piece of a new garment upon an old ;* ' or, as we should render it, recognizing the right of σχίσας to a place in the text, ' *No man, rending a piece from a new garment, putteth it on the old ;* ' for, as He goes on to say, '*if otherwise, then both the new maketh a rent, and the piece that was taken out of the new agreeth not with the old.*' The absurdity of such a course is here more strongly marked than in St. Matthew. There it is mainly, if not entirely, the destruction of the old which so unwise a patching would entail, that is urged ; but here that the new is also sacrificed, and this with no benefit thereby accruing to the old ; a truth to be brought out yet more vividly in the perishing of the wine and the bottles or wine-skins together. In St. Matthew it is but a piece of new cloth, new, as not having yet passed under the fuller's hands, which is lost ; while according to St. Luke a new garment is totally sacrificed, a portion cut out from it, that so this

---

[1] Bengel : Magnâ cum sobrietate et festivitate respondet Dominus ; a vestibus et vino (quorum usus erat in convivio) parabolas desumit jucundas ad confutandam quærentium tristitiam.

experiment, as profitless as wasteful, may be tried. The emphasis which the Lord lays on this reckless destruction of the serviceable for the sake of the unserviceable will come more plainly out when instead of, ' *if otherwise, then the new maketh a rent,*' we render as we ought, ' *if otherwise, he will also tear the new ;*'[1] he will ruin it, and that for the sake of the old, which after all is not advantaged thereby ; seeing that, after the patch is made, the two have no agreement together. The glaring contrast, the discord between old and new, rendering the garment such as no one would willingly wear, and therefore useless, is the point in the parable here ; not as in the earlier Evangelists, the energy with which the stronger new will inevitably tear itself clear of the weaker and failing old.

I return to the words as recorded by St. Matthew. As making room for their true exposition and that of those other which follow, it may be needful just to notice and set aside one strange misconception of their whole meaning and intention. I refer to theirs who understand by the ' *piece of new cloth* ' which no man ' *putteth upon an old garment,*' as by the ' *new wine* ' which ' *no man putteth into old bottles,*' the fasts and austerities of John's disciples and of the Pharisees ; which Christ would not venture as yet to impose on his own disciples, however John and the Pharisees might safely impose them upon theirs ; who were more inured and thus better able to bear them. It

---

[1] In the Greek, εἰ δὲ μή γε, καὶ τὸ καινὸν σχίζει (or better σχίσει), which Tyndale had rightly given ; '*for if he do, then breaketh he the new ;*' but which was rendered by Beza, who has not seldom exercised an injurious influence on our Version, Alioqui et illud novum findit vetus ; making τὸ καινόν a nominative, and supplying τὸ παλαιόν as an accusative governed by σχίσει.

is marvellous to find an interpreter like Hammond content thus to explain Christ's words: 'Young novice disciples that were not yet renewed by the coming of the Spirit upon them, and so were not strong enough for such, must not presently be overwhelmed with severe precepts such as fasting, &c., lest they fall off and be discouraged.' One is tempted to ask, Were the disciples of John and of the Pharisees ' renewed by the coming of the Spirit upon them,' that they could bear what Christ's disciples could not bear. Maldonatus, an interpreter of greater exegetical talent than Hammond—indeed of the very highest, where the necessity of maintaining at all costs Roman doctrine does not warp his interpretation—is here in the same hopeless confusion. It is not to be denied that there were some in old time who had shewn them the way in this the perversest of all interpretations. Yet these, of whom some are cited below,[1] were the exception; and for the most part the early interpreters grasped rightly the meaning of Christ's words. Thus in the Greek Church very distinctly Origen, Basil the Great,[2] Isidore, and

---

[1] Thus Tertullian of course (*Adv. Marc.* iv. 11): Humiliter reddens rationem quod non possent jejunare filii Sponsi, quamdiu cum eis esset Sponsus, postea vero jejunaturos promittens; nec discipulos defendit, sed potius excusavit; and yet he too has implicitly given the right explanation elsewhere, when speaking of the Lord's Prayer he says (*De Orat.* 1): Discipulis Novi Testamenti novam orationis formam determinavit; oportebat enim in hâc quoque specie novum vinum novis utribus recondi, et novam plagulam novo adsui vestimento. See too Theophylact has missed the meaning: ῥάκος οὖν ἄγραφον ἡ νηστεία καὶ οἶνος νέος· ἱμάτιον παλαιὸν καὶ ἀσκὸς, ἡ ἀσθένεια τῶν μαθητῶν. It is curious to find Beza consenting to this explanation: Istâ vero utrâque similitudine significat Christus haberi humanæ infirmitatis rationem a Deo, qui non sinat nos supra vires tentari, ideoque paulatim militiæ laboribus suos assuefaciat, quod in ipsis etiam apostolis præstitit.

[2] The regeneration, as he rightly implies, with the daily renewal which the regeneration alone renders possible, constitutes the new vessel, capable of receiving the new wine (*Hom. in Ps.* xxxii.): οἱ μὲν οὖν ἀνακαινούμενοι

Cyril;[1] and in the Latin Hilary,[2] and Augustine.[3] The last sees the highest fulfilment of that word concerning the new wine in the new vessels in the gifts of Pentecost ; and loves to put this saying of the Lord in relation with that which was spoken by the mockers then, in whose mockery there was yet the utterance of deepest truth, ' These men are full of new wine ' (Acts ii. 13).[4]

The meaning, as these all are agreed, is this ; No man, that is, no man of prudence (for the very consequence which He indicates as sometimes following, shews that some men make this mistake), seeks to repair an old

ἡμέρᾳ καὶ ἡμέρᾳ καὶ τὸν καινὸν οἶνον ἀπὸ τῆς ἀμπέλου τῆς ἀληθινῆς χωροῦντες ἀσκοὶ εἶναι λέγονται ἐν τῷ Εὐαγγελίῳ καινοί.

[1] See Cramer's Catena, in loc.

[2] Pharisæos et discipulos Johannis nova non accepturos [dicit], nisi novi fierent.

[3] Thus *Serm.* 267. 2 : Isti ebrii sunt ; musto pleni sunt. Ridebant, et aliquid verum dicebant. Impleti enim erant utres novo vino. Audistis cum Evangelium legeretur, Nemo mittit vinum novum in utres veteres ; spiritalia non capit carnalis. Carnalitas vetustas est, gratia novitas est. Quantocumque homo in melius fuerit innovatus, tanto amplius capit quod verum sapit. Elsewhere (*Quæst. Evang.* ii. 18) Augustine seems to me less firmly to grasp Christ's meaning ; while Jerome strangely enough in the very same passage (in loc.) gives the two explanations, the wrong and the right, which indeed mutually exclude one another ; first the wrong : Quod dicit [Dominus], hoc est : Donec renatus quis fuerit, et veteri homine deposito per passionem meam, novum hominem induerit, non potest severiora jejunii et continentiæ sustinere præcepta. Presently, without any consciousness that he is altogether changing his ground, he passes on to the right : Veteres utres debemus intelligere Scribas et Pharisæos. Plagula vestimenti novi et vinum novum, præcepta Evangelica sentienda, quæ non possunt sustinere Judæi, ne major scissura fiat. Tale quid et Galatæ facere cupiebant, ut cum Evangelio Legis præcepta miscerent, et in utribus veteribus mitterent vinum novum.

[4] *Serm.* 26 : Utres novos utres veteres mirabantur ; et calumniando non innovabantur, nec implebantur. *Serm.* 267 : Utres novi erant ; vinum novum de cælo expectabatur, et venit ; jam enim fuerat magnus ille Botrus calcatus et glorificatus. So too in one of Adam of St. Victor's magnificent Pentecostal hymns (see my *Sacred Latin Poetry*, 2nd edition, p. 192) :

> Utres novi, non vetusti,
> Sunt capaces novi musti.

garment with a new patch; but when the garment is indeed worn-out (for ' *old* ' here can mean nothing short of this), he perceives that it would be no true economy to endeavour with a new piece, which would not match with the faded and threadbare old, and which moreover that worn-out texture would not have strength to retain, to fit it for use again.   On the contrary, if poverty do not hinder (for this is tacitly understood), he puts on a garment new altogether, and in this presents himself at the bridal feast.   They proceed to explain, that as such an ancient garment the great Author of all the economies in the Church of God would here characterize that elder dispensation, given by the hand of Moses ; whereof these obligatory fasts, which men were now seeking to thrust on his disciples, formed an integral part, and of the entire of which they stand here as the sign and symbol.   This likening of that elder dispensation to such a worn-out garment may seem harshly spoken ; yet the language is not stronger than that which St. Paul uses (Gal. iv. 3, 9), nor than that employed in the Epistle to the Hebrews (Heb. vii. 18), where the writer speaks of the disannulling of the commandment which went before ' for the weakness and unprofitableness thereof.'   ' It would profit nothing,' Christ would here say, ' to seek to attach my new as a supplementary patch to that old of yours.   They would not hold together.   My doctrine is something different from that which you would have it ; something more than a mere supplement to yours, to make that good, where it is defective ; to repair that, where it is out-worn. It is something which is all of a piece, not a righteousness of works, eked out and patched here and there with the righteousness of faith, but from head to foot a new garment for souls.' It was exactly such a piece of patch-work as Christ here denounces, which the Galatians actually attempted, and for attempting which St. Paul chid them so earnestly (Gal. iii. 2, and throughout).

And then, as that first comparison had chiefly to do with *things*, the other which follows, namely of the wine and the bottles, has mainly to do with *persons*; as that with *doctrine*, something therefore more external, even as a garment is worn on the outside of the body, this with *life*, that which is more inward, as wine is inwardly received.[1] For we must not regard this which follows as a mere saying over again what Christ has said already. Our Lord often repeats Himself (thus Matt. xiii. 31, 32 compared with ver. 33 ; and again ver. 44 with ver. 45, 46 ; or Luke xiv. 28–30 compared with ver. 31, 32 ; or xv. 4–7 with ver. 8–10), but never *merely* repeats Him-self ; it is the same, but in some novel point of view, in some deeper aspect. Still keeping close to the bridal feast, and to the images which it suggests, He goes on to say, ' *Neither do men put new wine into old bottles ; else the bottles break, and the wine runneth out, and the bottles perish* (cf. Job xxxii. 19) ; *but they put new wine into new bottles,*[2] *and both are preserved.*' No prudent man, who means to keep his wine for the feast, pours it new, and not as yet having worked off its fermenting strength, into skins old, and therefore weak and stiff, and not capable of expansion.[3] If the new piece of cloth was

---

[1] Bede : Vino siquidem intus reficimur, veste autem foris tegimur.

[2] See the *Dictionary of the Bible,* art. *Bottle.*

[3] Οἶνον νέον εἰς ἀσκοὺς καινούς, literally ' *new* wine into *fresh* skins.' For the distinction between νέος and καινός see my *Synonyms of the New Testament,* § 60.

the new *doctrine*, which Christ refused to make merely supplementary to the old, the new wine, as was just re-marked, will be the new *life*, which they only can contain, who are willing to become new vessels—I have said, willing to become; for spiritual things in this differ from things natural, that *all* are old vessels at the first, a Paul as much as a Caiaphas; only among these old vessels, some are willing to be made new, and thus continent of the new life; while others not only are old, but are determined to remain in their oldness, even after the renewing powers have been brought nigh them, and offered to them for their acceptance; Osheas that will not be Joshuas, Jacobs that will not be Israels, and Simons that will not become Peters. In the words, '*new bottles*,' we have in fact an allusion to the mystery of regeneration; and this language He only had a right to use who had power to say further, ' Behold, I make all things new ' (Rev. xxi. 5). There was a restricted sense, indeed, in which Christ's apostles were ' *new vessels*,' '*new*[1] *cloth*,' even when He chose them. They were far newer, that is, than those who had grown old in their frauds and hypocrisies, the Pharisees and their adherents; and if themselves having much to learn, yet having far less than those to unlearn.

There is another point in which this second comparison is in advance of the first. In that other, the new holds itself *passive* in regard of the old; we can hardly, that is, attribute to the new piece of cloth the power of itself

---

[1] A hint of this may lie in the ἄγναφος of St. Matthew and St. Mark; which our Translators have rendered ' *new*,' but have suggested ' *raw or un-wrought*'—' *undressed* ' would be still better—in the margin. Bengel gives the true intention of the word: Discipulos rudes, novos et integros, nullâ peculiari disciplinâ imbutos, sumsit Jesus,

actually tearing away the old, with which it is brought into contact, however such a rent might and would follow on the attempt to combine the one with the other. But in this second comparison the new wine puts forth an *active* power for the bursting, and thus destroying, of the old vessels.[1] Here a new aspect of the truth is presented to us, namely, the perilous power which mighty truths of God exert, when they are received by men who are not thoroughly renewed and transformed by them, who remain old men still ;—the imminent danger lest the truth, so far as these men are concerned, should be utterly lost, like wine spilt on the ground ; the men themselves, like the bursten vessels, perishing with it. What a key have we in these words to Peasants' Wars, Anabaptist and other antinomian excesses in old times and in new ! On how many a saddest page in the history of the Church, in the history too of innumerable souls that have made an utter shipwreck of faith, do these words throw light.[2]

[1] Gregory the Great (*Mor.* xxiii. 11): Quia sancti Spiritûs fervor non solum veteri sed etiam novâ vitâ vix capitur.

[2] An article in the *Zeitschrift für Lutherische Theologie und Kirche*, 1866, pp. 240–251, with the title, *Eine religiöse Bewegung in Finnland,* supplies as mournful a commentary on these words as could well be found. It is the miserable record of a religious awakening among the poor neglected Lapps and Finns some twenty-five years ago—which, for want of wise guidance being allowed to become merely subjective, and to divorce itself altogether from the Word of God as its rule, and from the order of the Church as explaining that rule, ended in blasphemous excesses which remind one of nothing so much as the frightful extravagancies of the Brethren of the Free Spirit in the twelfth and thirteenth centuries (see Gieseler, *Kirch. Gesch.* vol. ii. pt. ii. p. 629). It is indeed startling, and at the same time wonderfully instructive, as shewing the fixed and narrow limits within which error moves, to meet not merely the speculations, but not seldom the very phrases of those licentious pantheists, reproducing themselves among the rude and ignorant children of the North. A faithful Swedish pastor who sought, but when for the larger number matters were beyond remedy, to bring back these unhappy people to the Word and the Testimony, sets down in his Diary their retorts of a single day to his godly warnings. I omit a part, and the

Keeping in mind the mournful comment upon this saying which the history of Christ's Church has so abundantly supplied, we may better understand his gracious unwillingness to put the old vessels to this trial, lest they should burst and perish in the process of the new wine's fermentation. His words involve, as I cannot but believe, a recognition that even those whose service is not the highest, may yet be allowed by Him, that many lower forms of service besides the service in the freedom of the Spirit will yet find merciful acceptance with the Father. Many an earnest Pharisee, many a rigid disciple of John, many an elder brother of the parable, if only he has been true to the light which he had, and the 'more excellent way' has not been offered to him, and deliberately refused by him, shall not be rejected nor cast out.

I will only observe, before leaving these words, that in them are condemned as hopeless, declared to be bound

---

rest I prefer to leave in his own language : Um Gott fürchten zu müssen, muss man sündigen ; wir sündigen nicht, denn wer den Geist hat, braucht nicht zu sündigen ; wir fürchten daher auch Gott nicht. Wir sind die Glieder Gottes, welche Gott nicht strafen kann ; denn Er kann seine eigenen Glieder weder strafen noch verdammen. Wir sind gestorben und können nicht sterben. Wir haben nicht leibliche, sondern geistliche Glieder. Wir sind auf der neuen Erde wohnhaft ; wir sind geistlich, heilig, gerecht. Wir sind die Bibel, das neue Testament, der Sinai. Unser Leib ist das Gesetz ; daher haben wir auch das Recht zu urtheilen und zu verdammen. Wir sind Gott der Vater, Gott der Sohn und Gott der heilige Geist. Der Sohn hat seine Macht, die jetzt bei uns wohnt, verloren. Der Geist in uns hat die Macht zu tödten. Der Pfarrer, der nicht leugnet dass er Fleisch hat, ist sterblich und gehört dem Teufel. Wir können das Innere aller Menschen durchschauen und wie Christus sagte, ' Hebe dich weg von mir, Satan,' so haben wir auch das Recht euch Teufel zu nennen und mit euch als solchen zu verkehren. Ihr lügt, wenn ihr sagt, ' Vater Unser, der du bist im Himmel ! ' Ihr solltet sagen, ' Vater Unser, der du bist in der Hölle,' denn so lange ihr unbekehrt seid, so ist der Teufel euer Vater. Die Kinder sollen ihren Eltern fluchen, damit der Fluch auf diese Weise sich rückwärts zu unseren Stammeltern verpflanzen könne—with not a little more to the same effect.

over to inevitable failure, not this attempt only, but all attempts to combine into one scheme and system heterogeneous materials, having no true affinity with one another. They refuse to coalesce; one proves too strong for the other. It has been often tried. There is such evident power and vitality in the great Christian ideas, that even those who have refused to accept Christianity as a whole have continually sought to borrow from it in part; to deck their own, which they will not renounce, with shreds and patches derived from it; to quicken with sparks from this higher source systems from which all proper life, if ever they had such, has long since departed. When the Neo-Platonists of the second and third centuries sought to give a new currency to the myths of an effete heathenism, by making them the vehicles of Christian ideas, of truths which would never have stirred in the thoughts of men, if Christ had not lived and taught and died, this was at once a sewing of the new patch upon the old garment with which it did not agree, and a pouring of the new wine into the old vessels which were quite incapable of containing it. The same results have in every case followed. As in the material world only substances which have affinity to one another will chemically unite, so the truth has ever attested itself to be the truth by refusing to combine with anything except itself.

But having thus justified Himself, and in Himself his disciples also, the Lord concludes in words which only St. Luke has preserved for us, ' *No man also having drunk old wine straightway desireth new: for he saith, The old is better.*' He graciously proceeds, that is, to make excuse for the disciples of John (He would scarcely have thought it necessary to make one, if the Pharisees only had been offended); explains how it came to pass that these took the offence that they did, could not at once find themselves in his doctrine and life. He throws his shield over them, lest his disciples, being delivered from the assault, should themselves be tempted to become assailants in their turn, and to manifest impatience with all who failed to recognize and accept at once and without hesitation their Lord's word and doctrine as the highest and the best. He will check any such intolerance and impatience on their parts. Was it to be expected that their own, to which these had been accustomed so long, should grow out of favour with them on the instant, even though He offered to them something better in its room? If the new wine did taste somewhat harsh and rough to their palates at the beginning, this was only in the natural and necessary order of things; no man used to the old *straightway* desireth the new, even though it be of a much higher quality. But let them have time and opportunity little by little to wean themselves from that old, and doubtless there would be found among them those who would grow into liking of this new, which indeed in a higher sense is the oldest of all (Gal. iii. 17; 1 John ii. 7, 8).[1]

Wonderful, and rare as it is wonderful, is the spirit of mildness and of toleration for all which is not absolutely sinful, so that it shall be allowed to endure till it drop away of itself, which speaks out in these words. St. Paul entered into his Master's spirit, and acted in practical conformity with it, when he would do nothing to force the Jewish converts to forsake their ceremonial law, earnestly as he must have desired to see this serious obstacle to an

---

[1] Bengel: *Paulatim* mutantur habitus animorum.

entire fusion of the Jewish and Gentile Churches, this perilous thing, liable to so much abuse, removed out of the way ; being content to wait patiently till it should fall off of itself—as a husk falls off, when its office is done, and the fruit which it has protected so long, is at length fully formed. Reverence for that which has been consecrated by time, with an acknowledgment of the mighty force which custom and habit exercise on the spirits of men, and at the same time a warning to the disciples not to overlook this in their impatient expectation that all men, whatever their past training and discipline may have been, should accept and embrace a more excellent way on the very first moment that it is presented to them, all this utters itself in these gracious words.

8. *THE TRANSFIGURATION*

Matt. xvii. 1–13; Mark ix. 2–13; Luke ix. 28–36.

THERE has been no little debate and difference of opinion on the relation in which the Transfiguration stands to the words of Christ which went immediately before, ' *Verily, I say unto you, There be some standing here, which shall not taste of death, till they see the Son of man coming in his kingdom,*' or, ' *till they have seen the kingdom of God come with power* ' (Mark); or, ' *till they see the kingdom of God* ' (Luke). The point in debate has been this— namely, how far the Transfiguration is to be itself regarded as a fulfilment of these words ; whether that was a coming of the Son of man in his kingdom, a coming of the kingdom of God with power; and, if accepted as such, in what sense it was such a coming. That the coming of which Christ here speaks is not the coming of the Son of man to judge the world, of which a little while before He spoke (Matt. xvi. 27), is evident; for He has said that there are those present who shall live to see it; that it shall fall within the lifetime of some of that generation who are the Lord's immediate hearers. To this coming, then, at the end of the world to judge the world He cannot refer.

But are we therefore compelled to find in the Trans- figuration the fulfilment of his statement, that some stand- ing there should not taste of death till they had seen Him

coming in his kingdom? There seem to me two most
serious objections to our doing so. The first is this.
Mighty event as the Transfiguration doubtless was,—and
it stands between the Temptation in the wilderness, and
the Agony in the garden, as the culminating point in our
Lord's ministry upon earth,—unutterably significant for
Himself and for the Church of all times, yet for all this
the transient glory of it fails to satisfy and exhaust
language so vast as this, '*the Son of man coming in his
kingdom*,' '*the kingdom of God coming with power*.'
Great as is the Transfiguration, it is hardly great enough
for such words as these. But, further than this, it seems
impossible to think that our Lord can have used such
language of an event removed from the moment at which
He utters it by no more than the interval of a week.
This is excellently put by Bishop Horsley,[1] little acceptance as his own explanation of the difficulty deserves to
obtain : ' If the time described as that when the Son of
man should be seen coming in his kingdom be understood to have been the time of the Transfiguration, what
will be the amount of the solemn asseveration in the
text? Nothing more than this—that in the numerous
assembly to which our Lord was speaking, composed,
perhaps, of persons of all ages, there were some,—the
expressions certainly intimate no great number,—but
some few of this great multitude there were, who were
not to die within a week ; for so much was the utmost
interval of time between this discourse and the Transfiguration. Our Lord and Master was not accustomed to
amuse his followers with any such nugatory predictions.
The like argument sets aside another interpretation, in

[1] *Sermons*, vol. I. p. 39

which our Lord's Ascension and the mission of the Holy
Ghost are considered as the " coming in his kingdom " intended in the text.   Of what importance was it to tell a
numerous assembly (for it was not to the disciples in
particular, but to the whole multitude, as we learn from
St. Mark, that this discourse was addressed)—to what
purpose, I say, could it be, to tell them that there were
some among them who were destined to live half a
year ? '

For myself, I can find no satisfactory explanation of this
prediction except such a one as shall recognize its fulfilment
in that mightiest judgment act of the Son of man, which
the world has yet seen, which, so far as we can understand, it will ever see, until his final coming as the Judge
of quick and dead.   I refer to that tremendous catastrophe, the destruction of Jerusalem,—when, indeed, that
old Jewish economy passed away with a great noise ; and,
extricating itself from that wreck and ruin, there emerged
what it is not too much to call a new earth and a new
heaven ; when the things shaken were removed to the
end that Christ's saints might receive a kingdom which
could not be moved.   This event, when the Lord spake,
was some forty years distant, or more.   To men then of
full age it was not a mere nugatory prediction, that they
should live to see this event, at once so terrible and so
magnificent, the close of one æon, and the commencement
of another ; divided from them, as it was, by so many
years ; even as these words of Christ compel us to believe
that, if only for one apostle, yet for more than one of the
disciples then standing there, it was fulfilled.   The
passage will thus be brought into instructive relation to
other Scriptures, on which it will throw, and from which

it will receive, light. For example, what other explanation can that announcement, 'Verily, I say unto you,
This generation shall not pass, till all these things be fulfilled' (Matt. xxiv. 34), obtain? A consummation of all
things, not, indeed, the final and exhaustive one, in some
sort only a rehearsal of that, it is here declared should
find place before that whole generation in whose hearing
the Lord spake, should have died. Again, when speaking
concerning John, the Lord says to Peter, 'If I will that
he tarry till I come, what is that to thee' (John xxi. 22)?
this 'till I come' cannot be interpreted of the final
coming; for an 'If I will,' spoken by those lips, is very
much more than a mere expression of power, that He
could keep John in life if He chose. The words must be
accepted as expressing not merely what He could do,
but what He intended to do. It is clear, however, that
He did not intend this disciple whom He loved, to tarry
till his final coming; for, not to say that there would
have been something monstrous in a life protracted so, we
know the place and date of his death. It follows that his
'till I come' must receive another interpretation, and
that can be no other than one which will put that statement into closest connexion with this wherewith we are
dealing now. Let me observe, before leaving this subject, that, accepting the judgment on the Jewish Church
as a coming of the Lord,[1] all difficulty in respect of such
passages as Jam. v. 8, 9 will at once be removed. Yet a
litlte while, St. James reminds them to whom he writes,
and the tyrannous oppression which they endure from
Jewish adversaries will have for ever passed away; yet a

[1] Hammond has more than one able note upholding this interpretation,
thus here, and on Matt. xxiv. 3.

little while, and Christ will have sent his armies, Himself
their invisible Captain, and destroyed the city of those
murderers, and delivered his own from their tyranny for
ever.[1]

But is there then, it may be asked, no real connexion
whatever between these words of Christ and the Transfiguration, which in the three synoptic Gospels is brought
into such close and significant juxtaposition with it, which
by all three is declared to have followed on the seventh
day succeeding? A most real connexion. The Transfiguration was a prelude and a pledge of that which should
be hereafter. In that Transfiguration it was clearly shewn
that He spoke not at random, who spoke of a kingdom
which was his; that He had a kingdom to come in; a
glory ready at any moment to burst forth, however for

---

[1] It must be freely owned that nearly all the early expositors, the Fathers
and medieval interpreters, find in the glory of the Transfiguration that which
for them satisfies and fulfils the prediction that has just gone before, ' *There
be some standing here, which shall not taste of death, till they see the Son of
man coming in his kingdom.*' At the same time, when their statements are
closely examined, it will be found that in almost every instance they have
felt themselves obliged to moderate and temper these, so that the Transfiguration shall in fact be rather a prelude and prophecy of the coming in
glory than the very coming itself. I quote a few passages in proof. And
first one or two from the Greek Fathers. Thus Basil the Great (*Hom. in
Ps.* 44): εἶδον δὲ αὐτοῦ τὸ κάλλος Πέτρος καὶ οἱ υἱοὶ τῆς βροντῆς ἐν τῷ ὄρει, καὶ
τὰ προοίμια τῆς ἐνδόξου αὐτοῦ παρουσίας ὀφθαλμοῖς λαβεῖν κατηξιώ-
θησαν. Theodoret (*Ep.* 145), having spoken of the glories of our Lord's
person and vestment, goes on: ἐδίδαξε διὰ τούτων τῆς δευτέρας ἐπιφανείας
τὸν τρόπον. So too the Latin Fathers. Thus Augustine (*Exp. Ep. ad
Gal.* c. ii.): Ipsis tribus se in monte Dominus ostendit *in significatione regni
sui*, cum ante sex dies dixisset, Sunt hic quidam, &c. And Leo the Great
(*Serm.* 94): In regno suo, id est, *in regiâ claritate*. Anselm (*Hom.* 4): Venientem in regno suo viderunt eum discipuli sui, qui in eâ claritate viderunt
fulgentem in monte, in quâ peracto judicio ab omnibus sanctis in regno suo
videbitur. And in the modern Roman Catholic Church, Maldonatus: Christus Transfigurationem regnum suum vocat, non quia proprie regnum, sed
quia *futuri regni imago erat* . . . Illud ipsum regnum tres illi apostoli non
in ipso, sed in figurâ, non præsens, sed per transennam ostensum, viderunt.

the moment it might be covered and concealed from the eyes of men, from the eyes even of those who were in closest communion with Him. The Transfiguration is an earnest in hand of a glory hereafter to be revealed.

But while the relation in which it stands, and on which the Evangelists lay so marked an emphasis, to that memorable prediction of the Lord's, is worthy of our exactest study, it is not less important to observe another connexion in which they are all careful to place it, namely, with the first distinct announcement which the Saviour has made to his disciples, of his rejection, sufferings, and death (Matt. xvi. 21 ; Mark ix. 31 ; Luke ix. 22), an announcement which had so greatly startled, surprized, and dejected them. For indeed this connexion supplies us with a very weighty hint for the right understanding of this solemn scene, and of the ends which it was meant to serve, as a confirmation of their faith, and as helping them to confirm the faith of others. How deep and lasting an impression it had made on them we best gather from the fact that more than thirty years after, St. Peter refers to it as an evidence to himself, an evidence therefore to all who received his word, that in declaring to them 'the power and coming of our Lord Jesus Christ,' he had not followed cunningly devised fables (2 Pet. i. 15–19). To them who had just heard of the sufferings of Christ there was here vouchsafed a prophetic glimpse into the glory which should follow, that in the strength of this they might not be troubled nor offended at the prospect of these sufferings now, nor at the sufferings themselves which presently should arrive. Nor may we regard it merely as an act of gracious condescension to their weakness. This would be to rob the Transfiguration of very

much of its meaning. For the Lord Himself this preli-
bation of glory had doubtless its highest significance. It
was a mighty strengthening and refreshing of Him, no
less than of his disciples, against that coming day of
humiliation and agony. He did not merely manifest to
others that glory which should one day be his, but became more fully conscious of it Himself, and that He
already possessed it; however He might voluntarily defer
its full manifestation;—not to say that in this momentary
breaking forth of that inward splendour, for the most
part hindered and restrained by the sackcloth covering of
the flesh, there was a step in the progressive glorifying
of that humanity which He had assumed. But it will be
better not to anticipate what will find presently its fitter
place.

' *After six days Jesus taketh with Him Peter and James
and John.*' Not without a meaning is it so carefully
noted by all the Evangelists that it was ' *after six days* '
(Matthew, Mark)—the ' *eight days after* '[1] of St. Luke being
no contradiction, but only a different way of counting, leaving as it does the six complete days between—that the
Transfiguration found place. There are six days of the
world's work, which the seventh day's glory, of which we
have here a foretaste, is to follow. Three of his disciples
the Lord takes with Him, that in the mouth of two or three
witnesses every word may be established (Deut. xix. 15);
these three the flower and crown of the apostolic band, the
' coryphæi,' as Chrysostom calls them, and not now alone

---

[1] Gerhard (*Loci Theoll.* xxxii. 2): Post dies sex Christus coram discipulis
transfiguratur; sic exacto hujus vitæ sextiduo succedet æternum sabbatum,
in quo piorum corpora clarificabuntur. Quid tota hæc vita aliud est quam
sex dies laboris? illos sequetur quies sabbati, et piorum gloria æterna.

favoured above the rest (Matt. xxvi. 37 ; Luke viii. 51);
they are Peter, who loved Him so much (John xxi. 17),
and John, whom He loved so much (John xiii. 23), and
James, who should first attest that death could as little as
life separate from his love (Acts xii. 1) ; being the same
three who should hereafter be witnesses of the deepest
depth of his humiliation in the Agony of the garden, and
who therefore were thus fitly forearmed by what they now
beheld against what they should then behold.

Having taken these, He ' *leadeth them up into an high
mountain apart by themselves.*' The tradition which makes
Mount Tabor to have been this '*high mountain,*' though
for many ages not so much as called in question, does not
date farther back than the fourth century, Cyril of Jerusalem[1] being the first to mention it. Indeed there is an
earlier tradition still, which places the scene of the Transfiguration on the Mount of Olives, and thus in the immediate neighbourhood of Jerusalem,[2] but it is one which
seems to have obtained little acceptance. Tabor having
been once fixed on (it probably was so, as the highest and
goodliest mountain in Galilee, rising in an almost perfect
cone from the plain,[3] and, though unnamed in the New,
of frequent commemoration in the Old Testament ; thus
see Judg. iv. 6, 14 ; viii. 18 ; Ps. lxxxix. 12 ; Jer. xlvi. 18),
there were built churches, and presently monasteries, on
its summit—three of the former to correspond to the
three tabernacles which Peter was *not* permitted to build !
But while evidence in favour of Tabor there is absolutely

---

[1] *Catech.* xii. 16. In the Greek Church the festival of the Transfiguration
(Aug. 6) has derived its name, Τὸ Θαβώριον, from this tradition.

[2] Ritter gives in proof a reference, *Itin. Anton. Aug. et Hierosolytanum,*
ed. Parthey, 1848, which I have had no opportunity of verifying.

[3] Λόφος μαστοειδής Polybius (v. 70. 6) calls it.

none, that against it is strong, is indeed decisive. 'The historical data which we possess, shew that the summit of the mountain was employed without any intermission between the times of Antiochus the Great, 218 B.C., and the destruction of Jerusalem under Vespasian, as a stronghold, and was by no means the scene of peace and solitude whither one would flee, anxious to escape the turmoil of the world. The consecration which quiet and seclusion give was only reached after the fortresses which once crowned its summit had been laid low.'[1] It is impossible therefore that Tabor can have been that 'holy mountain,' to which the Lord retired that He with his three disciples might be there, '*apart by themselves.*' It may perhaps have been Hermon, or one of the spurs of the Antilebanon. But, whatever mountain it was, it certainly is not for nothing that this and so many other of the most memorable events in Holy Scripture are transacted upon mountains; as the offering of Isaac (Gen. xxii. 14), the giving of the old Law (Exod. xix.; Deut. xxxiii. 2), and of the new (Matt. v. 1), the last decisive conflict between Jehovah and Baal (1 Kin. xviii. 19), the apparition of the risen Lord (Matt. xxviii. 16); from 'a very high mountain' the vision of the New Jerusalem is vouchsafed to Ezekiel (xl. 2), and to St. John (Rev. xxi. 10). It was not by accident that in the days of his flesh the Lord was wont to withdraw to a mountain for prayer (Matt. xiv. 23; Luke xxi. 37; John vi. 15), even as, according to St. Luke, it was for prayer that He retired to this the mount of his Transfiguration. Towering above the smoke and

---

[1] Ritter, *Comparative Geography of Palestine*, English translation, vol. ii. p. 313; compare Robinson, *Bibl. Researches*, vol. iii. pp. 220-225; Herzog, *Encyclopädie*, art. *Thabor*.

stir of this dim and lower earth, advancing their heads into a purer atmosphere and one nearer to heaven, they have in them a sort of natural 'Sursum corda,' which constitutes them fittest spots for nearer commerce with God, for special communications from Him.[1]

Being there, '*He was transfigured before them.*' St. Luke, writing primarily for Greek readers, avoids this word, '*transfigured,*' or transformed ; ('metamorphosed' would be a still closer rendering), which St. Matthew and St. Mark do not shrink from employing. He avoids it, probably, because of the associations of the heathen mythology, which would so easily, and almost inevitably, attach themselves to it in the imagination of a Greek ;[2] and is satisfied with telling us '*that the fashion of his countenance was altered*;' adding indeed to this that it was '*as He prayed*' that this marvellous change came over Him (cf. 2 Cor. iii. 18, where the significant μεταμορφούμεθα occurs). It was a change not without its weaker analogies, and prophetic anticipations in other personages of Scripture, in Moses for example, when the skin of his face shone after he had come from talking with God upon the mount (Exod. xxxiv. 29–35); which circumstance therefore Hilary rightly calls a figure of the Transfiguration.[3] Another such figure, although that

---

[1] Witsius (*De Glorif. Jesu in Monte,* 7) : Sed et ipsa Transfiguratio videbatur montem poscere, eumque sublimem ; ut loci ratio responderet conditioni gloriæ in quâ tunc Christus conspiciebatur.

[2] Jerome warns against such an abuse of μετεμορφώθη here : Nemo putet pristinam eum formam amisisse ; non substantia tollitur, sed gloria commutatur. Anselm : Non formam humani corporis amisit, sed suam suorumque glorificationem præmonstravit. In naming this great event, the German theology, calling it 'die Verklärung,' or 'the Glorification' (it is frequently 'Clarificatio' in the early Lutheran divines), has seized this point, not exactly the same as our 'Transfiguration.'

[3] Figura transfigurationis.

not an anticipation, but a reminiscence of it, the martyrdom of St. Stephen affords, when those who looked
at him 'saw his face as it had been the face of an
angel' (Acts vi. 15); and how often at the departure of
holy saints and servants of God has some such gleam of
the coming glory been observed to light up their countenances even here.

But in the Lord of glory it was not the countenance
only, which thus wore a splendour different from the
common; in addition to this, '*his raiment was white and
glistering;*'[1] or, as St. Mark has it, '*became shining, exceeding white as snow*' (cf. Rev. i. 14), '*so as no fuller on
earth can white them.*' It was probably night, when this
marvellous spectacle was vouchsafed to the disciples.
Such an assumption best explains '*the next day*' of Luke
ix. 37. This, if it was so, must have infinitely enhanced
the grandeur of the vision; although no doubt before
that brightness the brightness even of the noonday sun
would have paled (Acts xxvi. 13). Indeed, all words
seem weak to the Evangelists, all images to fail them
here. St. Mark, whose words I have quoted, borrows

---

[1] Bengel: ἐξαστράπτων, ab intra, gloriâ corporis translucente, et poros
vestimenti permeante; compare the ἐκλάμψουσι, which the Lord ascribes
and promises to his saints, Matt. xiii. 43. Λευκὸς ἐξαστράπτων is not 'white
and glistering' (E. V.); but ἐξαστράπτων (cf. Ezek. i. 4, 7; Nah. iii. 3) is
the modal explanation of λευκός, '*white*,' and so white that it was '*glistering*'
as well. This last word is a happy one; 'effulgent,' which hardly existed
in the language when our Version was made, would not express it as well,
while 'fulgurant,' and 'effulgurant,' are too merely Latin words. As
'*glistering*' in like manner we are to understand the 'raiment *white* as snow'
of the angel at the empty tomb (Matt. xxviii. 3); not the garment of innocence, but of glory; the same angel being described in St. Luke as clothed
'in *shining* garments' (ἀστραπτούσαις); so too 'the great *white* throne' of
Rev. xx. 11 is equivalent to 'the throne *of glory*' of Matt. xxv. 31, for
light at the utmost intensity is white; from this, too, we may further explain
Dan. vii. 9; Rev. i. 14.

one image from the world of nature, another from that
of man's art and device; struggling by aid of these to
set forth and reproduce for his readers the transcendant
brightness of that light which now arrayed, and from
head to foot, the person of the Lord, breaking forth from
within, and overflowing the very garments which He
wore; until in their eyes who beheld, He seemed to clothe
Himself with light, which is ever the proper and peculiar
investiture of Deity (Ps. civ. 2 ; Exod. iii. 2, 4), as with a
garment. In the circumstance that his glory was not
one which was lent Him, but his own, bursting forth as
from an inner fountain of light, not merely gilding Him
from without; nor playing, like that of Moses, on the skin
and surface of his countenance ; perhaps also in its being
a glory which arrayed not his face alone, but his entire
person, we have those tokens of superiority, those prerogatives of the Master above the servants, which we are
evermore able to trace even in matters wherein one or
another of these may seem to have anticipated, and thus
to have come into some sort of competition with Him.[1]

I have lightly touched already, and shall have occasion

---

[1] Witsius (*De Glor. Jesu in Monte*, 11): Quorsum ea omnia ? Et Christi
causâ, et nostri. Christi intererat ut hæc ipsi evenirent, quippe quem Pater
hâc quâdam cælestis gloriæ anticipatione ad instans certamen animare con-
stituit. Quum difficultates *prophetici* muneris suscipiendæ essent, aperturâ
cæli, descensu Spiritûs, et compellatione Patris gratissimâ, mirabiliter
animatus est (Matt. iii. 16). Nunc quum instaret tempus quo se ut Pontifex
Patri oblaturus erat, æquum fuit ut splendidis vestibus exornatus, ex earum
ac faciei suæ fulgore experiundo disceret, quæ post sui oblationem gloria
ipsum maneret in cælis. Instabat hora, quâ controversia ipsi de *regno* con-
tumeliosissimum in modum movenda, et regni professio in crimen morte
piandum imputanda, regiaque ipsius dignitas infami ludibrio exponenda
erat. Sed insolitâ hâc plus quam regii splendoris exhibitione clarius demonstravit Rex cælorum quanto ipsum in honore haberet, quam Assuerus olim
Mardochæo, in omni isto invidiosæ pompæ apparatu, quem ei per Hamanem
præstari jussit.

to dwell further on some aspects, in which the Transfiguration may be regarded as designed to strengthen and
encourage the hearts first of those who witnessed it, and
then of all those to whom their witness should come. But
in addition to these it has ever been contemplated in the
Church as a prophetic intimation of the glory which the
saints shall have in the resurrection.[1] As was the body
of Christ, the first fruits of the new creation, on the
Mount, so hereafter shall their bodies be. It is difficult
not to recognize a direct reference to the Transfiguration
in the words of St. Paul, where he speaks of Christ's body
of glory to which hereafter the body of our humiliation
shall be conformed (Phil. iii. 21); while in passages out
of number we have hints of the luminous nature of the
future glorified bodies of the redeemed (Dan. xii. 3 ; Matt.
xiii. 43 ; 1 Cor. xv. 43 ; Col. iii. 4 ; 1 Pet. v. 1 ; Rev. iii.
4, 5 ; Wisd. iii. 7); all these Scriptures pointing to the
glorious conformity of their bodies hereafter, to all which
his body at this time was, who now shewed in Himself
what hereafter He should shew in all them that were his.

    ' *And behold* ' (wonder within wonder), ' *there appeared
unto them Moses and Elias, talking with Him.*'[2] The

---

[1] Leo the Great (*Serm.* xciv.): In transfiguratione illud principaliter
agebatur, ut de cordibus discipulorum scandalum crucis tolleretur; sed non
minore providentiâ spes Sanctæ Ecclesiæ fundabatur, ut totum corpus
Christi agnosceret quali esset commutatione dcnandum, ut ejus sibi honoris
consortium membra promitterent, qui in capite præfulsisset. Gregory the
Great (*Moral.* xxxii. 6): In transfiguratione quid aliud quam resurrectionis
ultima gloria nunciatur? So in the Greek service-books: δεῖξαι βουλόμενος
τῆς ἀναστάσεως τὴν λαμπρότητα.

[2] One of the best and soundest of the Mystics, Richard of St. Victor,
warning against visions, and urging the necessity of trying all such by the
Word of God, of making that the standard by which all subjective revelations should be tried, whether they were indeed of God, or only delusions
of the enemy, has some striking admonitions drawn from this presence of
Moses and Elias with the Lord in the Mount (*Benjamin Minor,* lxxxi.)

question, *How* the disciples knew these two to be Moses and Elias, is surely an idle one ; and the suggestion that they gathered their knowledge from the conversation which they overheard, or that they recognized the horns of Moses, or the ascetic garments of Elias, merely super-fluous. That elevation of their whole spiritual life, that ecstatic state of a divine *clairvoyance*, if we may venture to use this word, in which alone they could have seen these sights at all, will have left them in no doubt con-cerning those whom they now beheld in solemn conclave with their Lord. Their recognition of them we must re-gard as immediate and intuitive.[1] The same question is sometimes asked about St. Paul, namely, how he could see in a vision a man whose name he should know to be Ananias (Acts ix. 12). It is sufficient to answer that the vision which shewed him the man, imparted to him also the name of the man.

But while this question may thus be dismissed, we cannot so dismiss another, namely, why the two who appear should be exactly Moses and Elias, these, and no other ? It was not merely that among all the prophets and saints of the Old Testament they were the two, of

Sed si jam te existimas ascendisse ad cor altum, et apprehendisse montem illum excelsum et magnum, si jam te credis Christum videre transfiguratum, quidquid in illo videas, quidquid ab illo audias, non ei facile credas, nisi occurrant ei Moyses et Elias. Suspecta est mihi omnis veritas quam non confirmat Scripturarum auctoritas, nec Christum in suâ clarificatione recipio, si non assistant ei Moyses et Elias. Compare Thauler, *Homiliæ*, 1553, p. 540.

[1] As Sedulius (*Carm. Pasch.* 286) puts it well :

Ignotos oculis *viderunt lumine cordis.*

He proceeds with verses which are worth quoting, on the purpose of their appearing :

Ut major sit nostra fides, hunc esse per orbem
Principium et finem, hunc Alpha viderier, hunc Ω,
Quem medium tales circumfulsere prophetæ.

whom one had not died (2 Kin. ii. 11; cf. Ecclus. xlviii. 9),
and the other had no sooner tasted of death than probably
his body was withdrawn from under the dominion of
death and of him that had the power of death (Deut.
xxxiv. 6; Jude 9); the two, therefore, whose apparition
in glorified bodies before the day of resurrection had less
in it perplexing than that of any others would have had.
This was something; but much more that these two were
the acknowledged heads and representatives, the one of
the Law, the other of the prophets; in which Law and
prophets the whole Old Testament is commonly summed
up (Matt. vii. 12).[1]

'*And they were talking with Jesus.*' What the matter
of this august conference was St. Luke informs us, namely,
that '*they spake of his decease,*[2] *which He should accom-*

---

[1] It behoved the Lord, in Tertullian's words (*Adv. Marc.* iv. 22), cum
illis videri, quibus in revelationibus erat visus; cum illis loqui, qui eum
fuerant locuti; cum eis gloriam suam communicare, a quibus Dominus
gloriæ nuncupabatur; cum principalibus suis, quorum alter populi informator
aliquando, alter reformator quandoque, alter initiator Veteris Testamenti,
alter consummator Novi.   Augustine (*Serm.* 232): Evangelium testimonium
habet a Lege et prophetis.   Ideo et in monte quando voluit ostendere
Dominus noster Jesus gloriam suam, inter Moysen et Eliam stetit.   Medius
in honore ipse fulgebat; Lex et prophetæ a lateribus adtestabantur.   Cf.
Serm. 78: Hic Dominus, hic Lex et Prophetæ; sed Dominus tanquam
Dominus; Lex in Moyse, Prophetia in Eliâ; sed ipsi tanquam servi, tanquam ministri.   Ipsi tanquam vasa, ipse tanquam fons.   Moyses et Prophetæ dicebant, et scribebant; sed de illo implebantur, quando fundebant.
Cf. *De Doctr. Christ.* ii. 25; Leo the Great (*Serm.* 94): Quid hoc stabilius,
quid firmius verbo, in cujus prædicatione Veteris et Novi Testamenti con-
cinit tuba, et cum Evangelicâ doctrinâ antiquarum protestationum instru-
menta concurrunt?   Adstipulantur enim sibi invicem utriusque fœderis
paginæ, et quem sub velamine mysteriorum præcedentia signa promiserant
manifestum atque perspicuum præsentis gloriæ splendor ostendit.

[2] Τὴν ἔξοδον.   The word is not without its special solemnity.   He who
has an εἴσοδος (Acts xiii. 24) into the world, has also an ἔξοδος out of the
world.   St. Peter employs the same word of his own 'decease,' 2 Pet. i. 15;
cf. Wisd. vii. 6; for a similar use of ἔκβασις, see Heb. xiii. 7; of ἄφιξις, Acts
xx. 29.   Bengel: Vocabulum valde grave, quo continetur Passio, Crux,
Mors, Resurrectio, Adscensio.   The Latin excessus, which is an exact

plish at Jerusalem;' of that *'decease'* prefigured by the
types of the law (Num. xxi. 9; Exod. xii. 46), fore-
announced by the oracles of the prophets (Zech. xii. 10;
Isai. liii. 9).[1] *'Decease'* has now become so mere a
synonym for death, it has so much lost its proper sense
of departure, i.e. out of this life (decessus), that, as we
read in the English, we are in danger of missing, indeed
we can hardly help missing, an allusion which must at
once suggest itself to every reader of the Greek. We
fail to mark the relation, which the sacred historian could
scarcely not have intended us to recognize, between this
' exodus ' and an earlier ; we fail to recognize in this an
' *accomplishing* ' or fulfilling, as he is careful to note, by
the Saviour at Jerusalem of a ' *decease*,' departure or
' exodus ' (cf. Heb. xi. 22), which Moses and Joshua had
begun in Egypt and in the wilderness, but had *not* accomplished (Heb. iv. 6–9); the 'exodus,' that is, or going out
of God's people, their Captain and Commander leading
the way, from this present evil world.

The unity of the Old and New Covenant is wonderfully
attested by this apparition of the princes of the Old in
solemn yet familiar intercourse with the Lord of the New ;
and not the unity only, but with this unity the subordination of the Old to the New, that ' Christ is the end of the
law ' (Rom. x. 4), and the object to which all prophecy
pointed (Luke xxiv. 44 ; Acts x. 43 ; xxviii. 23 ; Rom.

---

parallel, has precisely the same more solemn use; thus Cicero (*De Rep.* ii.
30): Post obitum, vel potius excessum Romuli. It is noticeable that Chrysostom, for ἔξοδον twice reads δόξαν here; which is not a *mere* inadvertence,
for he comments on the word which he thus reads. There is no vestige of
any such reading having ever existed.

[1] Gerhard (*Harm.* 87): Institutum itaque fuit colloquium de illo ipso
articulo, quo apostoli paulo ante offensi fuerant; nimirum de passione et
morte Servatoris nostri, Jesu Christi.

iii. 21), that therefore the great purpose of these had now been fulfilled ; all which was declared in the fact that, after their testimony thus given, Moses and Elias disappear, while Christ only remains.   It need hardly be observed what strength there was here, and in the remembrance of this scene, for the disciples, when they should afterwards behold their Lord put to death as a breaker of the law of Moses, as a false snatcher to Himself of the words of the prophets.

'*But Peter and they that were with him were heavy with sleep; and when they were awake, they saw his glory, and the two men that stood with Him.*' These words are too often misunderstood ; indeed, until the translation is corrected, they can hardly fail to be misunderstood.   It is usual for commentators to take the disciples to task for this sleep of theirs at such a moment,[1] and to find a parallel to it in the sleep of the same three in the garden of Gethsemane (Matt. xxvi. 40–45).   The parallel is altogether misleading.   That was a somnolence not without its guilt ; while they were sleeping that untimely sleep, they should have been watching and praying, seeking strength for themselves and help for their Lord.   But the fact that the eyes of the disciples here '*were heavy with sleep*,' this might be, and was, an evidence of human infirmity, of the inability of this weak nature of ours to bear a weight of glory, when it is laid upon it, but of nothing more than this.[2]   The true parallels to the words

---

[1] Thus Gerhard (*Loci Theoll.* xxxii. 2) : Discipuli somno erant gravati, per quem denotatur nostra somnolentia, quod gloriam vitæ æternæ non satis æstimamus ac meditamur.

[2] Chrysostom has a right insight into the matter : ὕπνον ἐνταῦθα καλῶν [ὁ Λουκᾶς] τὸν πολὺν κάρον τὸν ἀπὸ τῆς ὄψεως ἐκείνης αὐτοῖς ἐγγινόμενον. And Ambrose : Somno gravati erant.   Premit enim incomprehensibilis splendor divinitatis nostri corporis sensus.

before us are Gen. xv. 12; Dan. x. 9; Zech. iv. 1; and we may add, as materially helping to illustrate what the condition of the three apostles was, Num. xxiv. 4. Theirs, as has been urged already, was the condition of a divine *clairvoyance*; their eyes heavy with sleep, but they not asleep; for having resisted all the temptations of this frail nature of ours to succumb under the burden of this glory —and what a burden it is to be the immediate recipient of any divine revelation Daniel has often told us (vii. 28; viii. 27; x. 8, 11, 16)—' *having kept themselves awake throughout*' (for this, and not ' *when they were awake,*' is the right rendering),[1] ' *they saw his glory, and the two men that stood with Him.*' The disciples saw this vision, as indeed it only could have been seen, ' in spirit ' or ' in a trance' (Acts x. 10; xi. 5; xxii. 17; 1 Cor. xiv. 15; Rev. i. 10); just as the witch of Endor, being within the circle of the supernatural manifestation, saw what Saul, who was outside of it, could not see, and could only learn from her lips (1 Sam. xxviii. 13, 14). Whether they saw that vision in the body or out of the body the disciples could not, any more than St. Paul in a later ecstasy (2 Cor. xii. 3), have told.[2] It is from this point of view, and keeping this in mind, that we must explain St. Luke's comment on Peter's proposal which presently follows—to wit, that the apostle made it, ' *not knowing what he said.*' Tertullian long ago gave the right explanation of these words,[3] which

---

[1] Διαγρηγορήσαντες, not vigilantes (Vulg.), nor cum evigilâssent (Beza), nor postquam experrecti sunt (Castalio), which all are in error. Διαγρηγορέω Rost and Palm rightly render durchwachen, and refer to Herodian, iii. 4. 8 : πασῆς τῆς νυκτὸς διαγρηγορήσαντες.

[2] Compare Philo, *Quis Rer. Div. Hæres*, § 53, who there and elsewhere has much to say on the true character of the Scriptural ἔκστασις, which word he found in his Septuagint at Gen. ii. 21; xv. 12.

[3] *Adv. Marc.* iv. 22 : In spiritu enim homo constitutus, præsertim cum

many have subsequently missed.[1]   They are no apology
upon the part of the Evangelist for St. Peter's untimely
suggestion, still less a judgment upon it.   Inopportune
that suggestion may have been, and beside the mark ;
and, even while testifying for his zeal and for his delight
in that heavenly communion, such in some sense it was.
This, however, is not what St. Luke is affirming ; but that
he so spake, being out of and beside himself ; not indeed
demens but *amens*, rapt into another world, a supernatural world of fear and wonder, into conditions altogether remote from those of our common existence ; as
appears still more plainly in the parallel statement of St.
Mark ; '*for he wist not what to say, for they were sore
afraid.*'

His proposal is this : ' *Lord, it is good for us to be here ;
if Thou wilt, let us make here three tabernacles, one for
Thee, and one for Moses, and one for Elias ;* ' he made it,
as the third Evangelist, again significantly completing the
earlier, informs us, ' *as they departed from Him ;* ' or
much better, ' *as they were divided from Him.*'[2]   It is
too brief a converse, too transient a glimpse and foretaste
of the heavenly glory.   He will fain detain these august
visitors.   Wherefore should all these marvels of the
higher world be shewn to them, only to be withdrawn
again in an instant?   ' *It is good for us to be here* '—

gloriam Dei conspicit, vel cum per ipsum Deus loquitur, necesse est excidat
sensu, obumbratus scilicet virtute divinâ . . . Interim facile est amentiam
[=ἔκστασιν] Petri probare.   Quomodo enim Moysem et Eliam cognovisset
nisi in spiritu ?

[1] Gerhard for example : Hanc vocem ex carnali inscitiâ profectum esse
Lucas testatur, Non enim noverat quid loqueretur.

[2] Ἐν τῷ διαχωρίζεσθαι αὐτοὺς ἀπ' αὐτου, on which Beza rightly comments,
e conspectu abrepti.

better, as no doubt he felt, than to be rejected of the Jews, better than to suffer many things of the Elders and Chief Priests and Scribes, and be killed (Matt. xvi. 21). But that holy retirement in which they were was '*good*,' as he esteemed it, not merely as a safe shelter and hiding place from all this evil, but also for the sweetness which he found in the communion and fellowship which it offered. 'But what,' exclaims Anselm in a sermon of extraordinary richness and beauty, from which I have already quoted one or two fragments, 'if the contemplation of Christ's glorified humanity so filled the apostle with joy that he was unwilling to be sundered from it, how shall it fare with them who attain to the contemplation of his glorious Godhead? and if it was so good a thing to dwell with two of his saints, how then to come to the heavenly Jerusalem, to the general assembly and Church of the firstborn that are written in heaven, and to God the Judge of all, and to these, not seen through a glass and darkly, but face to face?'

But abiding on that mountain top they will need, as the apostle conceives, some kind of shelter ; for so are things earthly confused with things heavenly in his mind. He, ever prompt for action, as ready with the labour of his hands as with the devotion of his heart, aided by the other two, will quickly prepare some slight booths of the branches of trees, or of whatever else may come to hand, in which they may tarry : '*Let us make here three taber- nacles, one for Thee, and one for Moses, and one for Elias.*' [1] That there is any allusion here to the Feast of Tabernacles, that St. Peter is measuring here the heavenly felicity by that poor earthly copy, I cannot for an instant

[1] Ambrose: Impiger operarius communis obsequii ministerium pollicetur.

believe ; and altogether it seems to me that he is very needlessly schooled and found fault with by modern commentators, and, indeed, by some ancient interpreters as well, for these words of his. There was a certain fault in them no doubt. He who would suggest this had scarcely maintained himself at the height of that great confession which he had so lately made (Matt. xvi. 16). However honourably he may have meant it for his Master, yet, putting those other two at all on the same level with Him, he plainly declared that he did not yet perceive how far that Master transcended all other, even the princes of the elder dispensation, how far higher a dispensation had begun with Him ;[1] he in this revealed his own need of the teaching of that vision and that voice, which was presently to be vouchsafed to him and to his fellows ; for we have a right to see in what immediately succeeds the answer from heaven to that word of his :[2] ' *while he yet spake, behold a bright cloud overshadowed them,*' not the disciples, but the legislator and the prophet, and perhaps also Him that was Lord alike of them both.

---

[1] Jerome : Erras, Petre, sicut et alius Evangelista testatur, Nescis quid dicas. Noli tria tabernacula quærere, cum unum sit tabernaculum Evangelii, in quo Lex et Prophetæ recapitulanda sunt. Nequaquam servos cum Domino conferas.

[2] Augustine (*Serm.* 78) : Videt hoc Petrus, et humana sapiens tanquam homo : *Domine, bonum est,* inquit, *nos hic esse.* Tædium patiebatur a turbâ, invenerat solitudinem montis ; ibi habebat Christum panem mentis. Utquid inde discederet ad labores et dolores, habens in Deum sanctos amores, et ideo bonos mores ? Bene sibi volebat esse ; unde et adjunxit, *Si vis, faciamus hic tria tabernacula : Tibi unum, Moysi unum, et Eliæ unum.* Ad hæc Dominus nihil respondit : sed tamen Petro responsum est. Hæc enim eo loquente, nubes lucida venit, et obumbravit eos. Ille quærebat tria tabernacula : nobis unum esse, quod humanus sensus dividere cupiebat, responsum cæleste monstravit. Verbum Dei Christus, Verbum Dei in Lege, Verbum in Prophetis. Quid, Petre, quæris dividere ? Magis te oportet adjungere. Tria quæris ; intellige et unum.

A cloud is the constant symbol, or, if not always this, yet the constant accompaniment or vehicle, of the divine presence (Exod. xiv. 19; xix. 16; xxxiii. 9; xl. 34; 1 Kin. viii. 10; Ps. civ. 3; Isai. xix. 1; Ezek. x. 3; Dan. vii. 13; Rev. xiv. 14). There is a manifest fitness in the symbol. The clouds of our lower world veil, sheath, render tolerable to mortal eyes the splendour of the heavens, the brightness of the sun, which otherwise we could not endure to behold. In the Old Testament, indeed, 'a ministration of condemnation' (2 Cor. iii. 9), the cloud is a dark cloud, a thick cloud (1 Kin. viii. 12); for God, though in part revealing, is also in part a God that hideth, Himself (Isai. xlv. 15); it is often a cloud charged with thunder and lightning, and all the dreadful artillery of heaven (Exod. xix. 16; Ps. xviii. 12); for there was in that dispensation the utterance of God's displeasure against the sins of men. But the cloud which now overshadows these is ' *a bright cloud,*' agreeable to the character of the dispensation which has now begun; yet, bright as it is, still serving the purpose of veiling the more intolerable brightness within, even that of God's very presence in this the Schechina or place of his dwelling; and making possible for mortal and sinful men that which else would have been impossible for them, namely, to stand in that presence and live (Exod. xxxiii. 20; Judg. xiii. 22; Isai. vi. 5).[1]

It may seem strange at first that to ' *a bright cloud*' such a power of overshadowing and concealing should be ascribed; yet it is not really strange; for light in its utmost intensity hides as effectually as the darkness

---

[1] Ambrose: Ut apostoli Dei loquentis majestatem interpositâ nube ferre possent.

would do.   God dwells in light inaccessible, whom therefore 'no man hath seen, nor can see' (1 Tim. vi. 16);[1]
and compare the words of Milton, ' dark with excess of
light ;' and of Wordsworth, 'a glorious privacy of light;'
in like manner Philo affirms of the highest light that it is
identical with darkness (γνόφος), even as it is the character of extremes evermore to meet.   They, that is, the two,
were hidden in that blaze of intolerable light from the
eyes of the disciples, who '*feared as they entered into the
cloud*' (Luke ix. 34), feared with that fear which evermore falls on sinful men when brought suddenly into immediate nearness to the pure and awful presences of
heaven.   They may have feared too that their Lord was
now about to be taken from them, to anticipate the day
of his Ascension, and to mount already the cloud-chariot
which should one day bear Him from their sight (Acts
i. 9); for the Transfiguration must have made plain to
them as to Himself that He needed not the painful passage of death by which to enter into glory; that if He
still laid down his life, it was not of necessity, but of
freest love.

And then it must have been fear upon fear, when
' *behold a voice out of the cloud*,' the same voice which
had once before been heard at the Baptism (Matt. iii. 17),
and which should salute Him again as He stood on the
threshold of his Passion (John xii. 28); and thus at the
beginning, at the middle, and at the close of his ministry,
' *This is my beloved[2] Son, in whom I am well pleased;*

---

[1] Anselm, quoting these words of St. Paul, and then the words of Moses,
'And Moses drew near unto the thick darkness where God was' (Exod. xx.
21), and bringing both passages into connexion with this present, says pro-
foundly, Illa caligo et ista nubes atque illa lux idem sunt.

[2] Ἀγαπητός in St. Matthew and St. Mark; but ἐκλελεγμένος (cf. ἐκλεκτός
Luke xxiii. 35) is now recognized as the true reading in St. Luke.

hear ye Him.' This voice is said by St. Peter to have come 'from the excellent glory' (2 Pet. i. 17); from Him, that is, who dwelt in the cloud, which was here at once the symbol and the vehicle of the divine presence.[1] In respect of the heavenly salutation itself, the emphasis should not be so much laid on '*This*' as on '*Son*;' for the true parallel to the present salutation of the Son by the Father, with the installation of the Son in the highest place of the kingdom, is to be found at Heb. i. 1, 2 : 'God, who at sundry times and in divers manners spake in time past unto the fathers by the prophets, hath in these last days spoken unto us by his Son.' He is to be heard above all others, because He is not a servant in the house of another, as were Moses and Elias, but a Son in his own (Heb. iii. 5, 6). In the words themselves of this majestic installation there is a remarkable honouring of the Old Testament, and of it in all its parts, which can scarcely be regarded as accidental; for the three several clauses of that salutation are drawn severally from the Psalms (ii. 7), the Prophets (Isai. xlii. 1), and the Law (Deut. xviii. 15); and, as we shall see, they do together proclaim Him concerning whom they are spoken to be the King, the Priest, and, the Prophet of the New Covenant. St. Peter therefore might very fitly declare that in this voice from heaven 'He received from God

---

[1] St. Peter in this same passage, looking back at the privilege vouchsafed to him and to the 'sons of thunder,' speaks of himself and them as ' eye-witnesses of the majesty' (ἐπόπται γενηθέντες τῆς μεγαλειότητος). Ἐπόπτης, a technical word, too weakly rendered ' eye-witness,' though it would not be easy to suggest a more adequate rendering, sets well before us the light in which the apostle regarded his and their relation to the things which they were permitted to behold. The ἐπόπτης is properly one admitted and initiated into secret and holy mysteries, the Eleusinian for example, or any other reserved from the common gaze. Such an initiation he would imply, into the secretest and holiest mysteries of all, had been theirs.

the Father honour and glory' (2 Pet. i. 17). And first, '*This is my beloved Son;*' but the King's Son is Himself the King; 'yet have I set my King upon my holy hill of Sion' (Ps. ii. 6). And then, '*in whom I am well pleased;*' holy, therefore, harmless and undefiled, fairer than the children of men (Ps. xlv. 2), the sceptre of whose kingdom is a sceptre of righteousness (Heb. i. 8), for in no other could God take a perfect pleasure; and thus the Priest who could and should offer Himself without spot to God (Heb. ix. 14; 1 John iii. 5). But then, further, He is the One whom all are commanded to obey: '*Hear ye Him;*' therefore henceforth the sole Prophet of his Church; Moses, or the Law, has passed away, for that was but the shadow and outline of good things to come (Col. ii. 17; Heb. viii. 5; x. 1), while in Him is body or substance of good things actually present; Elias, or the prophets, has passed away, for in Him all prophecy is fulfilled (Luke xvi. 16; 1 Cor. xiii. 8). They, belonging as they did to a merely preparatory and provisional dispensation, vanish; but Christ, who is the Head of an everlasting dispensation, after whom we do *not* look for another, remains; and this will explain how it came to pass that '*when they had lifted up their eyes, they saw no man, save Jesus only.*'[1]

---

[1] I have made more than one citation from a long and interesting passage on the Transfiguration in Tertullian (*Adv. Marc.* iv. 22). Marcion, in his assault upon the Old Testament and the old Economy, as having proceeded from another God than the author of the New, had found in this transaction, not Christ preferred to Moses and Elias, but Christ honoured and Moses and Elias dishonoured. Tertullian's reply is admirable throughout. Strange, he says, if this had been intended, that they should appear talking with Him, which is an evidence of familiarity; sharing in the same glory, which is an evidence of favour and acceptance; and he thus concluded: Itaque etsi facta translatio sit auditionis a Moyse et Heliâ in Christo, sed non ut ab alio Deo, nec ad alium Christum, sed a Creatore in Christum ejus, secundum

But before accompanying the Lord and his three disciples, as they come down from that Mount of Vision to this common workday world of ours, with all its labour and suffering and sin, we may pause for a word or two on a subject common to all the Evangelists, but on which St. Matthew dwells most in detail. All have told us of the fear which overcame the three, even while they felt it most good and blessed to be there. But amazing as had been the sights which they saw, it was not these so much as the voice from heaven, the awfulness of that direct speaking of God with man, which man is so little able to endure (cf. Hab. iii. 2, 16 ; Exod. xx. 19 ; Heb. xii. 19), that brought them to the extremity of their fear : '*And when the disciples heard it, they fell on their face, and were sore afraid*'—this fear of theirs uttering itself, as is so constantly its manner (Gen. xvii. 3 ; Num. xvi. 22 ; Josh. v. 14 ; Judg. xiii. 20 ; 1 Sam. xxviii. 14 ; 1 Chron. xxi. 16 ; Ezek. i. 28 ; iii. 23 ; ix. 8 ; xi. 13 ; xliv. 4 ; Dan. viii. 17 ; x. 9 ; Luke xxiv. 5 ; Acts ix. 4 ; Rev. i. 17 ; xix. 10 ; xxii. 8), in an attitude suggested by those moral instincts of awe, by that sense of his own utter unfitness to stand face to face with the holiness of God, which any near revelation of that holiness must inevitably awaken in the heart of man.[1] To hide the face is the first impulse

decessionem Veteris, et successionem Novi Testamenti. Tradidit igitur Pater Filio discipulos novos, ostensis prius cum illo Moyse et Heliâ in claritatis prærogativâ, atque ita dimissis, quasi jam et officio et honore dispunctis.

[1] Witsius (*De Glorif. Jesu in Monte*, 39) : Quoties enim cunque Deus suam animis nostris majestatem illustribus documentis ingerit, toties nostræ non vilitatis solum sed et impuritatis et omnigenæ indignitatis conscientia vivide expergiscitur ; unde fit ut ad tam sublimis puritatis et magnificentissimæ gloriæ præsentiam trepidemus. Neque id solis contingit improbis, quibus formidolosa semper vindicis Dei cogitatio est, sed et piis, imo et amicis Dei ac familiaribus, quibus eo venerabilior semper summi

and instinct of such a moment (Exod. iii. 6 ; 1 Kin. xix.
13 ; Ezra ix. 6) ; to fall on the face is the most effectual
way of so doing, and at the same time of outwardly expressing the inner conviction that for man there is no
standing in his own right before God.

' *And Jesus came and touched them ;* ' as He, now the
Incarnate Word, and once the Angel of the Covenant, had
touched Daniel (Dan. viii. 18 ; ix. 21 ; x. 10, 18), and
Jeremiah (Jer. i. 9), and Ezekiel (Ezek. ii. 2) ; as by the
hand of a ministering Seraph He had touched the lips of
Isaiah (Isai. vi. 7) ; as hereafter, the glorified Son of man,
walking among the golden candlesticks, He should, under
circumstances not unlike, touch or lay his right hand once
more upon one of these same three (Rev. i. 17). And
with that touch there goes also the reassuring word, that
' *Fear not,*' which even the holiest need so much, when
God had shewn them their unholiness, the depths of
their corruption, the abundant cause which as sinful men
they have to fear, cause so abundant that no other but
He can enable them to lay this fear aside (Judg. vi. 23 ;
Dan. x. 12, 19 ; Matt. xxviii. 5 ; Luke v. 10).[1]

Numinis majestas est, quo clarius conspicitur ejus bonitas; et qui nunquam
sibi ipsis magis sordent, quam cum in liquidissimâ se divinæ gloriæ luce
contuentur.

[1] Witsius (*Ibid.*, 42) : Non caruit successu ea Christi compellatio, quippe
quâ expergefacti velut a veterno aliquo apostoli, accurate omnia circum-
spexerunt. Sed quocunque oculos verterent, nihil eorum deprehenderunt
quæ nuper tam admiranda ipsis videbantur. *Neminem viderunt, nisi solum
Jesum*, suetâ formâ, solito amictu. Non decebat diutius in terrâ commorari
Mosem et Eliam, quorum ministerium neque cum Jesu magisterio, neque
cum apostolorum functione miscendum aut confundendum erat. Discessit
igitur Moses, discessit Elias ; imo siluit vox ipsa cælestis Patris, quæ semel
locuta est, ut semper audiatur Filius. Christus ipse depositâ nuperæ Transfigurationis gloriâ ad pristinum ervi statum habitumque rediit ; temporariam
enim eam gloriam esse decuit, quæ non nisi præludium æternæ fuit ;
multaque adhuc perpetienda restabant Christo, antequam æternâ illâ poti-
retur.

An important discourse follows, which the Lord held with the three favoured disciples, as they were descending from the Mount, and leaving all its mysterious marvels behind them. And first the charge to silence, the seal which He set upon their lips, not to be removed till after the Resurrection: '*And as they came down from the mountain, Jesus charged them, saying, Tell the vision*[1] *to no man, until the Son of man be risen again from the dead.*' The three Evangelists here remarkably complete one another. St. Matthew, thus mentioning the injunction to silence, does not mention how well the disciples obeyed it; while St. Luke, mentioning the *fact* of silence —'*they kept it close, and told no man in those days any of those things which they had seen*' (ix. 36),—does not state that this was in obedience to an express command; only St. Mark, with his own characteristic fulness of detail, records both the express command given by the Lord, and the keeping of it by the disciples (ix. 9, 10). That '*Tell the vision to no man,*' implies that they were forbidden to reveal what they had seen even to their fellow-apostles themselves—a hard precept, yet one which was obeyed by them. At the same time, however strict the silence which they kept, we cannot imagine that even so the vision was only for themselves, and altogether lost upon the others. There must have pierced through the

---

[1] Ὅραμα, not in use distinguishable from ὀπτασία (Luke i. 22; Acts xxvi. 19; 2 Cor. xii. 1), nor from ὅρασις (Acts ii. 17; Rev. ix. 17), is exactly '*a vision;*' what a man most truly sees, but sees because God enables him to see it, because it is shewn to him; which he sees, as the three disciples saw this vision, ἐν πνεύματι, as contrasted with ἐν νοΐ (1 Cor. xiv. 15, 16). So invariably in the Acts, where alone, with the exception of this one passage, it occurs in the New Testament; but there no less than eleven times (vii. 31; ix. 10, 12; x. 5, 17, 19; xi. 5; xii. 9; xvi. 9, 10; xviii. 9; cf. Gen. xv. 1; Dan. ii. 19; Exod. iii. 3).

whole demeanour of these three, as they returned to fellowship with the others, evident tokens that they had not been for nothing on that holy mountain. The others, in one way or another, must have felt certain that they had seen sights and heard words which had strengthened and reassured their faith, and must have found in this conviction a strengthening and reassuring of their own.

But out of what motive shall we explain this charge to silence, not to be broken until after the Resurrection (cf. Matt. xvi. 20, 21)? We may, perhaps, best explain it thus: The mystery of Christ's Sonship should not be revealed to the world till it had been attested beyond all doubt; not till He had been ' declared to be the Son of God with power by the resurrection from the dead ' (Rom. i. 4), and by that Ascension, which was, so to speak, the necessary complement of his Resurrection. It could only be a matter of dispute, and, resting as it did on his miraculous conception, only too easily of profane discussion, till then. A little more light upon this point might have increased their guilt who rejected and crucified Him, but would have done nothing to bring them to the obedience of faith.

St. Mark does not merely connect, and bind into one, the two statements of his fellow Evangelists; he also adds what they have wholly passed over, namely, the perplexity which this language of their Lord occasioned them: ' *They kept that saying with themselves, questioning one with another what the rising from the dead should mean* ' (cf. John xx. 9). Not the rising from the dead, but the death which must have gone before, and which could alone render a rising from the dead necessary or possible, it was this which, running counter to all their prejudices

and preconceptions, perplexed them so much (Luke xxiv.
22–24 ; John xii. 24). Yet on this point they do not
venture to ask any explanation ; but on something else
closely connected with all which they had just beheld.
' *And his disciples asked Him, saying, Why then say the
Scribes that Elias must first come?* ' That momentary
glimpse which had been vouchsafed to them of Elias
reminded them of the place which he occupied in the
economy of salvation (Mal. iv. 5, 6). They had seen
him, but only for an instant. That transient glimpse
could not satisfy the largeness of prophetic announcements about him. How are they to understand his
disappearance, that they are returning with their Master
alone ? How was this to be reconciled with a cardinal
point in the Jewish theology, namely, that Elias should
go before the Messiah ? nay, how was it reconcilable with
their Master's claims to be the Messiah at all ? Their
reference to what the Scribes said on this matter, leads us
to gather that these urged, as a capital and decisive objection against his Messiahship, that no Elias went before
Him ; while yet the prophecies of the Old Testament had
solemnly closed with a pledge that Elias, going before,
should prepare the way of the Lord. This stumbling-block
to their faith the Scribes may have laid in the way of the
disciples. Will their Lord graciously remove it out of
their path ?

The great Interpreter of prophecy gives right to that
interpretation of the prophetic word which the Scribes
maintained : ' *Elias truly shall first come, and restore
all things. But I say unto you, That Elias is come already,
and they knew him not, but have done unto him whatso-
ever they listed. Likewise shall also the Son of man suffer*

*of them.   Then the disciples understood that He spake
unto them of John the Baptist.'* Elias *had* first come.
Whether he had *so* come in the person of John the
Baptist, as that he should not hereafter come in his own,
whether the prophecy of Malachi found in him its *exhaustive* fulfilment, and not a partial and initial one only,
is a question than which few in modern times have more
divided interpreters ; but one upon which it is unnecessary
here to enter, as not immediately belonging to the matter
in hand.   Enough, that in John the Baptist that word
which cannot be broken had found *a* fulfilment ; whether
a further fulfilment awaits it, this still remains to be seen.

9. *JAMES AND JOHN OFFERING TO CALL FIRE FROM HEAVEN ON THE SAMA-RITAN VILLAGE*

Luke ix. 51–56.

WE have here one of the memorable incidents of our Lord's last journey to Jerusalem, whereof St. Luke has preserved for us so careful a record. *'And it came to pass, when the time was come that He should be received up, He stedfastly set his face to go to Jerusalem.'* I should prefer to render the second clause of this sentence, ' *when the days of his Assumption*[1] *were fulfilled.'* Such a rendering would not lose nor dissolve, as does our present, the word at once so solemn and so sweet, with which the Evangelist mitigates, even as imagination in these things is so potent to mitigate, the bitterness of his Lord's passion and death;

---

[1] Some understand by our Lord's ἀνάληψις, which is spoken of here, his ready acceptance among men; and make the Evangelist to say that the days of this his acceptance were completed, had now come to an end; which he proceeds to illustrate and to prove by the churlish refusal on the part of the Samaritans to receive Him now, as contrasted with the glad acceptance which He found from them at an earlier date (John iv. 39-42). But this is certainly a mistake. It is true that ἀνάληψις occurs only here in the N. T., so that its meaning in Scriptural Greek cannot be fixed by a comparison of other passages where it appears; but ἀναλαμβάνεσθαι is the solemn word everywhere employed to express our Lord's taking up into heaven (Mark xvi. 19 ; Acts i. 2, 11, 22 ; 1 Tim. iii. 16), and in like manner to express that which was, so to speak, the rehearsal of this, namely, the rapture of Elias in the Old (2 Kin. ii. 10; 1 Macc. ii. 58 ; Ecclus. xlviii. 9); and in the same sense an apocryphal Jewish book bears the title, 'Ανάληψις Μωσίως. See Suicer, *Thes.*, s. v. ἀνάληψις.

looking on as he thus does to the issue and the end, to
the taking up of Christ into heaven, to his reception in
his heavenly home and into his Father's glory. In that
' *stedfastly set his face* '[1] is implied that He addressed
Himself to this work, as One whom no threatenings of
his adversaries should arrest, no difficulties nor dangers
turn away from the accomplishment of his purpose.
The disciples at first followed trembling, as we plainly
gather from Mark x. 32. He Himself, as there described,
' went before them,' after the manner of some leader who
heartens his soldiers by choosing the place of danger for
himself.[2]

' *And sent messengers before his face,*' probably ' two
and two,' as He afterwards sent the Seventy 'into every city
and place, whither He Himself would come ' (Luke x. 1);
and yet, seeing that He was not Himself sent but to the
lost sheep of the house of Israel, these messengers will
not now have gone forth to prepare his spiritual way, but
simply as harbingers, to use that word in its most proper
sense. ' *And they went, and entered into a village of the
Samaritans, to make ready*[3] *for Him ; and they did not
receive Him, because his face was as though He would go
to Jerusalem.*' This refusal of theirs was no piece of
ordinary inhospitality, such as the Samaritans were wont
to shew to Galilæan pilgrims on their way to the feasts at
Jerusalem.[4] It was not merely as such a pilgrim, that

---

[1] Ἐστήριξε τὸ πρόσωπον: cf. Jer. xxi. 10; Ezek. vi. 1; xxviii. 21. So
τάσσειν τὸ πρόσωπον (2 Kin. xii. 17); ἑτοιμάζειν τὸ πρόσωπον (Ezek. iv. 3);
ἐφιστάναι πρόσωπον (Lev. xvii. 10). But St. Luke makes probably here
especial allusion to Isai. l. 7: ἔθηκα τὸ πρόσωπόν μου ὡς στερεὰν πέτραν.

[2] More intrepidi ducis, as Grotius puts it well.

[3] Ἑτοιμάσαι, to which we may supply ξενίαν, this phrase ἑτοιμάζειν
ξενίαν, to prepare a lodging, occurring Philem. 22.

[4] The enmity even to these ordinary pilgrims reached often much further

they shut their doors against Him ; but this, we must remember, was Christ's solemn progress from Galilee to Judæa as Messiah, with these messengers everywhere announcing Him as such. But, as the Samaritans esteemed it, a Messiah going to Jerusalem to observe the feasts there, did by this very act proclaim that He was no Messiah ; for on Gerizim, as they believed, the old patriarchs had worshipped [1] (John iv. 20), consecrating it to be the holy mountain of God—which therefore, and not Jerusalem, the Christ, when He came, would recognize and honour as the central point of all true religion.

There is no need to suppose the two apostles who are so eager to avenge this repulse to have been themselves the ' *messengers*,' or harbingers, in the strictest sense of this word, who endured it. The sons of Zebedee were more probably with their Lord forming part of his immediate retinue, at the moment when some others brought back the tidings of the village which, refusing to receive Him,

than to a mere refusal of these common rights of hospitality. Josephus (*B. J.* ii. 12. 3-7) relates at full the bloody retaliations with which, during the governorship of Quadratus, some of the fiercer sort of the Jews avenged the murder of a Galilæan pilgrim, or of several Galilæan pilgrims, as he states it in another account (*Antt.* xx. 6. 1), wasting a whole district with a slaughter which spared none, and, as the sons of Zebedee would fain have here done, destroying with fire the villages of these hateful schismatics. The treacherous lyings in wait on the part of the dwellers in Samaria which called forth these bloody revenges will have begun very early, if, as St. Jerome's Hebrew teacher assured him, they were already denounced by the prophet Hosea (vi. 8, 9) : Quorum quum intelligentiam quærebam ab Hebræo, ita nobis expositum est. Sacerdotes Bethel, imo fanatici Bethaven, temporibus Paschæ et Pentecostes et Scenopegiæ, quando per Sichem eundum erat ad Hierosolymam, ponebant in itinere latrones, qui insidiarentur pergentibus, ut magis vitulos aureos in Dan et Bethaven quam in Hierosolymis et in templo adorarent Deum. Wetstein (on John iv. 20) gives some specimens from Jewish books of the courtesies by word of mouth which were wont to be exchanged between the Samaritans and the Jewish pilgrims who passed through the land on their way to Jerusalem.

[1] See p. 110.

had missed the opportunity of entertaining, not angels but the Lord of angels, unawares. Upon this provocation all their suppressed and smouldering indignation against the schismatics through whose territory they were journeying, breaks forth. At this instance of contempt shewn to their Lord and to themselves (for no doubt a feeling of personal slight mingled with their indignation, however little they may have been aware of it themselves), the 'sons of thunder,'—sons of thunder indeed, as Jerome exclaims,[1]—will fain play Old Testament parts. They feel that a greater than Elias is here ; for they are fresh from the Mount of Transfiguration, where they had seen how the glory of the foremost prophet of the Old Covenant paled and waned before the brighter glory of Him whom they served, the Lord of the New (ver. 28–36); an outrage against Him, and a rejecting of Him, should therefore not be less terribly avenged.

Out of their sense of this, ' *they said, Lord, wilt Thou that we command fire to come down from heaven, and consume them, even as Elias did ?* ' These last words ' *Even as Elias did,*' which one would very unwillingly let go, have many ancient authorities in their favour, but are omitted by many. Supposing them to have a right to a place in the text, there is certainly a reference here, and even if this is not the case, there is probably a reference here, to the destruction of the two scornful captains with their fifties by the fire which Elijah called down upon them (2 Kin. i. 10, 12). If he spared not those of his own people, should they shrink from executing judgment on heretical Samaritans ?[2] With all of carnal and sinful

---

[1] And Ambrose: Quid enim mirum, filios tonitrui fulgurare voluisse?

[2] Jerome (*Ad Algas.* 5): Si ad servi Eliæ injuriam ignis descendit de cælo, et non Samaritas sed Judæos consumsit incendium, quanto magis ad contemptum Filii Dei in impios Samaritas debet flamma venire ?

which mingled with this proposal of theirs, yet what insight into the dignity of their Lord, and the greatness of
the outrage which was an outrage against Him, does it
reveal ; what faith in the mighty powers with which He
was able to equip his servants ! How mighty a power this
was in the eyes of one of these two is evidenced from the
fact that, when in the Apocalypse he records the great
wonders and lying signs of the false prophet, the only
sign which he specially names is, that ' he maketh fire
come down from heaven on the earth in the sight of
men ' (Rev. xiii. 13 ; cf. Lev. ix. 24 ; 1 Kin. xviii. 38 ;
1 Chron. xxi. 26 ; 2 Chron. vii. 1). And yet it might
almost seem as though, with all this confidence of theirs,
there was a latent and lurking sense upon their part of a
certain unfitness in this their proposal ; and thus, out of
no desire to intrude into their Lord's office, but only out
of a feeling that this avenging act might not exactly become *Him*, they proffer *themselves* as the executors of the
judgment. It will become the servants, though it would
not perfectly become the Lord.

Already, as would seem, He who was the pattern of a
perfect patience had turned to go, that He might seek
in another village the hospitality denied Him in this.
They meanwhile had lingered behind, hardly enduring
that the guilty village should escape the punishment
which was its due. But now on this word of theirs,
' *He turned, and*' turning ' *rebuked them : Ye know not
what manner of spirit ye are of.*'[1] We must beware

---

[1] The emphasis in the English sentence should be on the second ' *ye.*'
The emphatic position of the ὑμεῖς at the end of the sentence, which it
would have been hard to reproduce in English, which our Version has not
attempted to reproduce, and, indeed, its introduction at all, sufficiently indicates this. Bishop Andrews well: ' Vos is no idle word. It makes a

here of extenuating these words of our Lord, as though '*what manner of spirit*' did but signify 'what temper;' of paraphrasing thus, as some do,—'You know not that you are speaking out of your own hasty passionate temper, being hurt as much by the slight upon yourselves as that put upon Me,[1] even while you suppose yourselves zealous for my glory and for nothing else.' But '*spirit*' here means not the spirit of a man, but the spirit of God; and the saying is a far weightier one than such an extenuation of its sense would leave it. 'You are missing,' Christ would say, 'your true position; which is, having been born of the spirit of forgiving love, to be ruled by that spirit, and not by the spirit of avenging righteousness. You are losing sight of the distinction between the Old Covenant and the New, missing the greater glory of the latter, and that it is the higher blessedness to belong to it.' Thus Hammond rightly: 'Christ tells them they know not of what spirit they are, that is, they considered not under what dispensation they were.' [2]

plain separation between them and Elias. You, why you are of my spirit. The disciple and the Master are of one spirit. But if ye be of my spirit, my spirit is *in specie columbæ*, not *aquilæ*; not of the eagle that carrieth Jupiter's thunderbolt, but of the dove that brings the olive-branch in her bill.'

[1] Thus Corn. a Lapide: Nescitis quis spiritus vos impellat; putatis enim vos a Spiritu Dei agi, cum agamini spiritu humano impatientiæ et vindictæ.

[2] The εἶναί τινος of the original, expressing as it does a relation of dependence of one upon the other, Augustine (*Con. Adimant.* 17) gives rightly, cujus spiritûs *filii* estis. This whole clause, οὐκ οἴδατε οἵου πνεύματός ἐστε ὑμεῖς, is wanting, as is well known, in many, indeed in most, of the primary authorities, in A, B, and C, being therefore omitted by Lachmann and Tischendorf. I cannot for all this believe it to have no right to a place in the text. It is found in D, in several early Versions and Fathers; and not to urge, Who could have ventured,—we may confidently ask—Who would have been able, to invent words so exactly touching the central point of the whole matter as these do? This marvellous fitness of theirs seems of itself to preclude the notion of an unauthorized insertion; while, on the

It behoves us to see clearly that there is no slight cast here on the spirit of Elias. Both spirits, that which breathed through and informed the prophets and saints of the Old Covenant, as well as that which should inform the disciples of the New, are divine.[1] The difference between them is not of opposition, but only of time and of degree. The spirit of the Old Testament was a spirit of avenging righteousness ; God was teaching men by terrible things in righteousness his holiness. But the spirit of the New Covenant, not contrary but higher, is that of forgiving love ; in it He is overcoming man's evil with his good. There was, indeed, pardoning grace in the Old (Mic. vii. 18 ; Exod. xxxiv. 6 ; Num. xiv. 18 ; 2 Kin.

other hand, the temptations were many to an unauthorized omission of them. Hastily and superficially regarded, they might seem to favour a Manichæan antagonism between the Old Testament and the New, to involve a slight on Elias, as though his spirit was *contrary* to the spirit of Christ and to that which Christ's disciples ought to entertain. It is possible that to some such feeling as this, the words of the verse preceding, ὡς καὶ 'Ηλίας ἐποίησε, may owe their omission in so many MSS. Add to all this that such an abrupt termination as στραφεὶς δὲ ἐπιτίμησεν αὐτοῖς is nearly, if not quite, inconceivable. Christ cannot but have put his disciples in a right point of view for understanding the error into which they had fallen. Yet, if we omit this clause, we must then conclude with these words, ' *And He turned and rebuked them ;*' seeing that those which follow, '*for the Son of man is not come to destroy men's lives, but to save them,*' do certainly possess no right to a place in the text, having been brought in from Matt. xviii. 11 ; Luke xix. 10.

[1] The severity of the God of the Old Testament on that occasion, and the lenity of Christ on this, with his distinct refusal to do, or to suffer his servants to do, ' *as Elias did,*' was one of Marcion's favourite *antitheses*, or contradictions between the Old Testament and the New, by the aid of which he sought to prove that they could not have proceeded from the same Author. Tertullian (*Adv. Marc.* iv. 23) replies : Agnosco Judicis severitatem ; e contrario Christi lenitatem increpantis eandem animadversionem destinantes discipulos super istum viculum Samaritarum. Agnoscat et hæreticus ab eodem severissimo Judice promitti hanc Christi lenitatem : Harundinem quassatam non comminuet, et linum fumigans non extinguet. Talis utique multo magis homines non erat crematurus. Nam et tunc ad Heliam, Non in igni (inquit Dominus), sed in spiritu miti.

vi. 21, 22), even as there is avenging justice in the New ;
fire does come down from God out of heaven and consume
his enemies (Rev. xx. 9; cf. xi. 5); in it too ' God is a
consuming fire' (Heb. xii. 29); and that same Lord who
spake these words shall Himself 'be revealed in flaming fire,
taking vengeance on them that know not God' (2 Thess.
i. 8 ; Matt. xxii. 7 ; Luke xix. 27); even now severity and
goodness go hand in hand.[1] At the same time each
economy has one predominating tone, from which it
takes its character.[2]

The two apostles, however, were for the moment failing
to recognize this. In a confusion of the Old and the
New, and not knowing of '*what manner of spirit*' they
were, they had fallen back on the rudiments of God's
education of his people, when it was their privilege to go
on unto perfection, and to teach the world the far greater
might of meekness and of love; even as it is deeply interesting to remember that it was one of these very two
who brought somewhat later to the cities and villages of
Samaria the perfect gifts of the Holy Ghost (Acts viii. 14,
25 ; cf. 2 Cor. xiii. 10). They did not understand that
there was blood which should speak better things than that
of Abel (Heb. xii. 24). The blood of Abel cried well, when
it cried for vengeance (Gen. iv. 10), since vengeance, or
in other words, the violent restoration of the balances
of justice, which have been violently disturbed, is the

---

[1] Grotius : Habet quidem et Evangelium sua ultimæ necessitatis tela, quæ
in Ananiam Petrus, in Elymam Paulus exercuit ; sed usi iis sunt apostoli, ubi
nulla esse suspicio poterat iracundiæ semet sub Dei obtentu vindicantis ; usi
sunt in præfractæ malitiæ homines, quibus nulla species ignorantiæ patro-
cinabatur.

[2] Augustine (*Con. Adim.* 17): Nam hæc est brevissima et apertissima
differentia duorum Testamentorum, timor et amor. Illud ad veterem, hoc
ad novum hominem pertinet; utrumque tamen unius Dei misericordissimâ
dispensatione prolatum atque conjunctum.

Lord's (Rom. xii. 19); but the blood of Christ spake even better things, for it spake of pardon and forgiveness, of a pardon and forgiveness which should include even them by whom that blood had been shed. In their missing of all this there was a fault and matter of blame, yet blame by no means so severe as some are disposed to find.[1] They were rebuked for choosing that, which perfectly good in its own time, was only not good now, because a better had come in, for returning to the lower level of the Old Covenant, when Christ had lifted them up, if only they had understood this, to the higher level of the New. I quote from a sermon of Bishop Andrews— it is one of those referred to in the last note: ' Elias' spirit, I hope, was no evil spirit. No; but every good spirit, as good as Elias', is not for every person, place, or time. Spirits are given by God, and men inspired with them, after several manners, upon several occasions, as the several times require. The times sometimes require one spirit, sometimes another. Elias' time, Elias' spirit. As his act good, done by his spirit, so his spirit good in his own time. The time changed; the spirit, then good, now not good. But why is it out of time? For " *the Son* " of man is come. As if He should say, Indeed, there is a time to destroy (Eccles. iii. 3); that was under the law, *ignea lex*, the fiery law, as Moses calls it; then a fiery spirit would not be amiss. The spirit of Elias was

---

[1] This incident furnished a favourite text to the English divines of the seventeenth century for sermons on the anniversary of the Gunpowder Treason. Andrewes, Jeremy Taylor, Allestree, Tillotson, and many more, have found here their argument. Yet, faulty as the two disciples were, their fire from above resembled so little the fire from beneath which the incendiaries of the Gunpowder Plot would have kindled, that one must needs think they are used somewhat hardly in being brought, with whatever explanations, into any comparison with them.

good till the Son of man came; but now He is come, the date of that spirit is expired. When the Son of man is come, the spirit of Elias must be gone; now specially, for Moses and he resigned lately in the Mount. Now no lawgiver, no prophet, but Christ.'

' *And they went to another village ;* ' probably not this time a Samaritan one,[1] and found, as we gather from the narrative, the hospitality there, which had been refused them in the other.

---

[1] It is ἑτέραν, not ἄλλην.

10. *THE RETURN OF THE SEVENTY*[1]

Luke x. 17-20.

SOME have supposed that for the convenience of his narrative St. Luke omits, or rather defers, various intermediate events, and links the return of the Seventy directly with their sending forth.   Others, who will not allow that there is any such overpassing of intervening incidents, assume that the return of some at least of their number may have followed closely on their sending forth, so closely that nothing which the sacred historian desired to record happened in the interval.   The question is not a very important one, nor is it easy to come to any decision about it.   But whether sooner or later, these ambassadors of Christ '*returned again with joy, saying, Lord, even the devils are subject unto us through thy name*' (cf. Mark xvi. 17).   It will be observed that in his charge to the Seventy (ver. 2–16) our Lord had given them no distinct commission to cast out devils, as he had to the Twelve (Matt. x. 8 ; Luke ix. 1) ; but some tentative efforts of theirs, some ventures of faith in this direction, even without distinct authority, had been crowned with success. An acknowledgment that this surpassed at once their

---

[1] I have called this 'The Return of the Seventy ; ' yet it may very well be a question whether both at ver. 17 and also at ver. 1 for 'Seventy' we should not rather read 'Seventy-two' (cf. Exod. xxiv. 1, 9; Num. xi. 16, 25, 26) ; but in a matter on which experts are disagreed, I do not count it necessary to marshal the evidence on the one side and the other.

commission and their hopes seems to lie in that utterance of theirs, ' *Lord, even the devils are subject unto us;* not diseases only, over which Thou gavest us power (ver. 9), but the devils as well. The work, in which a little while ago apostles themselves were foiled (ix. 40), has not lain beyond the limits of our powers, has not baffled us.'

Such exultation was most natural ; yet was there in it something of peril for those who entertained it, and for their own spiritual life. One need not exactly affirm that ' *through thy name* ' comes in only as a formal and a saving clause at the end, and that the entire emphasis of the passage lay really on what preceded—'*are subject unto us;*'[1] still there may have been something of this. It could scarcely have been otherwise ; for, indeed, there is no more perilous moment for any man than that when he first discovers that he too can wield powers of the world to come ; that these wait upon his beck ; lest he should find in this a motive to self-elation, instead of giving all the glory to God. The disciples at the present moment were exposed to this temptation, as we might conjecture even if we had only these words of theirs ; but as is certain, when we read these words in the light of that earnest warning which the Lord presently ad-dresses to them (ver. 20), suggesting to them a safer and a truer joy than that which they were now too incau-tiously entertaining.

Yet while we must needs recognize a certain self-satisfaction and self-elation, which mingles with this report

---

[1] Augustine (*Enarr. in Ps.* xci.) : Redeuntes dixerunt, Domine, ecce dæ-monia nobis subjecta sunt. Dixerunt quidem, in nomine tuo ; sed ille videt in eis quia in ipsâ glorificatione gaudebant et extollebant se, et ibant inde in superbiam, et ait illis, conservans nomina illorum apud se, Nolite gaudere in hoc ; gaudete autem quod nomina vestra sunt scripta in cælis.

which they bring back of the successes of their ministry, and makes itself felt as an undertone throughout it, this will not warrant the interpretation made by some, of Christ's words which follow : '*And He said unto them, I beheld Satan as lightning fall from heaven.*' Here, they urge, is a warning to the disciples against that sin of pride which their Lord detected in them; as though He had said, 'Be not lifted up; beware of the first beginnings of a sin, which may end in so fearful a catastrophe as that which I once beheld'—beheld, that is, in his preexistent glory and before the world was—the fall, namely, of one through pride even from the height of heaven itself. 'Swift and sudden as the descent of the lightning was that fall, from the highest to the lowest, from a throne of light even to the blackness of darkness for ever. And even such a casting down may be yours, if you forget your humility, and are lifted up in heart.'[1] I cannot so take the words. The warning I believe to be reserved for ver. 20, the Lord for the present freely sharing in their joy, even as his own presently breaks forth at these tidings of the mighty works which they had wrought (ver. 21 22). Any interpretation of this passage seems to me altogether at fault, which makes it say other than what the Saviour on another occasion said, '*Now* is the judgment of this world, now shall the prince of this world be cast out' (John xii. 31), or, 'cast down,' as some read, which would

---

[1] So Gregory the Great (*Moral.* xxiii. 6): Mire Dominus, ut in discipulorum cordibus elationem premeret, mox judicium ruinæ retulit, quod ipse magister elationis accepit; ut in auctore superbiæ discerent, quid de elationis vitio formidarent. Compare Ambrose, *De Fugâ Sæc.* 7; Bernard, *In Ded. Eccles. Serm.* v. 6; Stella: Quare Dominus Jesus, ut optimus medicus animarum, ut roboraret suorum discipulorum animos adversus pestiferum morbum inanis gloriæ, proponit exemplum Luciferi, qui ob superbiam a tantâ et tam supremâ felicitate dejectus est, quia de donis a Deo acceptis insolenter gloriatus est.

bring that passage into yet closer verbal connection with this.[1]

Others, who agree with these interpreters in taking the Lord to allude here to that great original fall of the ' son of the morning,' anterior to the fall of man, yet do not accept the words in the same sense. They too find in them a check to the undue elation of the disciples, but from another point of view; 'Think not so much of these petty exorcisms which you have been permitted to achieve.[2] I have seen another sight; the very prince of the whole kingdom of wickedness, and him in whose defeat the defeat of each one of his subordinate ministers was involved, cast out from heaven itself,'—with, of course, the underthought of having been Himself the victorious author of his defeat.

The supporters of these expositions commonly urge that no other satisfies the words ' *from heaven*; ' Satan, they say, may at a later moment have fallen into a deeper depth than before, but how fallen ' *from heaven* ' in the days of Christ's flesh ? how could He speak in this language of any fall of Satan which He was only now beholding, seeing that long since, at the instant of his first sin, he had been cast out from his first habitation (Jude 6), from his place among the ' sons of God ' (Job xxxviii. 7), in the heavenly places ? It is sufficient to reply to these, that their difficulty arises from giving an emphasis to the word ' *heaven*,' which it was not intended to bear, and

---

[1] Κάτω βληθήσεται, instead of ἐκβληθήσεται : but there is no sufficient reason for disturbing the received reading.

[2] So Theophylact : μὴ θαυμάζετε εἰ δαίμονες ὑμῖν ὑποτάσσονται· ὁ γὰρ ἄρχων αὐτῶν πάλαι κατέπεσεν ἀπ᾿ οὐρανοῦ· εἰ γὰρ δὲ τοῖς ἀνθρώποις οὐχ ἑωρᾶτο τοῦτο, ἀλλ᾿ οὖν ἐμοὶ ἐθεωρεῖτο τῷ τῶν ἀοράτων θεωρῷ. Ὡς ἀστραπὴ δὲ κατέπεσεν, ἐπεὶ φῶς ἦν, καὶ ἀρχάγγελος, καὶ ἑωσφόρος, εἰ καὶ σκότος γέγονε.

which in this very chapter there is plain evidence that it need not have ; for see ver. 15 : ' And thou, Capernaum, which art exalted *to heaven*, shalt be thrust down unto hell.' For the right understanding either of that passage or of this we must dismiss the more solemn use of ' *heaven*,' in which it signifies the holy place, the more immediate seat and habitation of God and of the blessed spirits, and only associate with the word the notion of elevation and preeminence—so that in fact Christ would be saying here, ' I beheld Satan fall from the high places of his pride and power.' [1] What this fall of his might mean, and what the subjection of the devils to the Seventy had to do with it, may presently be considered ; but it will be desirable first to confirm this interpretation of ' *heaven* ' here by one or two further quotations. Isaiah, describing the fall of the king of Babylon, the type of a mightier enemy of the Church of God, exclaims, ' How art thou fallen *from heaven*, O Lucifer, son of the morning ! ' (xiv. 12 ; cf. Rev. ix. 1) ; and if it be urged that ' from heaven ' is a figure there, justified and explained by the comparison of the king to the morning star, it may be rejoined that there is quite as much justification in the comparison of Satan here to the lightning. Then, too, at Ephes. vi. 12, the warfare of the faithful is declared at this present time to be with ' spiritual wickedness in high places,' or, as it might be still more accurately translated, ' in *heavenly* places ' (ἐν τοῖς ἐπουρανίοις), which can only mean, as our Translators have rightly understood it, in high seats of authority. And then further, the passage in Rev. xii. 7–11, ' There was war *in heaven*,' is referred by all good

---

[1] Compare Cicero (*Phil.* ii. 42): Collegam *de cælo* detraxisti,—robbed him, that is, of the splendour and honour which before were his.

expositors to that destroying of the works of the devil, which was the consequence of the triumphant life and death and ascension of the Son of God. *There* is described in its full consummation what the Lord is here with prophetic eye already beholding as begun.

But if Christ be not here speaking of that original fall of Satan, in which he left his first habitation, but rather, as I am persuaded, of some fall within the fall, some present dejection of Satan from those seats of his power and his pride, which during the four thousand years of his domination he had reared and constructed anew, and from which he was now being thrust out again—what reason, it may be asked, had the Lord for in spirit beholding this at the present moment? These few and petty exorcisms, were they not far too slight and insignificant a matter to justify so magnificent a saying? Assuredly, if contemplated as the *efficient* cause of that fall; but not, if seen as its evidences and accompaniments. As Christ drew proofs of a victory over Satan, which must have been accomplished by Himself, from his own expelling of devils (Matt. xii. 28, 29), so He found proofs of the same victory in like works done by his disciples. The power of the strong man could not but indeed be broken, when not merely the Stronger Himself could spoil his goods at his pleasure, but the very weaklings among his servants could go in and out of his domain, and do there at their will.[1] The Lord in no way links the headlong and shameful fall of Satan from on high with what they had wrought, as if that had anything to

---

[1] Corn. a Lapide : Non novam mihi rem narratis, nam cum vos nuper mitterem ad evangelizandum videbam dæmonem suâ potestate a me privatum quasi de cælo cadere, ac per vos magis casurum.

do with effecting it. That fall, that new stripping him of so large a part of the power and strength which he still retained, was the fruit of the Incarnation, of the life and death and exaltation of the Son of man. These successes of theirs were tokens, but nothing more, of the triumphant progress of the work.

But this great triumph of the kingdom of good over the kingdom of evil in their respective heads, which Christ evermore in the spirit saw, at certain moments of his life He realized with intenser vividness than at others. And this moment of the return of the Seventy was one of these solemn and festal moments of his life. He employs the imperfect tense (ἐθεώρουν), to make clear that He had foreseen the glorious issue even when He sent them forth. This which they now announce to Him is even as He had surely expected : 'I saw, as I sent you forth, Satan fall like lightning from heaven.' Already He beheld the whole idol-worship of the heathen world, whereof Satan was the soul and informing principle (1 Cor. x. 20), giving way, its splendour departing, its oracles dumb, its temples forsaken—till, instead of riding on the high places of the earth, and claiming the homage of the great and noble and learned of the world, it should creep into obscure corners, and after surviving awhile as the despised superstition of 'pagans' or villagers, expire altogether. This and much more of the same kind, the putting down of how many of the enormous wickednesses of the world, the casting down of how many strongholds of evil, was implied in the power which his disciples put forth. See-ing the greatest in the least, He saw a pledge of the great exorcism of the heathen world in these slighter cures which his disciples had been strong to effect.

He proceeds : ' *Behold, I give unto you power to tread on serpents and scorpions, and over all the power of the enemy ; and nothing shall by any means hurt you.*' The reading, ' *I have given you,*' arose from a misunderstanding of the passage. Hitherto He had not given them this power ; they, as we have seen, had in faith anticipated some portion of it ; and He, finding they were the men to make the right use of it, now imparts it to them in all its fulness, according to that law of his kingdom, ' To him that hath shall be given.' In the form of the promise there is manifest allusion to Ps. xci. 13 ; perhaps also to Isai. ix. 8 ;[1] and, whether directly so intended or not, we may certainly recognize here a very gracious reading backward and reversing of a threatening made under the elder Covenant, ' Behold, I will send serpents, cockatrices, among you, which will not be charmed, and they shall bite you, saith the Lord ' (Jer. viii. 17). The physical consequences of man's sin, which may be traced through all regions of lower life, do in the animal world concentrate themselves with an especial malignity in the poisonous adder, in the stinging scorpion ; which therefore are fitly used as the symbols and representatives of all that has most power and most will to hurt and to harm ; of all forms of deadliest malice exercised by Satan and his servants against the faithful (Ezek. ii. 6). Amid all this deadliest malice of the enemy they should go, themselves unharmed ; and, shod with the preparation of the Gospel of peace, should tread it all under their feet : ' *and nothing sh ll by any means hurt you.*' And yet, while we thus transfer, and rightly, the serpent and scorpion into the region of spiritual wickedness, and

---

[1] Compare the παιδίον νήπιον (LXX.) there with the νήπιοι of ver. 21.

see here a pledge and promise that the faithful should
be kept from the powers of evil, we must not so exclusively do this as to leave out a literal fulfilment as
well ; such as found place when St. Paul shook the viper
from his hand (Acts xxviii. 5), when St. John, if that
indeed was so, drank of the poison-cup ; and in this
respect the passage contains a promise of the same character as that made by the Lord after his resurrection
(Mark xvi. 18).

But with the enlarged commission, for it is ' *all the
power of the enemy* ' which it is now given them to prevail against, comes also, and as I believe comes for the
first time in this discourse, the word of warning : ' *Notwithstanding in this rejoice not, that the spirits are subject
unto you ; but rather rejoice, because your names are written
in heaven.*' They were not forbidden altogether to rejoice
in these mighty powers as exercised by them, forbidden
only to make them the chiefest matter of their joy.
The reason is obvious. These a man might possess, and
yet remain unsanctified still (Matt. vii. 22, 23 ; 1 Cor.
xiii. 2) ; these at best were the privilege only of a few,
they could not therefore contain the essence of a Christian's
joy. There was that wherein they might rejoice with a
joy which should not separate them from any, the least of
their brethren, a joy which they had in common with all.[1]
There was that in which they might rejoice without fear,

---

[1] Augustine (*Enarr. in Ps.* cxxx.) : Redierunt apostoli, et dixerunt Domino,
cum missi essent a Domino, Ecce, Domine, in nomine tuo etiam dæmonia
nobis subjecta sunt. Vidit Dominus quod tentaret eos superbia ex potentiâ
miraculorum ; et ille, qui medicus venerat sanare tumores nostros, continuo
ait, Nolite in hoc gaudere, quia dæmonia vobis subjecta sunt, sed gaudete
quia nomina vestra scripta sunt in cælo. Non omnes Christiani boni dæmonia
ejiciunt ; omnium tamen nomina scripta sunt in cælo. Non eos voluit
gaudere ex eo quod proprium habebant, sed ex eo quod cum ceteris salutem
tenebant. Inde voluit gaudere apostolos, unde gaudes et tu.

namely, in the eternal love of God, who had so loved as
to ordain them unto everlasting life. This mention of
' *names written in heaven* ' (cf. Isai. iv. 3 ; Heb. xii. 23,
' the Church of the firstborn, which are written in
heaven ') is the nearest allusion to ' the book of life,'
' the Lamb's book of life,' ' the book of God,' ' the book
of the living,' or simply ' the book,' which anywhere
occurs in the Gospels ; but the image is one which elsewhere runs through all Scripture (Exod. xxxii. 32, 33 ;
Ps. lxix. 28 ; Ezek. xiii. 9 ; Dan. xii. 1 ; Phil. iv. 3 ;
Rev. iii. 5 ; xiii. 8 ; xx. 12 ; xxi. 27 ; xxii. 19). It
expresses under an image what St. Paul expresses without
one, where he speaks of God's eternal purposes of love
toward his saints (Ephes. i. 4, 5).

The Lord has administered, where He saw this was
needed, a wholesome rebuke to that pride, of which He
detected the germs in his disciples; but this does not
hinder Him from rejoicing in this new victory of the
kingdom of light over the kingdom of darkness,—a matter
of the greater joy, that it was these ' *babes* ' by whose
hands this victory had been won : they of the household
were dividing the spoil. ' *In that hour Jesus rejoiced* [1] *in*

---

[1] The forms ἀγαλλιάω (for ἀγάλλω), and ἀγαλλίασις, belong to sacred
Greek exclusively, being found only in the N. T., the Septuagint, and in
writings dependent upon these ; ἀγαλλίαμα, which is also found in the
Septuagint, does not occur in the N. T. Ἀγαλλιᾶσθαι is often there joined
with χαίρειν, as at Matt. v. 12 ; Rev. xix. 7 ; cf. Tob. xiii. 13 ; in the
Septuagint oftener with εὐφραίνεσθαι. It is stronger than χαίρειν, for this
last may be in spirit and with no external manifestations ; but ἀγαλλιᾶσθαι
is to exult, so to rejoice as with outward tokens to testify the inward joy,
as an old expositor, Stella, here puts it well : Non est intelligendum quod
antea in gaudio interiori non fuerit, sed interioris gaudii quædam signa nunc
exterius demonstravit ; ideo convenientissime dixit, Exultavit. Exultatio
namque dicitur quasi extra se saltatio, quando videlicet ex abundantiâ gaudii
interioris signa lætitiæ foras erumpunt.

*spirit, and said, I thank Thee, O Father, Lord of heaven
and earth, that Thou hast hid these things from the wise
and prudent, and hast revealed them unto babes : even so,
Father ; for so it seemed good in thy sight.'* Precisely the
same words with a slightly different introduction occur
at Matt. xi. 25, 26; where they cannot possibly be the
record of the same discourse; for they have the same
perfect fitness there as here; they are embedded in one
narrative quite as deeply as in the other. A careful
comparison of the two passages can, I think, leave no
doubt on our minds that Christ did from time to time
repeat Himself in nearly or quite the same words; which,
after all, is not at all so wonderful in Him, each of whose
utterances being perfect, could never be changed for the
better.

The all-important character of that which He is uttering here may well explain its repetition; setting, as He
does, his seal to that word of the prophet, 'Woe unto
them that are wise in their own eyes, and prudent in
their own sight' (Isai. v. 21 ; cf. Prov. iii. 5, 7), and, be
it noted, not merely thanking God for what He has revealed, but also for what He has hidden, that the same
things revealed by Him to some, were by Him hidden
from others. There is, then, if these words mean aught,
such a thing as a punitive hiding and a penal blindness.
The hand of the Lord may be upon those who withstand
the truth, so that they shall not be able to see the Sun of
righteousness (Acts xiii. 11). That there are those from
whom God hides his truth in displeasure may be a very
terrible fact; but a fact may be very terrible, and yet true
notwithstanding ; and here is one of which we can only
get rid by dealings the most violent with this and with

other plainest statements of Scripture (Isai. vi. 10 ; xxix. 10; lxiii. 17 ; Matt. xiii. 11–15 ; Luke xix. 42 ; John ix. 39 ; xii. 39, 40 ; Rom. xi. 8). Christ here thanks his Father for two things, first, that He has hidden from the wise and prudent ; and, secondly, that what He has hidden from them He has revealed to babes ; the hiding and revealing being recognized by Him as alike his Father's work, and the judgment and the grace alike matters for which He renders thanks. The words of St. Paul. 1 Cor. i. 26–29, supply a remarkable parallel to this whole saying; while the early history of the Church, from which Scribes and Pharisees, the Gamaliels, and all or nearly all of the disputers of this world, stood aloof, fishermen meanwhile and publicans, and men ignorant and unlearned, finding their place therein, furnishes the best commentary.

11. *THE PHARISEES SEEKING TO SCARE THE LORD FROM GALILEE*

Luke xiii. 31–33.

THE LORD lingers too long in Galilee; so, at least, to his adversaries it seems. He is in comparative security there; in the midst of friends and adherents; adding every day to the number of these; confirming his word by signs following (Matt. xv. 28; John iv. 46); his reputation growing; all men holding Him for a prophet (Matt. viii. 27; ix. 8, 33); hardly to be reached there by the uttermost malice of his foes. Gladly would these scare him from the shelter of that safe retreat into the toils which have been set for Him at Jerusalem (Mark xi. 18; Matt. xxi. 46). And even if they do not quite succeed in this, it will be something if they can deliver themselves from his unwelcome presence in Galilee, and at the same time involve Him in the discredit of an ignoble flight. It was *that* if possible, *this* at any rate, which they proposed to themselves, when they made to him the communication which follows.

' *The same day there came certain of the Pharisees* '— came, no doubt, with a friendly and confidential mien, and as men to whom, whatever secondary differences might divide them, his safety was dear,—'*saying unto Him, Get Thee out, and depart hence, for Herod will*

kill Thee.' The words curiously remind us of another
similar plot and intrigue, by which it was sought, and
equally in vain, to terrify a prophet of the Old Covenant
from the appointed sphere of his labours ; Jeroboam playing there the part of Herod here ; Amaziah, the priest of
Bethel, of the Pharisees ; and the prophet Amos sustaining there the part which our Lord sustains here.   There
too Amaziah, with apparently no unfriendly meaning
although he had just before denounced the overbold
prophet to the king (had the Pharisees done the same in
the present instance ?), came to Amos, saying, ' O thou
seer, go, flee thee away into the land of Judah, and there
eat bread, and prophesy there; but prophesy not again
any more at Bethel, for it is the king's chapel, and it is
the king's court ' (Amos vii. 10–17 ; cf. Isai. xxx. 10, 11 ;
2 Tim. iv. 3).   As the Pharisees here, so the priest of the
Calves there takes nothing by his move, but goes utterly
baffled and defeated away.

We may with tolerable certainty affirm that Herod
Antipas entertained no such design of killing Jesus as by
these Pharisees is ascribed to him here.   He had enough
of prophet's blood on his hands in the murder of John
the Baptist, and can scarcely have wished to have more.
A vain, frivolous, voluptuous prince,[1] yet he is nowhere
charged in Scripture with seeking to compass the Lord's
death.   Even the crime of the Baptist's death, who came
into far more direct collision with him, he had been
entangled in unawares.   When he heard of the fame of
the Lord, he satisfied himself with saying to his servants,

---

[1] Very far the best account which I anywhere know of the whole
Herodian family is to be found in Keim, *Jesu von Nazaro,* vol. i. pp. 173–207;
for the character of Herod Antipas, see p. 203.

'This is John the Baptist; he is risen from the dead, and therefore mighty works do shew forth themselves in him' (Matt. xiv. 2); he devised no plots of open or secret violence against Him. The report of Christ's *miracles* appears to have excited his curiosity (for his *doctrine* he cared nothing), so that when Pilate sent Jesus to him, ' he was exceeding glad, for he was desirous to see Him of a long season, and he hoped to have seen some miracle done by Him' (Luke xxiii. 8); but it is plain, both from this account and from his conduct in sending the Lord back unharmed to Pilate, with nothing worthy of death done to Him (Luke xxiii. 15), that he had no enmity against Him for the past, nor fear of Him for the future. And then further, had he cherished that murderous thought in his heart by the Pharisees imputed to him, ' *that fox* ' is not the style with which he would have been characterized by the lips of truth; but if the Lord had been pleased to designate him by any title of the kind, He would have styled him ' that wolf,' or ' that leopard,' by the name of some animal, of which bloodthirstiness, and not cunning, is the prevailing feature. Add to all this, that if Herod had been known really to entertain such designs, the Pharisees, who were now in deadliest conflict with the Lord, would have been the last to warn Him of his danger, or in any way to assist Him in escaping from the snares which were being laid for his life.

The only point upon which it is possible to raise a question seems to me to be this, namely, whether this was a gratuitous invention on the part of the Pharisees, devised with the purpose of terrifying the Lord from those quarters; and suggested possibly by some flying rumours, to which they gave no credit themselves, of Herod's ill will to Christ—such rumours as the Baptist's murder might easily have occasioned ; or whether they and Herod understood one another, and he, possibly disquieted at this period by the growing number of Christ's adherents, may have been willing to use their assistance, and to allow them to use the terror of his name, so to induce the Lord quietly to withdraw to some other part of the land. Those who are disposed to see such an understanding here, urge that in the words of Christ's reply, ' *Go ye, and tell that fox*,' there is an intimation that such a collusion existed, and that it had not escaped Him.   The bringers of this warning professed to be his friends, and to bring it of goodwill to Him, and meaning to defeat the purpose of Herod ; but bidding them to return to him with that message, the Lord will have implied that He perfectly apprehended the relation in which they and Herod stood to one another ;—how the king was waiting to learn from their lips the issue of their joint stratagem, and what success was likely to attend it : ' This is my answer to him that sent you, whose emissaries you have condescended to become—to *that fox*, who thinks with his paltry wiles and transparent devices to scare the lion from his own domain.'

Yet I cannot but believe that they have more rightly apprehended the situation, the many interpreters, ancient and modern, who have seen in this report which the Pharisees bring to Jesus a fiction wholly of their own devising. They did but pretend the malice of Herod, who, if he had desired to rid himself of the Lord's presence, had other means at his command ; and who certainly was on no such friendly terms with the Pharisees as to make very probable any understanding between them.

Nor need the words, '*Go ye, and tell that fox,*' or '*this fox*'—for such would be the more accurate rendering— cause any difficulty here. The Lord, in that spirit of finest irony which is not alien from the spirit of deepest love and loftiest truth, so far fell in with, or seemed to fall in with, the aspect of the matter which they presented to Him, and to be deceived by it, that He used its language —not at the same time failing to let them perceive that their intrigues, covert and close as they thought them, were manifest to Him. The '*fox*' was really in their own hearts, and to this '*fox*' He indeed addresses Himself.[1] Some of the early interpreters ingeniously urge in this sense the words ' *this fox,*' as of one actually present, rather than ' *that fox,*' as of one at a distance,[2] which might have be- forehand been expected. It was they, the Pharisees, who were themselves offended at his continued presence in the land ; who would fain drive Him from it ; it was to their own selves they should indeed carry back their message. This explanation has the further advantage, that so the decorum which our Lord ever preserved in regard of the powers that be, however unworthily these might be represented, will be perfectly maintained ; which decorum might seem violated, if the message had been really intended for Herod, and not rather to stop short with these intriguing Pharisees themselves.

But the reply which they were to carry back to ' *this fox,*' or in other words, to accept themselves, is not with-

---

[1] Maldonatus : Christus non Herodem, sed Pharisæos ipsos qui Herodem sibi minabantur, vulpem appellavit. Non quod hæc verba de Herode non dixerit, sed quod in personâ Herodis, quam illi sibi induebant ut ipsum deterrerent, eos notaverit atque refellerit.

[2] Thus Theophylact : οὐ γὰρ εἶπε, τῇ ἀλώπεκι ἐκείνῃ, ἀλλὰ ταύτῃ. If there be anything in this, it has been missed by the Vulgate, which has '*vulpi illi,*' no less than by our Translators.

out its obscurity : *Behold. I cast out devils, and I do cures to-day and to-morrow,*[1] *and the third day I shall be perfected.'* Its general meaning is not hard to catch : ' So far from being interrupted in my ministry by any tidings of the kind you bring, be they false or true, by your wish, or by Herod's wish, to be rid of my presence at once, I shall proceed on my way, I shall do as before I have done, I shall put forth my beneficent powers, casting out devils, healing the sick for the present (" *to-day* "), for the future (" *to-morrow* "), and only at a remoter period (" *the third day* ") will my life and course reach their appointed term.'[2] The words are exactly parallel to others spoken on a later and not a very dissimilar occasion, when his disciples, trembling for his life and for their own, would have dissuaded Him from affronting the dangers of Judæa : ' Are there not twelve hours in the day? If any man walk in the day he stumbleth not, because he seeth the light of this world' (John xi. 9; cf. ix. 4). *' To-day and to-morrow and the third day'* will here exactly correspond to the ' twelve hours ' there, signifying as they do a fixed and appointed time. Nor is this of necessity a very brief time, but rather the contrary ; for the intention upon his part to make his further sojourn in Galilee a brief one was exactly that which the Pharisees would have been delighted to hear, while it is very far from his desire at all

---

[1] Σήμερον καὶ αὔριον : cf. Josh.; and for a similar method of counting backward to the third day, Susan. 15; 2 Kin. xiii. 5, LXX.

[2] Cajetan : Per hodie et cras et tertiam diem universi temporis requisiti ad opus suum perfectio significatur. Calvin : Hodie et cras defungar munere mihi divinitus injuncto ; ubi ad finem stadii ventum fuerit, tunc in sacrificium offerar. There is frequently a certain solemnity about this indication of the third day ; such as is scarcely wanting here ; thus see Gen. xxii. 4 ; xxxi. 22 ; xxxiv. 25; xl. 20; xlii. 18; Exod. xix. 11, 16; 1 Kin. xii. 12; 2 Kin. xx. 5; Hos. vi. 2.

to gratify them by the announcement which He is making.[1]
Least of all do these words signify—which would be a
meaning utterly trivial—that the time of his actual tarrying in Galilee should extend over two literal days, ' *to-day
and to-morrow*,' and that on '*the third day*' He should
quit it, even as the verse following can as little mean that
He would occupy three such actual days in the journey
from that spot to Jerusalem. What He means is this :
' There is for Me a predetermined time, during which I
shall labour unhindered. No malice nor intrigues of my
enemies shall prevail to abridge that time.[2] Instead of
fleeing, as you suggest, I will leisurely accomplish my
work this day and to-morrow ; and then when the third
day comes, *I shall be perfected*, I shall finish my course :
the things concerning Me will have an end ; which, however ' (for all this is implied in the word), ' shall be no
abrupt nor premature one, no cutting off of my life
in the midst of my days, with my work unfinished, in an
obscure corner of a remote province ; but a death which
shall be the solemn and fit conclusion of my life, the com-
pletion and consummation of all which I came into the
world to accomplish.'[3]

---

[1] Maldonatus : Non id agebat Christus, ut Pharisæos consolaretur ; quod
profecto fecisset, si illis significâsset brevi se post tempore moriturum. Quid
enim erat quod illi magis optarent ? sed volebat potius augere materiam
invidiæ atque doloris.

[2] Stella : Fallimini, si creditis vos aut Herodes quod versutia humana
possit aliquid contra potentiam Dei et ejus voluntatem. Vos dicitis quod
Herodes mortem mihi molitur, et vos non moleste fertis; sed inanis est
deliberatio ejus, quia non est in manu ejus mors mea, quia nemo tollet
animam meam a me. Potestatem enim habeo ponendi animam meam, et sic
cum voluero ponam eam et moriar.

[3] To make τελειοῦμαι a middle verb, completing it with τὰ ἔργα, and finding as the meaning, ' *on the third day I finish*,' i.e. ' *my works*,' sadly mars the
force of this passage. It is not for nothing that the two active verbs which
go before are exchanged for this passive. Our English, ' *I shall be per-*

There may seem a slight contradiction between the statement of the verse which has just been considered, and of that which now follows : ' *Nevertheless,*[1] *I must walk to-day, and to-morrow, and the day following ; '* for here the Lord speaks of ' *the third day* ' as one of the days of his walking, while there He contemplated it as the day on which He should be perfected and finish his course. But there is no real contradiction. He contemplates his death as being, in fact, the crowning work of his life. As little does this ver. 33 merely repeat the statement of that which went before. Hitherto He has but stated the fact that his ministry should continue ; now He is giving the grounds in the divine order and fitness of things why it should continue, why he should walk and work unlet and unhindered. ' This my cutting off here in this remote Galilee, with which you threaten Me, is impossible ; for *it cannot be that a prophet,* and therefore least of all He who is the chief of the prophets, *perish out of Jerusalem.* That city which has been the mur-

---

fected ' (in the Vulgate, Consummor), is very good ; a vast improvement on ' *I make an end,*' of the earlier Versions. Compare, for similar uses of τελει-οῦσθαι, Phil. iii. 12 ; Heb. v. 9 ; xii. 23. More than once Augustine transfers this word from Christ to Christ's Church, and finds in it a prophecy of the three stages of the spiritual life through which He causes it in each of its members to pass, namely, the forgiveness of sins, the restoration to health, the consummation in glory ; thus *Con. Jul. Pelag.* vi. 19 : Ecce, inquit, ejicio dæmonia, et sanitates perficio hodie et cras, et tertiâ die consummor. Expulsio quippe est dæmoniorum remissio peccatorum ; perfectio sanitatum, quæ fit proficiendo post baptismum ; tertia consummatio est, quam suæ quoque carnis immortalitate monstravit,incorruptibilium beatitudo gaudiorum. Cf. *Enarr. in Ps.* cx. 46.

[1] What the exact force of this ' *Nevertheless* ' (πλήν) is, expositors have often not troubled themselves to consider ; it seems to me best given by Maldonatus, whose whole commentary on this difficult passage is masterly : Refertur non ad omnia præcedentia, sed ad illud tantum ultimum, *et tertiâ die consummor,* quasi dicat quamvis tertiâ die moriturus sim, tamen interim nemo me impedire poterit, quominus hoc intermedio tempore miracula faciam.

deress of all the prophets from the beginning (Isai. i. 21),
which has ever claimed this dreadful prerogative to herself, as she is chief in favours, to be also chief in guilt,
she shall not forego it now ; she shall continue to the
end the seat of all the deadliest enmity to the kingdom
of God ' (Matt. xxiii. 34–37). But the words reach much
further than this, much further than to the stating merely
of such a general fact as this. They have a direct reference to those with whom the Lord is speaking now, and
contain the finest irony on their affected interest in his
welfare : ' You have come, expressing your alarm for my
safety, should I tarry longer here. You may lay aside
your apprehensions. My danger is not in Galilee, nor
yet from Herod. I shall not perish here, but in Jerusalem, your seat, your head-quarters, the city where you
reign supreme. When the day of my death, or of my
consummation, shall arrive, you, and not Herod, will be
the authors of the murderous deed.' [1]

---

[1] Calvin: Vosne ut ab Herode mihi caveam monetis, quos video meos
fore carnifices ?

12. *THE UNFINISHED TOWER AND THE DEPRECATED WAR*

Luke xiv. 25-33.

OUR LORD on more than one occasion during his earthly ministry found a multitude in his train ; loosely attached to Him ; but such as would inevitably have detached themselves from Him and fallen away, so soon as ever a day of temptation had arrived. Nothing could be further from his desire than such a following as this. 'They that are with Him are called and chosen and faithful' (Rev. xvii. 14); and such, and such only, will abide with Him unto the end. But not so these ; to whom therefore He turned, and spake words repelling rather than inviting. They who would enlist recruits for the warfare of this world, commonly keep out of sight what of hard, painful, and dangerous the work to which they invite them will bring with it ; but not so He, who desired that none should join themselves to Him without a clear knowledge beforehand of all to which they were engaging themselves. To a Paul, on the very threshold of his conversion, He will shew what great things he must suffer for his name's sake (Acts ix. 16). Ezekiel at his first commission is told with the utmost plainness to what manner of men, to such as could be likened only to thorns, briars, scorpions, he is sent (Ezek. ii. 6). And to this multitude Christ addressed one of his hard sayings—one after the hearing of which we can hardly doubt that many went back and walked no more with Him (cf. John vi. 66). A sad consummation, yet better far than that they should throw in their lot with Him, afterwards to be offended, and to fall from Him, in that day of trial which was sure before long to arrive (Matt. xiii. 21).

We read then that ' *there went great multitudes with Him; and he turned, and said unto them, If any man come to Me, and hate not his father, and mother, and wife, and children, and brethren, and sisters, yea, and his own life also, he cannot be my disciple.*' Let us here notice, by the way, the profound confidence in a guiding, interpreting Spirit, who should be ever at work in his Church, which these words of Christ reveal. Take them literally, and they stand in direct contradiction to the whole teaching of the rest of Scripture, in contradiction to the teaching of Moses, of the prophets, of the apostles, of Christ Himself elsewhere ; they enjoin an immorality ; they require of men to hate those whom it is their prime duty to love. And yet Christ spake the words notwithstanding, satisfied to leave to that interpreting Spirit to put them in harmony with all which elsewhere is commanded in the Scripture, or written by the finger of God on the heart of man.

But in other ways also the unparalleled boldness of Christ's teaching, the tremendous claims which He makes on those who offer to join themselves to Him, may well fill us with marvel and with awe. How intolerable the pride and presumption of any less than the greatest, lower than the highest, to impose the conditions of discipleship which He here imposes, to demand of men the sacrifices which He here demands ; and this, be it

observed, not in the name of Another, whose messenger
He is ; but in his own ; setting forth Himself the object to
whom all this measureless devotion of all men is justly
due, who, claiming it all, claims nothing but that which
is his own by right.   When I ask myself what are the
proofs of Christ's divinity which the Scripture affords,
when I enquire whether He did Himself there claim to
be God, I find evidence of this not so much in texts
where this in as many words is asserted—though these
are most needful—but far more in the position toward
every other man which He uniformly, and as a matter of
course, assumes.   What man, that was not man's Maker
as well as his fellow, could have required that father and
mother, wife and children, should all be postponed to
himelf ; that, where any competition between his claims
and theirs arose, he should be everything, and they nothing ? that not merely these, which, though very close
to a man are yet external to him, but that his very self,
his own life, should be hated, when on no other conditions
Christ could be loved.   It is nothing strange or unreason-
able that man's Creator, the author of his being, the
supreme and absolute Good, should demand all this of his
creatures (Exod. xxxii. 27 ; Deut. xxxiii. 9) ; but that
Jesus of Nazareth should challenge the same unreserved
devotedness on the part of all men, should require that
every other duty of every other man should yield to the
duty to Him, that every other love should subordinate
itself to the love of Him ; how could this be, except as
He also stood in the place of God, and was God ?

But these are thoughts which, followed out as they
deserve, would lead too far from the subject immediately
in hand.   Christ has spoken of the absolute renunciation

of all, even of a man's own life, that last citadel of selfishness, as he who ought best to know, had long since proclaimed (Job ii. 4), that citadel, where it may still make itself strong when every outwork has been abandoned [1]— He has spoken of this as the condition without which no man could be his disciple. But this self which needs to be renounced is oftentimes a very subtle one, the self of him who proposes to serve God, but to serve Him in his own strength, and not in God's; and thus to have wherein to glory; who may have renounced much, but has not renounced a vain confidence in his own powers, and that these will enable him to carry to a successful end a service thus undertaken. Christ uses two similitudes, borrowed from two enterprizes, the one grave to a private man, the other even to a king; by aid of the first he warns his hearers, and in them all who should come after, of the shameful close which may attend a service in this spirit begun; while in the second He points out to all the only wise course for the avoiding of such perils as would thus lie before them. This is the first :—'*For which of you, intending to build a tower, sitteth not down first, and counteth the cost, whether he have sufficient to finish it? Lest haply, after he hath laid the foundation, and is not able to finish it, all that behold it begin to mock him, saying, This man began to build, and was not able to finish.*' And this the second: '*Or what king, going to make war against another king, sitteth not down first, and consulteth whether he be able with ten thousand to meet him that cometh against him with twenty thousand? Or*

---

[1] As Gregory the Great here says well, and in the very spirit of his great master Augustine (*Hom.* xxxii.) : Nec tamen sufficit nostra relinquere, nisi relinquamus et nos.

else, while the other is yet a great way off, he sendeth an ambassage, and desireth conditions of peace.' [1]

The comparison of the Christian life, sometimes that of the individual, sometimes that of the collective Church, to the carrying up of a building is frequent in Scripture (Matt. vii. 24–27 ; Ephes. ii. 20–22 ; 1 Cor. iii. 9 ; 1 Pet. ii. 4, 5) ; and not less frequent the likening of it to the waging of a war (1 Cor. xvi. 13 ; 1 Thess. v. 8 ; Ephes. vi. 11–17 ; 2 Tim. ii. 3, 4 ; iv. 7). But the fitting in of these words to their place here, the making them to illustrate the matter directly in hand, is not so easy as is often carelessly taken for granted. Indeed the current interpretation of this passage is far from satisfactory ; and we have only to look a little closely at it to perceive the very serious difficulties with which it is encumbered. I believe, indeed, that by that interpretation words among the most profound and far reaching which our Lord spake upon earth, are made to take comparatively a slight and trivial meaning. That interpretation may be stated as follows. Christ would have the candidates for admission within the inner circle of his disciples to consider diligently with themselves, and accurately to weigh, whether they have strength and means to carry them triumphantly through the arduous enterprize which they meditate ; and if, as the result of this calculation, they discover that they have not, then to renounce the enterprize altogether ; and not, as some foolish builder, to begin the tower of the Christian life, which they will prove unable to crown and complete ; like some rash king, to challenge to the conflict

---

[1] Ἐν δέκα χιλιάσιν. See for the same idiom, indeed for exactly the same words, 1 Macc. iv. 29 ; and with the συμβαλεῖν εἰς πόλεμον compare συμβαλεῖν εἰς μαχήν, Josephus, *Antt.* VI. 5. 2.

powers, the powers, that is, of the kingdom of darkness, which are twice as strong as they are, with which therefore they cannot hope to wage a successful war.

This explanation labours under a double defect. In the first place, according to all the other teaching of Scripture, the disciple who indeed builds and completes the tower, is not one who has counted the cost, and found that he *has* sufficient; he whose warfare is crowned with victory is not he who has calculated the opposing forces, and found that those at his command are more and mightier than any which can be brought against him; but he rather who, having counted the cost, has found that he has *not* enough, that the outlay far exceeds any resources at his command, that he begins and must continue a bankrupt to the end; having nothing in himself, that so he may possess all things in God; who, having taken the measure of his own forces and of those of the adversary, has understood that this warfare is one not to be waged at his own charges, has learned to cry, 'Who is sufficient for these things?' and sought to a mightier for aid. All other Scripture teaches us, in the glorious words of Charles Wesley's hymn, to be 'strong in self-despair,' and not in self-confidence; that emptiness is indeed the one condition of fulness; that, however sad a thing it may be in this world to end with being a bankrupt, in the spiritual world it is the best thing which can happen to begin with being such; a man's poverty being there his riches, and his weakness his strength, and his ignorance his wisdom; for such are the strange paradoxes of the kingdom of heaven.

This is one blemish, and a most serious one; but there is another behind. Granting that this objection could be set aside, is it conceivable that Christ should counsel in such a case, and having made such a discovery, not so much as to begin the too costly tower, but to leave it altogether unattempted;[1] or, more marvellous still, not so much as to provoke the too potent foe, but rather to make terms with him, to engage not to molest *him*, if he will not molest us, whom to defy to the uttermost is our first duty and only safety (1 Pet. v. 9; Ephes. vi. 11–16), whose works to destroy was once the work of Christ in his own person, will be his work through his Church to the end? What sort of peace would that be? Can we imagine that the Lord would give the allowance of his word to such abject resolves as these? for what, after all, are they who leave off to build, who, in place of challenging, make conditions with the enemy, but the Demases who forsake not Paul only, but Paul's Lord, having loved this present world (2 Tim. iv. 10); who, when tribulation comes or even threatens, straightway are offended and fall away (Matt. xiii. 21); who see the wolf coming and flee (John x. 12)? 'The fearful' of Rev. xxi. 8, the 'traditores,' the 'turificati,' in the early days of the Church's suffering, all these did in that sense count the cost, and give over to build; having challenged the king of the dark kingdom, shrunk from encountering him in battle. But can we suppose that Christ had a word of allowance for these? that they could plead that they were acting on his advice? and yet, adopting the common interpretation, how could we avoid so doing?

But it is not so. These sayings of our Lord contain a

---

[1] As Maldonatus asks well, who sees the difficulty, but not the way out of it, Deinde quomodo nos Christus dehortaretur ne Christiani efficeremur? Quomodo cum Diabolo, cum quo, susceptâ lege Christi, bellum gerere parabamus, pax nobis facienda est?

far different lesson from this, one in far closer agreement
with the other teaching of Scripture. What that teaching is, the words with which Christ follows up and
applies all which He has here said, sufficiently declare :
' *So likewise, whosoever he be of you that forsaketh not all
that he hath, he cannot be my disciple.*' In that ' *forsaketh* '
(ἀποτάσσεται), or ' renounceth,' ' biddeth good by to,'
' taketh farewell of,' lies the key to the whole passage.
Christ sees the multitudes addressing themselves to his
discipleship with one manner of furniture and preparation
for it ; such as He knows will utterly fail them, when the
stress of the trial comes ; He warns them of their need of
quite another. It is the poor, those who, counting up
their means, discover that they have *not* enough to carry
through and complete the work, and that of their own
they never will have enough, and who therefore renounce
all that they have, it is these, and not the rich, not, that
is, they who walk in a vain conceit of their own riches
(Rev. iii. 17), who are able to finish this tower.[1] How it
fares with the others, what a swift and shameful coming
to the end of all their fancied resources inevitably awaits
them, how total a bankruptcy, this Christ puts vividly
before our eyes in the verses which follow (ver. 29, 30).
He gathers up in these the world's judgment upon them
who, professing to forsake it, were yet of it all the while,
and who sooner or later reveal that they were so. The
world cannot pardon that they should ever have affected
any higher service than its own; and, even while it
receives back its prodigals, receives them with taunt and

---

[1] Gregory the Great (*Hom.* 37) : Hoc enim inter terrenum et cæleste
ædificium distat, quod terrenum ædificium expensas colligendo construitur,
cæleste vero ædificium expensas dispergendo. Ad illud sumtus facimus,
si non habita colligamus; ad istud sumtus facimus, si et habita relinquamus.

with scorn; the salt which has lost its savour is trodden under foot, not of God, but, doom more ignominious far, is trodden under foot *of men* (Matt. v. 13). Nor are worldly and wicked men the only mockers. The scorners here include, as more than one in olden times has urged, not these *men* only, well pleased when any scheme of higher service, such as threatened to put them and their meaner lives to rebuke, has come to nought; but fallen spirits as well, the angels to whom men are a spectacle (1 Cor. iv. 8); who, so far as they can rejoice in aught, rejoice in dishonour done to God; and who, being first our tempters, are afterwards, when we have succumbed to their temptations, our mockers and scorners as well:[1] '*This man*' (the contempt makes itself still more felt in the original), '*began to build, and was not able to finish.*'

Such uncompleted buildings, open to all the winds and rains of heaven, with their naked walls, and with all which has been spent upon them utterly wasted, are called in the language of the world, which often finds so true a word, This man's, or that man's, Folly; arguing as they do so utter a lack of wisdom and prevision on their parts who began them. Such, for example, is Charles the Fifth's palace at Granada, the Kattenburg at Cassel. They that would be Christ's disciples shall see to it that they present no such Babels to the ready scorn of the scornful; beginning, as though they intended to take heaven by storm, to build up a tower which should reach even thither, and anon coming to an end of all their resources, of all their zeal, all their patience, and leaving

---

[1] Gregory the Great (*Hom.* 37): Ipsos irrisores patimur quos ad malum persuasores habemus.

nothing but an utterly baffled purpose, the mocking-stock of the world, even as those builders of old left nothing but a shapeless heap of bricks, to tell of the entire miscalculation which they had made. Making mention of ' *a tower*,' I cannot but think that the Lord intended an allusion to that great historic tower, the mightiest failure and defeat which the world has ever seen, that tower of Babel, which, despite of its vainglorious and vaunting beginning, ended in the shame and confusion of all who undertook it (Gen. xi. 1–9).[1]

It is well worthy of remark, and indeed I have briefly

---

[1] A characteristic passage in Jeremy Taylor's Sermons, *Of Lukewarmness and Zeal*, contains no direct reference to these words of our Lord, yet such can scarcely have not been intended : ' So have I seen a fair structure begun with art and care, and raised to half its stature; and then it stood still by the misfortune or negligence of the owner, and the rain descended, and dwelt in its joints, and supplanted the contexture of its pillars ; and having stood awhile like the antiquated temple of a deceased oracle, it fell into a hasty age, and sunk upon its own knees, and so descended into ruin : so is the imperfect, unfinished spirit of a man ; it lays the foundation of a holy resolution, and strengthens it with vows and arts of prosecution, it raises up the walls, sacraments and prayers, reading and holy ordinances; and holy actions begin with a slow motion, and the building stays, and the spirit is weary, and the soul is naked, and exposed to temptation, and in the days of storm takes in every thing that can do it mischief; and it is faint and sick, listless and tired, and it stands till its own weight wearies the foundation, and then declines to death and sad disorder, being so much the worse because it hath not only returned ' to its first follies, but hath superadded unthankfulness and carelessness, a positive neglect, and a despite of holy things, a setting a low price to the things of God, laziness and wretchlessness : all which are evils superadded to the first state of coldness, whither he is with all these loads and circumstances of death easily revolved.' Shakespeare too must have had this passage in his eye when he applies this comparison to one who undertakes greater changes in the State than he is able to carry through :

> ' Like one that draws the model of a house
> Beyond his power to build it; who, half-through,
> Gives o'er, and leaves his part-created cost,
> A naked subject to the weeping clouds,
> And waste for churlish winter's tyranny.'
>
> 2 Henry IV. Act I. sc. 3.

remarked already (p. 183), how greatly our Lord loves
to bring out some truth which He would very earnestly
enforce and commend to men, by two successive images;
like, and yet unlike; approaching it from different quarters; the second oftentimes going deeper into the heart
of the matter than did the first, at all events presenting
it in some aspect under which the first did not, perhaps
in the nature of things could not, present it; the two in
this manner mutually completing one another. It is thus
for example with the parables of the mustard-seed and
the leaven (Matt. xiii. 31–33); the former setting forth
the outward development, the second the inward operation,
of the truth; it is thus again with the Hid Treasure and
the Pearl (Matt. xiii. 44–46), the first putting before us one
who unexpectedly lights on the kingdom of heaven, the
second one who has found, but who before was engaged
in the seeking of, the same. So too, as we have seen, the
new wine in the old vessels is something more, and
contains a profounder lesson, than the new patch upon
the old garment (Matt. ix. 16, 17). Another example
we have here of the same, where the king, measuring
beforehand his own forces and the forces of the adversary
whom he is tempted to provoke to the conflict, tells us
something which the builder, sitting down to count the
cost of the tower which he is planning to erect, would
not have told. There is sometimes a further gain in a
duplicate illustration such as this; and such gain in the
present instance we have. Any misgiving as to the cor-
rectness of the interpretation just put upon the first
similitude must, I am persuaded, disappear with a careful
study and comparison of the second.

That in the sphere of things natural the course which

Christ here recommends is the only wise one, this is self-evident. Any other would be fraught with uttermost hazard, with almost inevitable ruin, to him who pursued it. War indeed is sweet, as the ancient proverb assures us, to those who have never tried it; [1] and examples out of number of kings who, committing themselves to an unequal struggle, have drawn down ruin on themselves and on their kingdom, history sacred and profane will alike supply. Crœsus in profane history, Amaziah (2 Kin. xiv. 8–12) and Josiah (2 Kin. xxiii. 29, 30) in sacred, will suggest themselves at once; while within the last three years we have had a more memorable example of the catastrophe which may follow than any among all these. Hezekiah, on the contrary, wise betimes, and knowing how much overmatched he would prove in conflict with the great king of Assyria, sends an ambassage, while the other is yet at a distance, desiring conditions of peace : ' I have offended; return from me; that which thou puttest on me will I bear' (2 Kin. xviii. 14).

But it is with the spiritual counterpart of this wisdom that we have here to do. The exposition which I have felt bound to reject, that, I mean, which makes the king who might come with his twenty thousand against him who with ten thousand should imprudently provoke a war, to be the devil, altogether paralyses ver. 32; for what can be the meaning of sending an ambassage to him, and desiring of him conditions of peace ? How can we conceive, as has been urged already, counsel such as this issuing from the lips of the Lord? Lange, who clings to the common interpretation, can only evade the difficulty which it offers in this way : ' peace here, accord-

---

[1] Γλυκὺς ἀπείρῳ πόλεμος.

ing to the sense of the image, can only mean a truce, and the request for peace only the avoiding of a *premature* conflict, to which the Christian as yet is unequal.' It is a still poorer escape to urge, as does Calvin, that all parts of such a parabolic saying as this must not be pressed, that in the interpretation some, being the drapery and not the very image of the truth, may be very well allowed to fall away. This in itself is most true ; yet what part could be pressed, if this, in which the whole teaching evidently culminates, might not be so ?[1]

How profound, on the contrary, is the lesson here, when we recognize in this king who might come against us with his twenty thousand, with a might altogether overpowering ours, no other than God Himself. He is a true fighter against God, a θεομάχος quite as truly, though in another way, as the openly ungodly, who would fain *be* anything in his sight, who, face to face with God, would assert *himself* at all ; who does not renounce all that he hath, and, as that which is the dearest to him, and cleaves closest to the natural man, his own righteousness the first of all.[2] The book of Job will supply the amplest and

---

[1] Gerhard (*Harm. Evang.* 120) in like manner owns that not merely we must not press this part of the similitude, but in the application go quite counter to it, which it is difficult to think was the Lord's intention : Tantum hoc observemus in hâc militiâ, quo a propositâ parabolâ discedimus : ut quandoquidem hic hostis nunquam nobis honestas pacis conditiones proponit, nos etiam nunquam cum ipso paciscamur, nec ullam pacem vel otium ab ipso expectemus, quamdiu mortalem hanc vitam in his terris degimus.

[2] Bengel : Hæc igitur rogatio pacis exprimit odium animæ propriæ [ver. 26], quo quis, omni suitate abnegatâ, meræ se gratiæ committit. Ædificator pecunias, belligerator copias, discipulus parentes et caritates omnes abnegat et impendit. Illi habent apparatum positivum, hic negativum. Maldonatus, who has almost always something valuable on the harder passages in Scripture, sees clearly that the king coming with his twenty thousand cannot be Satan, with whom we never must have peace, nay rather a πόλεμος ἄσπονδος : but only doubtfully suggests that by him God Himself may be

richest materials for the illustration of these words; these words in return doing much to explain that book. The patriarch himself was sorely tempted to be such a fighter against God, with his ten thousand to challenge Him who would come against him with his twenty thousand. Early indeed in that terrible and decisive struggle of his life he has glimpses more than one of the madness of provoking to the conflict of righteousness such an Adversary; as, for instance, when he exclaims, 'How should man be just with God? If he will contend with Him, he cannot answer Him one of a thousand' (ix. 2, 3); and again, 'If I wash myself with snow-water, and make my hands never so clean, yet shalt Thou plunge me in the ditch, and mine own clothes shall abhor me' (ix. 30, 31); but at other times he is very far from having renounced all that he has; thus see xxiii. 3–5, and indeed that chapter throughout, with much in his other discourses rashly spoken by him. It is only at the last that he altogether does so, lays his hand upon his mouth, confesses that he has nothing with which to answer God (xl. 4), and abhors himself in dust and ashes (xlii. 5, 6); demands, that is, conditions of peace, and, having demanded, obtains them (xlii. 7–17). St. Paul would have been another such fighter against God, if those things which he once counted gain he had resolved to count gain to the end; if, refusing to submit himself to the righteousness of God, he had stood out upon a righteousness of his own (Phil. iii 3–9).

---

intended: Mittere vero legationem et rogare quæ pacis sunt non est a diabolo, hoste capitali nostro, pacem petere, quocum perpetuum nobis bellum gerendum est, nec pacem unquam licet pangere. Nam et in pace vincimur; hoc enim pejus et turpius; quod in bello quidem, ut milites decet, repugnantes atque resistentes, in pace volentes, sine vulnere, sine sanguine, superamur.

But he also on the way to Damascus learned better ; and when, with his face to the earth, he asked, ' What wilt Thou have me to do ? ' he, too, was exactly falling in with that which Christ here declares to be the only wisdom for every man ; he was demanding conditions of peace from that far mightier King, with whom it is impossible for flesh and blood, for sinful man, to contend.[1]

We may take an example from the opposite side. The Pharisee in the parable (Luke xviii. 9–12), when he enumerated the long catalogue of his virtues, was precisely one who was refusing to forsake all that he had, rather was hugging this all as closely as he could. He was calculating his means, and finding that he had enough to finish the tower ; he was mustering his forces, and so disastrously overrating their strength, that he did not fear to set himself in battle-array against Him, who resisteth the proud, and giveth grace only unto the humble. The

---

[1] I know none in the ancient Church, and only Bengel and Stier among modern interpreters, who have grasped the meaning of this portion of Scripture with at all so firm a hand as Gregory the Great has done. It is the more remarkable that he has done so, seeing that his exegesis is for the most part so dependant on that of Augustine. I have already quoted words of his on the only way in which the necessary cost for the building of the tower is to be got together. He too has apprehended rightly what so few have apprehended, namely, that the king who might come against us with his twenty thousand, with whom therefore it is our only wisdom to make terms betimes, is not Satan, but God ; thus *Hom.* 37 *in Evang.* : Rex contra regem ex æquo venit ad prælium, et tamen, si se perpendit non posse sufficere, legationem mittit, et ea quæ pacis sunt postulat. Quibus ergo non lacrymis veniam sperare debemus, qui in illo tremendo examine cum Rege nostro ex æquo ad judicium non venimus ? quos nimirum conditio, infirmitas, et causa inferiores exhibet . . . . Quid ergo agendum est, fratres, nisi ut dum nos cum simplo exercitu contra duplum illius sufficere non posse conspicimus, dum adhuc longe est, legationem mittamus, et rogemus ea quæ pacis sunt ? Longe enim esse dicitur, qui adhuc præsens per judicium non videtur. Mittamus ad hunc legationem, lacrymas nostras, mittamus misericordiæ opera, cognoscamus nos cum eo in judicio non posse consistere, pensemus virtutem ejus fortitudinis, rogemus ea quæ pacis sunt. Hæc est nostra legatio, quæ Regem venientem placat.

publican, on the contrary, in the same parable, avowed
that for the carrying up of the tower he had *not* enough
he had nothing; that this was a war in which he could
not so much as look his mightier Adversary in the face;
and therefore exclaiming, 'God be merciful to me a
sinner,' he threw down his arms, and sought, while there
was yet time, ' *conditions of peace.*'

Let me observe, before quitting this matter, that there
is a certain fine irony in our Lord's falling in so far with
man's dream of being something and being able to hold
his own even in the face of God, as to speak of him
as a king over against another king, king against king—
in his so far falling in with man's dream of self-righteous-
ness, and estimate of his own powers, as to speak of
the ten thousand which he could bring against the twenty
thousand of God, as though he were only overmatched
in the proportion of two to one; while, indeed, a day
will arrive, when he who in Christ's school has learned
anything which he ought to learn, will be ready to cry,
' I cannot answer Thee one thing in a thousand.'

I ought not to leave unnoticed that some modern
Roman Catholic expositors, and some medieval interpreters as well, have sought in the following way to
escape the difficulties which cleave to the common interpretation of Christ's words. They have urged that these
sayings are *not* addressed to the whole body of disciples
or candidates for discipleship, but only to as many as
might be meditating whether they should undertake or
not the so-called ' counsels of perfection.' These are
warned that they should accurately consider beforehand
whether they have strength sufficient for the fulfilling of
these; and, if they discover that they have not, should

not so much as attempt them.[1]   All this, as may be seen
in words quoted below, is ingenious enough ;[2] and undoubtedly some difficulties would so be evaded ; but
such an explanation contains no help for us, who believe
that *all* Christians are invited to be perfect, as their
Father in heaven is perfect (Matt. v. 48), and who further
can trace no intimation that these exhortations were
addressed to a select few, an inner circle, but on the
contrary a statement than which none could be more
distinct, that they were spoken to ' great multitudes '
(ver. 25)·

---

[1] So Bernard (*De Convers., ad Cler.* c. 21) : Utinam turrim inchoaturi,
sedentes computarent, ne forte sumptus non habeant ad perficiendum. Utinam
qui continere non valent, perfectionem temerarie profiteri, aut cælibatui dare
nomina vererentur.   Sumptuosa siquidem turris est, et verbum grande quod
non omnes capere possunt.

[2] Cajetan : Significatur regis nomine professurus statum perfectioris vitæ.
Bellum adversus alium regem est perfectior vita ad superandum mundum,
quantum ad licita communiter aliis, puta, habere agros, vacare humanis
negotiis, et reliqua hujusmodi, hominibus quidem licita, apostolicæ autem
perfectioni interdicta.   Et describitur mundus duplicatâ potentiâ adversus
profitentem vitam perfectiorem, quia et pugnat communi impugnatione,
trahendo ad illicita communiter omnibus, et pugnat speciali impugnatione,
trahendo ad interdicta apostolicæ vitæ.   Si enim, consideratâ proprii animi
dispositione, imparem se videt tanto prœlio, sapienter prævenit, rogans ea
quæ pacis sunt, non aggreditur statum perfectioris vitæ, contentus statu
communi.

13. ZACCHÆUS

Luke xix. 1-10.

THE LORD is on his way to Jerusalem, on that last journey thither, which was so rich in incidents, and whereof St. Luke has preserved for us so accurate a record. '*And Jesus entered and passed through Jericho. And behold there was a man named Zacchæus, which was the chief among the publicans.*' [1] It was only natural that Jericho, from its position close to the fords of Jordan (Josh. ii. 7), and as the frontier city on entering the land from Peræa, set, too, as it was in the richest plain of Palestine, and that which abounded most in the choicest productions of that favoured land, in the rare and costly balsam above all,[2] should be the seat of an officer of a somewhat superior rank, who should there preside over the collection of the revenues of the state.

Such an officer was Zacchæus; one too who had suc-

---

[1] His superior dignity probably suggests ἀνήρ, not ἄνθρωπος, twice used in regard of him (ver. 1, 7). Whether he was one of the publicani, the farmers of the revenue, or held some intermediate rank between these and the portitores, the actual collectors of the customs and taxes, is uncertain; but the latter is the more probable supposition. The fact that the publicani were generally Romans, and Roman knights, would not indeed of itself be decisive on the matter; for Josephus tells us that Jews sometimes attained to this dignity. Yet is it more probable that the ἀρχιτελώνης belonged himself to the τελῶναι, although, as the name implies, having many subordinate officers under him.

[2] Pliny, *Hist. Nat.* xii. 54. There is a beautiful description of Jericho in Keim, *Jesu von Nazaro,* vol. iii. p. 17.

ceeded in winning that wealth, in the quest of which he
had been content to brave the contempt of his fellow-
countrymen, to come under that mingled scorn and hate
with which they visited the traitors to the national cause,
who for filthy lucre's sake were content to gather for the
Roman treasury that tribute which was the most humilia-
ting token of their subjection to a Gentile yoke (Matt.
xxii. 17). And yet, rich as he was, he had not, as the
sequel shews, incurred the woe of those rich who are full,
and who have so received their consolation here, that all
longings for a higher consolation are extinct in them
(Luke vi. 24). We may take, as an evidence of this, the
fact that '*he sought to see Jesus,—who He was;*' not
'*who He was*' in the sense of 'what manner of person;'
but, '*which He was*' of that confused multitude, to distinguish Him from his company.[1] And he sought this,
as the issue proves, out of no mere curiosity, such as
Herod's (Luke xxiii. 8); but much more nearly in the
temper of those Greeks who at the feast desired to see
Jesus (John xii. 21).[2] He may not have known or given
any account to himself, out of what motives this anxiety
to see the Lord had its rise ; yet assuredly there were
yearnings here, unconscious they may have been, of the
sick man towards his Healer, of the sinner towards his
Saviour.

It was not easy for him to accomplish his desire. '*He
could not*' see Him '*for the press, because he was little of*

---

[1] Maldonatus : Quis esset eorum quos in confertâ et confusâ videbat
turbâ.

[2] Augustine (*Serm.* 174): Noli te extollere ; pusillus esto, Zacchæus esto.
Sed dicturus es, Si Zacchæus fuero, præ turbâ non potero videre Jesum.
Noli esse tristis ; adscende lignum, ubi pro te pependit Jesus, et videbis
Jesum ; with much other profitable adaptation of the words.

stature.' So earnest, however, is he in the matter, that,
rather than be defeated of his longing, he devises a way
for the satisfying of it, which will involve, indeed, a
certain compromise of his dignity, but from which he
does not therefore shrink. Many, no doubt, would
wonder that he, a rich man, and of some official position in the city, should climb up, like one of the populace,
into a tree, the better to gaze upon a spectacle below.[1]
But there is that in him which will not allow such respects
as these to have any weight at the present. He has not,
or, if he has, he overcomes, that false pride, through
which so many precious opportunities, and oftentimes in
the highest things of all, are lost.[2] Jericho and the
neighbourhood was famous for its palms ('the shady city
of palm trees,' as the poet Vaughan has called it; cf. Deut.
xxxiv. 3; Judg. i. 16; iii. 13; 2 Chron. xxviii. 15).
No stately palm-tree however, but a sycomore, a tree of
much humbler name, plays its part in this story. The
sycomore would now be sought in vain in the plain of
Jericho, although found elsewhere in the Holy Land
(Robinson); but they were common once (1 Kin. x. 27;
1 Chron. xxvii. 28; Ps. lxxviii. 47); and one of these did
on this occasion bear fruit of the noblest kind; so that
Fuller with good right exclaims, 'Who dares say syco-
mores are always barren? See one here loaden with

---

[1] Die Unwahrscheinlichkeit einer Baumklettirung des Mannes von Geld
and Stellung, is urged by Keim as a proof of the unhistoric character of this
story of Zacchæus.

[2] Calvin : Signum enim vehementis desiderii fuit, arborem conscendere,
quum divites ut plurimum sint fastuosi, seque specie gravitatis venditent.
Neque enim Christi conspectum sine cælesti instinctu tantopere expeteret.
Sic Dominus sæpe priusquam se hominibus manifestet, cæcum illis affectum
inspirat, quo feruntur ad ipsum adhuc latentem et incognitum.

good fruit.' [1]   For into one of these Zacchæus has climbed ;
hoping, it may be, for he has run before the multitude,
effectually to conceal himself in its leafy screen, before
the throng of the crowd come by ; not to say that these
will be the less likely to remark him, as their attention
will be turned in quite another direction.

If this *was* at all his expectation, he is disappointed
in it ; for ' *when Jesus came to the place, He looked up ;* '
and He, who knows how to discover his own in places
the most unlikely, a Matthew at the receipt of custom,
a Nathanael under the fig-tree, with sure and unerring
glance detected Zacchæus in the sycomore, and at once
laid bare his hiding-place ; addressing him by his name,
for ' He calleth his own sheep by name ' (John x. 3) ; and
drawing him forth from his concealment with that word,
' *Zacchæus, make haste, and come down.*'   This his dealing with Zacchæus reminds us of the gentle violence by
which he compelled another, however reluctant, to come
out of the crowd, and to confess before all that she had
touched Him, and why (Luke viii. 45–47).   Like that, it
is meant for the overcoming of a false shame ; and the
summons is not without a certain delicate rebuke that he,
inwardly drawn, as no doubt he was, to the Lord, should
have been content with that far off sight of Him, instead
of coming boldly forward, and joining himself to his
disciples.   Yet that faint rebuke is at once made good by
the words which follow : ' *for to-day I must abide at thy*

---

[1] *A Pisgah Sight of Palestine*, ii. 12. Fuller has here taken for correct
the old derivation of συκομωραία, finding μωρός foolish, and not μῶρον the
mulberry tree, in the latter half of the word : Porro sicomorus ficus *fatua*
dicitur, eo quod inanes ficus generat (Stella ; and so Augustine, *Serm.*
174, § 3). This, it need hardly be said, is an error, the sycomore deriving
its name from a resemblance to the fig in its fruit, to the mulberry in its
leaves.

house ;' [1] words of an extraordinary grace, for while the Lord *accepted* many invitations into the houses of men (Luke vii. 36 ; xi. 37 ; xiv. 1), yet we do not read that He honoured any but this publican by thus offering Himself to his hospitality. 'Adopting the royal style,' as the author of *Ecce Homo* puts it well, 'which was familiar to Him, and which commends the loyalty of a vassal in the most delicate manner, by freely exacting his services, He informed Zacchæus of his intention to visit him, and signified his pleasure that a banquet should be instantly prepared.'

The word of gracious command was not spoken in vain. Zacchæus in the sycomore tree was as ripe fruit, which dropped into the Saviour's lap at his first and lightest touch : '*he made haste, and came down, and received Him joyfully.'* [2] Each had found what he was looking for, the Saviour and the sinner ; the Shepherd had found his sheep, and the sheep its Shepherd. Some, as usual, were displeased—as many, that is, as conceived that the Christ should be a prince of Pharisees, rather than a Saviour of sinners. These, '*when they saw it, all murmured, saying, That He was gone to be a guest with a man that is a sinner.'* [3] Could He not have chosen some other for his host ? Jericho was a city of priests, as well as a city of publicans. The Talmudists assure us that there were almost as many priests there as at Jerusalem itself ; so that it is a stroke from the life to introduce

---

[1] Augustine (*Serm.* 113) : Volebas videre transeuntem ; hodie hic apud te invenies habitantem.

[2] Ambrose (*Exp. in Luc.* ix. § 90) : Zacchæus in sycomoro, novum novi temporis pomum.

[3] Augustine (*Serm.* 184) : Hoc erat, reprehendere quod in domum ægroti intravit medicus.

in the parable of the Good Samaritan the priest and the Levite, as passing exactly along that road which led from one of these cities where they dwelt to the other where their duties lay (Luke x. 31, 32). With such a choice of hosts from whom to select, would it not have better become a preacher of righteousness to select some other than this sinner, whose house to honour with his presence? Surely it was ill done by a favour so signal to reverse that just sentence of social excommunication under which the publicans, and Zacchæus among the number, lay (Luke xv. 2).

Probably the murmurers, with these words of discontent on their lips, with these thoughts of displeasure in their hearts, followed to the house of Zacchæus. But they meet there with a practical refutation of their discontent; there it is plainly shewn that the Lord had chosen well, when He chose this man for his host and entertainer. He was one who was as smoking flax, which they would have quenched outright, but which the Lord with only a breath of his mouth fanned into a light flame. Christ's presence in *his* house forms a parallel by way of contrast to his presence in the house of the Pharisee (Luke vii. 36 ; cf. xiv. 1). There He could bring no blessing, for there was there no sense of need ; there the Pharisee esteemed that he was honouring the Lord, not that he was being honoured by Him.

What follows is placed by some on the next day. They assume the Lord to have tarried a night under the roof of Zacchæus, and that on the following morning, perhaps as his divine guest was about to depart, Zacchæus stood forth and made this profession of a new life, with a making good, so far as this might be, of the faults of his

old. But '*to-day*' of ver. 5 is too clearly taken up by
'*this day*' of ver. 9, to admit of such an interpretation.[1]
Rather the meal was ended at which he had been permitted to entertain his Lord ; and he then stood forth,
making that practical answer to these murmurers, which
ought to have silenced, and perhaps did silence some of
them ; for it shewed that he had not received the grace
of God in vain; it shewed what the condescending love
of the Saviour could effect, how it could separate a man
for ever from his old conversation, to walk henceforward
in newness of life. In the presence then of them all (see
ver. 11) '*Zacchæus*,' who had so long, like another Levi,
sat at the receipt of custom, '*stood*,' or stood forth, '*and
said unto the Lord ; Behold, Lord, the half of my goods I
give to the poor ; and if I have taken anything from any
man by false accusation,*[2] *I restore him fourfold.*' The
present, '*I give*,' expresses the fixedness of his resolve ;
for however this distribution of his goods is still in the
future, that future to him is as though actually present. To

---

[1] Nothing can be built on καταλῦσαι, as though, which some urge, this
must imply the tarrying for a night. We have in Xenophon (*Anab.* I. 10.
19), καταλῦσαι τὸ στράτευμα πρὸς ἄριστον.

[2] The verb συκοφαντεῖν occurs in the N. T. only here and at Luke iii. 14.
It is rendered there, ' to accuse falsely ; ' here, ' to take anything by false
accusation ; ' and in the Geneva, ' to take by forged cavillation.' The use
of the word as to defraud or to wring out by chicane is not uncommon in
the Greek orators. Rettig (*Theoll. Stud. und Krit.* 1838, p. 775) observes
that, while the story of the forbidden export of figs from Attica, and of the
συκοφάντης as one who denounced this, is, as all now admit, a later invention to explain the word, still it is so manifestly connected with σῦκον and
φαίνειν, that in them the key to unlock its meaning must be looked for.
He suggests that the συκοφάντης was originally one who informed against
him who made to the State too small returns of his property for the
purposes of taxation ; and, the figtree being a chief source of wealth in
Attica, informed against him who returned the number of these, or the
crop derived from them, below the mark. He observes that σικόβιος, an
informer, and συκάζειν (= συκοφαντεῖν) both point in the same direction.

make it stand for a past, and to accept this ' *I give*,' and
' *I restore*,' as the expression of his past conduct in the
stewardship of this worldly mammon, as though Zacchæus
had been another Cornelius, ' a devout man, which gave
much alms to the people ' (Acts x. 2), is a curious missing
and marring of the whole point of this incident, in fact
a most notable piece of Pharisaic exegesis.[1] Zacchæus
might, and would even then, have needed the higher
righteousness of Christ, but he would scarcely have been
until this day one of the ' *lost*.' Salvation would not on
that day have first come to his house. But it is not thus.
All this which he now announces of a giving of his own,
and a restoring of that which is another's, is to be taken
as the blessed results of Christ's visit, as the outward utterance of the mighty inward change that had passed upon
him. Now is he a righteous man according to that rule
of the prophet (Ezek. xviii. 21, 22; xxxiii. 15), and his
name and he are agreed.[2]

But at the same time, while, ' *If I have taken anything
from any man*,' must not be looked at as expressing only
a possible case, which the speaker regards as very impro-
bably an actual, neither must it be pressed too far in the
other direction. It is not, indeed, such a confident clearing

---

[1] Maldonatus: Aliqui interpretantur quasi antequam ad ipsum Christus
venisset, solitus fuisset dimidiam bonorum suorum partem pauperibus dare,
et si quid quem defraudâsset, quadruplum reddere. Cyprian (*De Op. et
Eleem.*) is one of these: but many more adhere to the true interpretation,
as Irenæus (*Con. Hær.* iv. 12), who sees in this to which Zacchæus adjudges
himself, solutionem præteritæ cupiditatis; Tertullian (*Adv. Marcion.* iv. 37)
and Gregory the Great (*Hom.* 27), who encouraging to repentance by various
examples of those who through it obtained pardon, speaks thus: Alius
avaritiæ æstibus anhelans aliena diripuit. Aspiciat Zacchæum, qui, siquid
alicui abstulit, quadruplum reddidit.

[2] נִצְדַּק =justus. Without restitution, as Augustine (*Ep.* liv. *ad Maced.*)
says well, pœnitentia non agitur, sed fingitur.

of himself as Samuel's (1 Sam. xii. 3) ; yet neither, on the other hand, is it to be accepted as the confession and admission of an habitual unrighteousness, of a free allowing of himself hitherto in chicane and wrong. Zacchæus had been hitherto no extortioner. Had he been so, had he been conscious that his were in the main ' treasures of wickedness,' gotten together by fraud and wrong, it would have been ridiculous to offer as a gift half of them to the poor, while as yet it was not seen whether the whole would satisfy the demands of justice, might not be swallowed up in acts of restitution, with such addition as the law required. Without, however, having been this extortioner, he yet feels that, according to that higher standard of right which he recognizes now, some of his gains may prove to have been unfairly acquired ; for, as the Italian proverb has it, there is seldom a large river into which some turbid water has not entered. Any such injustice he will abundantly make good, even to a fourfold restitution, calmly adjudging against himself that which David in his extreme indignation adjudged against him who had taken his neighbour's lamb (2 Sam. xii. 6) ; imposing a maximum of penalty on himself ; much more indeed than the law save in some exceptional cases required (Exod. xxii. 1 ; Ezek. xxxiii. 15).

The words that follow are spoken *to* Zacchæus, but in the hearing of the multitude, and *for* them no less than for him. This appears in the third person, under which he is addressed. As meant for him, they are an allowance, on the Lord's part, of this offering of his goods as the true expression of a higher offering, even of a dedication of himself to God : ' *This day is salvation come to this*

house.' [1] As addressed to the multitude, they contain a
further justification of the grace shewn to this man that
was a sinner. Sinner as he is, salvation has yet come
to his house, '*forasmuch as he also is a son of Abraham*'
(cf. xiii. 16); one therefore to whom this mercy was due;
for their view, as may here be fitly observed, is worthy
of no acceptance who assume Zacchæus to have been a
heathen, and the Lord therefore to style him '*a son of
Abraham*' only in an ethical sense, a follower, that is, of
the faith of Abraham (Matt. iii. 9; Rom. iv. 12). It is
well known that some, both in ancient and modern times,
have so understood it, or at least have suggested this as
possible,[2] but in the face of all evidence alike external
and internal. Zacchæus (Zaccai) is a Jewish name, occurring Ezra ii. 9; Nehem. vii. 14; 2 Macc. x. 19, and in
the Talmud. Had he been not merely '*a sinner,*' but '*a
sinner of the Gentiles,*' the murmuring multitudes would
assuredly have urged as the head and front of Christ's
offending, not '*that He was gone to be a guest with a
sinner,*' but with '*a Gentile*'—which, indeed, would
have been in their sight so enormous an aggravation of
the offence, that it would have been impossible they
should pass it over without notice. Neither did it belong
to the proprieties of the Lord's earthly life, '*a minister*'
as He was '*of the circumcision, to confirm the promises

---

[1] On the words '*to this house,*' rather than '*to this man,*' Grotius deli-
cately remarks, ut ostendat relatam hospitii gratiam. Yet hardly so; the
parallel is to be rather found in such passages as Acts xvi. 33, 34. It is
doubtless for the sake of this verse that this Scripture supplies in the
Roman Catholic Church the Gospel for the service on the occasion of the
dedication of churches.

[2] Thus Tertullian (*Adv. Marc.* iv. 37: Zacchæus, allophylus fortasse),
Cyprian, Chrysostom, Maldonatus, Stella, and others. Some, on the other
hand, have identified him with Matthias, the future apostle; Clement of
Alexandria (*Strom.* iv. 6) for example.

made unto the fathers' (Rom. xv. 8), that He should violate the ordinances and customs of the Jews, which, so acting, He would have done (Acts x. 28 ; xi. 2, 3 ; Gal. ii. 12). As little can any argument be founded on that word '*lost*,' as applied to Zacchæus; for elsewhere the Lord speaks of 'the *lost* sheep of the house of Israel' (Matt. x. 6); and if, as surely is the case, the gulf between what a man is, and what he was intended to be, is often-times the truly tragic thing in his destinies, is that which alone furnishes the proper measure of his loss and of his fall, who, then, so '*lost*' as a son of Abraham, *that*, *not being a heathen*, was yet sunk down to a level with the heathen ? Such was Zacchæus ; and such '*lost*' as he was the Son of man declares that He was come '*to seek and to save*' (Ezek. xxxiv. 11).

This said, He seems to have moved forward without further delay on his journey toward Jerusalem, leaving that '*house*' poorer in this world's riches, certainly by one half, and probably by more than one half, than if He had never entered into it ; and yet, as He Himself declares, how immeasurably richer too ; for One bringing salvation had lodged within it ; and, though He was now quitting it for ever, the salvation which He had brought with Him remained behind.

14. *THE TRUE VINE*

MANY interpreters have thought it necessary to look in the external world for some object which will have suggested this similitude to the mind of the Lord. Some, for example, who suppose that his 'Arise, let us go hence,' with which the preceding chapter concluded, was not acted on at once, but that He lingered still, have imagined to themselves a spreading vine, whose branches found their way into the chamber in which He and his disciples had just celebrated their last supper together (Ps. cxxviii. 3). But surely those words of his, 'Arise, let us go hence,' leave no room for this supposition. On the part of the disciples there could have been no tarrying, after they had received such a summons ; and when the Lord used these words, He must have intended what He said. When others suggest that passing, as He may very well have done, through a vineyard on his way to the brook Kedron, He found his motive there, one can only reply that this and every other suggestion of like kind appear merely and altogether superfluous ; that it becomes us far better to believe that, as all worlds, natural and spiritual, lay ever open before Him, and the innermost essences of things, so He drew freely from this inexhaustible storehouse whatever was most adapted to his present need. There was quite enough to suggest this image of closest union between Him and his people in that sacrament of union, which had just been instituted by Him, and in which He had declared of the fruit of the vine, of the ' pure blood of the grape ' (Gen. xlix. 11 ; Deut. xxxii. 14), blessed and consecrated by Him, ' This is my blood of the New Testament, which is shed for many for the remission of sins.' We may dismiss then, as unnecessary, all speculations on the external motive which He found for this discourse.

At the same time when our Lord affirms of Himself, ' *I am the true vine*,' with what, it may be very fitly asked, does He liken Himself, over what assert a superiority ; for in that ' *true* ' He manifestly claims Himself actually to be what some other persons or things falsely pretended to be ; or if not all this, claims to be fully and perfectly what they only partially, inadequately, and most imperfectly were? The word which He employs is decisive that it is the latter which He intends ;[1] to keep which in mind will help us much to understand what follows. And first, He certainly does *not* liken Himself, which is Lampe's suggestion, to that golden vine of exquisite workmanship, a symbol no doubt of the theocracy, which was the chief ornament of Herod's temple,[2] nor avouch Himself as ' *the true vine*,' by comparison with it. And if not to that dead work of man's art and device, as little does He name Himself ' *the true vine*,' as contradistinguished from

---

[1] For the distinction between ἀληθής and ἀληθινός see my *Synonyms of the New Testament*, § 8. Ἀληθής (= verax) is the true as set over against the false (Rom. iii. 4) ; ἀληθινός (= verus) is the true as set over against the imperfect, the inadequate, that which has at best but types, shadows, and outlines of the truth ; as Origen puts it well, πρὸς ἀντιδιαστολὴν σκιᾶς καὶ τύπου καὶ εἰκόνος (cf. John i. 9 ; vi. 32 ; Heb. viii. 2).

[2] Josephus, *Antt.* xv. 11. 3.

the natural plant. Not a few have understood Him thus; Tholuck, for example : ' The Saviour would intimate here that the relation which finds place between the vine and its branches is one which reveals itself in its highest potency in the spiritual relation between the Saviour and them that believe on him ; the kingdom of nature being a prophecy of the kingdom of grace, so that in this last are found continually the fulfilments of the prophecies of the kingdom of nature.'[1] This last, being most true, and earth the shadow of heaven, and the things on earth the copies of things in the heavens, is yet not the truth of this passage. An antagonism far deeper, and moving far more distinctly in the region of moral and spiritual things, the Lord would indicate here. The key to the right understanding of this statement lies, as was long ago noted by Grotius,[2] in some words of Jeremiah (ii. 21), ' Yet I had planted thee a noble vine; wholly a right seed ; how then art thou turned into the degenerate plant of a strange vine unto Me?'[3] and Christ, claiming to be ' *the true vine*,' claims perfectly to realize in Himself that divine idea which Israel after the flesh had altogether failed to fulfil. Planted as this ' right seed,' it had become ' an empty vine,' which brought forth fruit to itself (Hos. x. 1), and none to God ; and should end in becoming that ' vine of the earth,' the clusters of whose grapes should be cast into the winepress of the wrath of God (Rev. xiv. 18–20). In confirmation of this view it is hardly

---

[1] So Maldonatus : Quia melius et perfectius homines in se per fidem natos nutrit, quam sarmenta sua naturalis vitis.

[2] Ergo cum se illam veram vitem vocat, intelligit sibi demum excellenter competere ista epitheta, Jer. ii. 21. Genuina, non fera vitis.

[3] Ἐγὼ δὲ ἐφύτευσά σε ἄμπελον καρποφόρον, πᾶσαν ἀληθινήν· πῶς ἐστράφης εἰς πικρίαν, ἡ ἄμπελος ἡ ἀλλοτρία ; (LXX.)

necessary to observe that not in these passages only, but
continually in the Old Testament the Jewish Church is
set forth as a vine or vineyard (Ps. lxxx. 8–16; Isai. v.
1–7; Cant. viii. 11; Ezek. xix. 10–14), is rebuked for
not being a true vine, for bearing grapes of Gomorrah,
bitter fruit or none (Isai. v. 4; Deut. xxxii. 32, 33; cf.
2 Kin. iv. 39), our Lord taking up the same language in
the New (Luke xiii. 6; Matt. xxi. 33). But what Israel
should have been, and was not, this Christ, the true Israel,
was.

'*And my Father is the husbandman.*' [1] This was a
very favourite passage with the Arians; as many slight
allusions or longer discussions on the part of those who
took share in the Church's great conflict with these gainsayers, abundantly attest. The reason is obvious. The
doctrinal statement of this verse, not qualified by other
statements, was capable of being made to imply an entire
subordination on the part of the Son to the Father, the
relations in fact of a creature to a Creator. Augustine
and other theologians before him are careful to reply that
it is in his humanity that Christ is '*the true vine.*' It was
of the very essence of his mediatorial work, of the days-
man who should lay his hands upon both, that as on the

---

[1] The word which our Lord uses here is γεωργός, not ἀμπελουργός. It is
true that ἀμπελουργός would more directly designate the actual cultivator
of the vine, whose own hands dress and prune it; yet at the same time
his office is altogether a subordinate one (see Luke xiii. 7); while γεωργός,
by Philo distinguished from γεωπόνος or the actual labourer, in no way
marks out a humble social status, as is sufficiently shewn by such a passage
as 2 Chron. xxvi. 10, where of King Uzziah it is said that he was a 'husbandman' (γεωργὸς ἦν). Noah in like manner is called ἄνθρωπος γεωργὸς γῆς
(Gen. ix. 20). So too by the γεωργοί of Matt. xxi. 33–41 are intended the
chiefs and leaders of the Jewish theocracy. Not that the γεωργός need in
the least be assumed to '*purge*' or prune only by the hand of others. The
labour of the vineyard is exactly of that lighter kind, in which the pro-
prietor may be well pleased himself to take a share.

onc side He could say, ' I and my Father are one,' so
upon the other, ' I and my brethren are one ; ' and He
is here asserting the latter relation, not excluding the
former.[1] But while the vine and the vine-branches must
thus both be partakers of the same nature, for He that
sanctifieth and they that are sanctified must both be of
one (Heb. ii. 11), He will presently challenge for Himself, as Augustine does not fail to notice, a share in the
work of the husbandman, an office, which, only as He is
one with the husbandman of this allegory, He could have
any right to challenge for his own.[2] He too has power
to ' *purge* ' or cleanse through his word (ver. 3). Neither,
when we affirm that in his humanity He was ' *the true
vine*,' may we leave out of sight for a moment, that it was
a divine humanity in which He was this, in a humanity
united to his divinity, ennobled, and, as one may say,
deified, through this union ; for only so could it have
become a life-giving humanity to the world.[3]

Affirming his Father to be ' *the husbandman*,' He
excludes *none* from his Father's husbandry—not even, as

---

[1] Ambrose (*De Fide*, iv. 12): Illud quoque ad separandam Patris et Filii
divinitatem objicere consueverunt, quia Dominus dixit in Evangelio, Ego
sum vitis vera, et Pater meus agricola est ; agricolam et vitem diversæ esse
naturæ dicentes, et vitem in agricolæ esse potestate. Ambrose answers
rightly : Dominus vitem se esse dixit, incarnationis suæ significans sacra-
mentum. Basil the Great (*Con. Eunom.* iv. 3) puts the argument of the
Arians : εἰ ἄμπελος, φασίν, ὁ Σωτήρ, κλήματα δὲ ἡμεῖς, γεωργὸς δὲ ὁ Πατήρ· τὰ
δὲ κλήματα ὁμοφυῆ μὲν τῇ ἀμπέλῳ, ἡ δὲ ἄμπελος οὐχ ὁμοφυὴς τῷ γεωργῷ, ὁμοφυὴς μὲν ἡμῖν ὁ Υἱός, καὶ μέρος ἡμεῖς αὐτοῦ, οὐχ ὁμοφυὴς δὲ ὁ Υἱὸς τῷ Πατρί,
ἀλλὰ κατὰ πάντα ἀλλότριος. Basil replies as Ambrose.

[2] Augustine : Denique cum de Patre tanquam de agricolâ dixisset, quod
infructuosos palmites tollat, fructuosos autem purget, ut plus afferant fructum ; continuo etiam seipsum mundatorem palmitum ostendens, Jam vos,
inquit, mundi estis propter sermonem quem locutus sum vobis. Ecce et ipse
mundator est palmitum, quod est agricolæ, non vitis, officium.

[3] Augustine : Quamvis autem Christus vitis non esset, nisi homo esset,
tamen istam gratiam palmitibus non præberet, nisi etiam Deus esset.

Chrysostom will have it, Himself, the vine, any more than his disciples, the vine-branches. He too learned obedience by the things which He suffered. All the trial and temptation of his walk upon earth, all 'the contradiction of sinners' which was allowed to come upon Him, all in which it pleased the Father to bruise Him and put Him to grief (Isai. liii. 10), all the awaking of the sword against Him, Jehovah's fellow (Zech. xiii. 7), this was throughout the discipline of his Father's love ; to which He was submitted the first, that He might so become a pattern to all those who came after. 'Wonder not,' He would implicitly say to his disciples, 'at the sufferings which are coming upon Me ; they are part of my Father's husbandry ; still less wonder at your own ; for " if these things be done in the green tree, what shall be done in the dry ? " '—all being 'dry trees' when brought into comparison with Him. That suffering which to flesh and blood is always so unwelcome He sets here in how comforting a light. It is an evidence of the watchful care with which the heavenly Husbandman tended first the vine, and now is tending the branches of the vine.

'*Every branch in Me that beareth not fruit He taketh away.*' There are then branches *in Him*, which are unfruitful, and which therefore are removed. Christ here anticipates the future condition of his Church ; He contemplates a Church in which men shall find themselves *in Him* ; as all infants baptized into Christ are in Him ; planted together in the likeness of his death ; but for whom it remains themselves to determine whether by believing and obeying, they shall make the potential blessings of this position actually their own ; whether that fellowship with Christ, which has been so freely given to them in baptism, shall unfold itself into the new creation, into the whole Christian life; whether faith shall keep open the channels through which the power and grace and strength of Christ may flow into the soul, or unbelief shall stop them. The branches which shall have through unbelief doomed themselves to unfruitfulness ' *He taketh away.*' In the natural world branches of the vine, which are not good for that to which they were specially ordained, namely for the bearing of fruit, are good for nothing. There are trees which may be turned to secondary uses, if they fail to fulfil their primary. Not so the vine. As timber it is utterly valueless (Ezek. xv. 2–4). It is with it exactly as with the saltless salt, which, having lost its savour, is fit only to be cast out of doors (Matt. v. 13); both of them being meet emblems of the spiritual man who is not spiritual, who is good neither for the work of this world nor of a higher. But on this ' *He taketh away* ' what further might be fitly said may be better reserved for ver. 6, where the doom of the barren branches is more in detail set forth.

'*And every branch that beareth fruit, He purgeth*[1] *it, that it may bring forth more fruit.*' [2] They assuredly are right who refuse to recognize in this ' *He purgeth* ' any direct, but only a secondary, allusion to temptations and afflictions, as the means by which this cleansing is effected. It

---

[1] Αἴρει, καθαίρει: suavis rhythmus, as Bengel observes; but it is nothing more, for the words are not related to one another.

[2] Pliny (*Hist. Nat.* xiv. 14): [Numa] ex imputatâ vite libari vina diis, nefas statuit; ratione excogitatâ ut putare cogerentur, alias aratores, e t pigri circa pericula arbusti; cf. c. xxii. From whomsoever this remarkable prohibition came, it had, we may be quite sure, a much deeper meaning than that merely economical which the Roman naturalist (naturalist in bot h senses of this word) ascribes to it here; has its points of contact with H eb xii. 5–11, its dim reachings-out after a symbolic setting forth of the truth which there is declared.

is the whole process of sanctification, the circumcision of the Spirit, by whatever discipline brought about, of which Christ is speaking, and to which He pledges his Father here. At the same time, seeing that afflictions play so large, so necessary a part in this process of sanctification, it is in a secondary sense most true that there is here a reference to these. Regarded as a means of this purifying, as an evidence of the intention of the heavenly husbandman that the fruit-bearing branches shall be more fruitful still, these may be welcomed, may be contemplated in some sort as rewards of obedience. St. James bids the faithful to welcome them, for the blessing they bring with them (i. 2–4, 12), and compare Heb. xii. 11 ; Rom. v. 3–5. To how many dealings of God with his own, mysterious, inscrutable, inexplicable otherwise, will this, kept properly in mind, furnish us with a key. Oftentimes the fine gold of some saint appears to us as if cleansed from all its dross; but the inexorable refiner, who sees with other eyes than ours, and detects remains of dross where we see nothing but gold, flings it again into the furnace, that so it may be purer yet. Augustine has a striking image in illustration. Many a time, he observes, a portrait seems perfect in the judgment of all eyes save those of the artist who drew it. Others would fain see him now to hold his hand; they count that he cannot improve it, perhaps may mar it ; but he returns it to the easel, touches and retouches still. And why ? Because, being this artist, there floats before his mind's eye an ideal perfection, to which hitherto his work has not attained ; but to which he would fain see it approach more nearly yet.

'*Now ye are clean through the word which I have spoken*

unto you '—' *clean* ' and yet needing to be ' *cleansed.*' [1] We
have a hint here of the mystery of that double relation
in which every believing man stands to God, of that
double relation which is more fully and dogmatically
stated in some of the Pauline epistles; but which is yet
distinctly anticipated here, and at John xiii. 10. The
faithful in Christ Jesus are ' *clean,*' being by faith justified
from all things, and having thus a standing-ground before
God; which yet is in some sort an ideal one,—their actual state, although ever approximating to this, yet still
failing to correspond to it,—they therefore needing by
the same faith to appropriate ever more and more of
that sanctifying grace, those purifying influences, which
continually stream forth from Him on all them that are
his; and by aid of which He is bringing them to be all
that, which for his sake his Father has been already
willing to regard them,[2] however the absolute identity of
what they are and what they are counted to be, is reserved
for another state of existence.

---

[1] Καθαροί, and yet of those whom the husbandman καθαίρει (ver. 2). Here
there is a real connexion between the words, which we would gladly have
seen reproduced in our Version. Augustine : Mundi scilicet atque mundandi.
Neque enim, nisi mundi essent, fructum ferre potuissent; et tamen omnem,
qui fert fructum, purgat agricola, ut fructum plus afferat. Fert fructum,
quia mundus est; atque ut plus afferat, purgatur adhuc. Quis enim in hâc
vitâ sic mundus, ut non sit magis magisque mundandus ?

[2] Gerhard (*Harm. Evang.* 177): Quia dixerat Patrem purgare palmites
fructuosos Christo insitos, ideo docet duplicem esse purgationem, videlicet
purgationem primam, quæ est ipsa justificatio in remissione peccatorum
consistens, atque insitionem in Christum, veram illam vitem, indivulso nexu
conjunctam habens; et purgationem secundam, quæ consistit in quotidianâ
renovatione ac veteris Adami mortificatione, quæ non semel tantum fit, sicut
regeneratio et in vitem insitio, sed singulis diebus repetitur, et per totam
vitam continuatur. . . . Quia mundatio fit per verbum, ergo non immediate,
sed per ministros Ecclesiæ verbum prædicantes et sacramenta administrantes,
qui in hoc mundationis opere sunt Dei συνεργοί (1 Cor. iii. 9). . . . Christus
non dicit, Mundi estis propter sermonem, quem inspiravi vobis, sed, quem

' *Abide in Me, and I in you. As the branch cannot bear fruit of itself, except it abide in the vine, no more can ye, except ye abide in Me.*' Our Lord does not say here, as He is so often taken to say, ' If you abide in Me, I will also abide in you.' The second clause in this sentence is not promise, any more than the first; they are precept both : ' Take heed that ye abide in Me, and that I abide in you.'[1] The next verse, where the same words recur, and still more ver. 7, are decisive on this matter; see also vi. 56. It is of course only in a very restricted sense that the relations between Him and them are mutual. There is no correlation of forces. He is throughout and only a giver, they are throughout and only receivers.[2] The mystical use of this word ' to abide,' representing as it does the innermost fellowship and communion of the faithful with their Lord, and of their Lord with them, and occasionally representing a higher mystery still (John xiv. 10; xv. 10), is peculiar to St. John, but is very frequent both in his Gospel and in his Epistles, in the lan-

locutus sum vobis. Ergo verbo prædicato et audito vim mundandi tribuit, quam ipso actu exserit, si fide recipitur.

[1] We must not therefore complete κἀγὼ ἐν ὑμῖν with μενῶ, but with μείνω. Bengel gives it well : Facite ut maneatis in me, *et ut ego maneam in vobis.* Godet's words are worth quoting (*Comm. sur l'Évang. de S. Jean*) : *En moi* exprime l'état dans lequel le chrétien fait abstraction de tout ce qui est sa sagesse, sa force, son mérite propre, pour puiser tout en Christ, sous ces différents rapports, par l'intime aspiration de la foi. Et c'est là l'unique condition de l'activité de Christ en nous. Jésus le fait sentir en supprimant à dessein le verbe dans la proposition suivante, *Et moi en vous.* Par cette ellipse il enveloppe le second de ces deux faits dans le premier de telle sorte que là où le premier s'accomplit, le second ne peut manquer d'arriver. De cette manière l'action de Christ est mise hardiment sous l'empire de notre liberté, aussi bien que la nôtre propre.

[2] Augustine : Ita in vite palmites sunt, ut viti non conferant, sed inde accipiant, unde vivant; ita vero vitis est in palmitibus, ut vitale alimentum subministret eis, non sumat ab eis.

guage of his Lord, and in his own which he has learned from that Lord.[1]

' *I am the vine, ye are the branches.*' Our Lord willingly repeats great truths which He would deeply imprint on the minds of his disciples; thus see John iii. 3, 5; vi. 48, 51; but in those places, as in this, with a variation, with more fulness on the second occasion than on the first, or with some other modification, which sufficiently justifies the repetition. In the present instance He now for the first time explicitly calls the disciples ' *the branches,*' however as much may have been involved in words which He has uttered already. So, too, while He had already declared the abiding in Him to be the one condition of all fruit-bearing, He adds a promise now, that he who abides in Him shall not only bear fruit, but shall bear it abundantly: ' *He that abideth in Me, and I in him, the same bringeth forth much fruit; for without Me ye can do nothing.*'

It is a poor and inadequate interpretation of these last words to make them to mean, ' Ye can do nothing *until* ye are in Me, and have my grace.' It is rather, ' *After* ye are in Me, ye can even then accomplish nothing except as ye draw life and strength from Me; only through a putting forth of my power which is in you can ye commence, carry forward, or bring any work to a good effect. From first to last it is I that must work in and through you.' We have a warning here to the regenerate man that he never seek to do aught of himself; not a de-

---

[1] Besides the μένειν ἐν ἐμοί here, or ἐν αὐτῷ (1 Ep. ii. 6), we have also μένειν ἐν τῇ ἀγάπῃ (xv. 9); ἐν τῷ λόγῳ (viii. 31); ἐν τῷ φωτί (1 Ep. ii. 10); ἐν τῇ διδαχῇ (2 Ep. ix.); ἐν τῷ Πατρί (1 Ep. ii. 24); ἐν τῷ Θεῷ (1 Ep. iv. 16); all expressing, though from slightly different points of view, the same blessed and transcendant truth; and then, as the fearful contrast to all these, there is the μένειν ἐν τῇ σκοτίᾳ (xii. 46); ἐν τῷ θανάτῳ (1 Ep. iii. 14).

claration that the unregenerate is unable to do aught. Christ does not mean, ' Out of and apart from Me ye are powerless for good;' but, 'Being in Me, only through putting forth of my power, suffering Me effectually to work in and through you, can you accomplish anything'— a truth which needs to be evermore repeated, for it is evermore in danger of being forgotten by us. The words are frequently appealed to by Augustine and others engaged in controversy with the Pelagians of old ;[1] even as in the formularies and symbolic books of the Reformed Churches they constantly appear as a *dictum probans* against all open or covert Pelagianism.

' *If a man abide not in Me, he is cast forth as a branch, and is withered* ' (cf. Ezek. xvii. 24 ; Matt. iii. 10 ; vii. 19 ; xxi. 19 ; Mark xi. 20, 21 ; Luke xxiii. 31). Some will fain have it that in giving these words their spiritual significance we must reverse their order, urging that the branch, because withered, is therefore cast forth, and not, because cast forth, therefore withered. But it is not so, either in the natural world or the spiritual ; and there is no sufficient reason for deserting the actual sequence of Christ's words, which only the strongest necessity should compel us to abandon. So far however from such necessity existing, the declaration, as it now stands, yields a lesson the most solemn, one which, changing the order of the words, we should in good part miss. An unfruitful

---

[1] Thus Augustine (*Con. duas Ep. Pelag.* ii. 8): Dominus autem ut responderet futuro Pelagio, non ait, Sine me difficilè potestis aliquid facere, sed ait, Sine me nihil potestis facere. Et ut responderet futuris etiam istis in eâdem ipsâ Evangelicâ sententiâ, non ait, Sine me nihil potestis perficere, sed, facere. Nam si perficere dixisset, possent isti respondere, non ad incipiendum bonum, quod a nobis est, sed ad perficiendum, esse Dei adjutorium necessarium. Dominus cum ait, Sine me nihil potestis facere, hoc uno verbo initium finemque comprehendit.

branch is not ' *withered*,' when broken off from its paren stock and stem ; on the contrary, it retains a deceitful greenness and freshness for a little while ; deceitful, because upon all this the sentence of death has irrevocably passed. Churches, which, through abandonment of the Catholic faith, individuals who, by unbelief and by the sins which spring from unbelief, have separated themselves off, and in the awful but secret judgments of God have been sepa- rated off, from Christ their Head, may keep for a while the show and semblance of life, may deceive others, may deceive even themselves—so long, that is, as any residue of that good thing which they have gotten from Christ remains. But little by little, sooner or later, they come to an end of all which they carried away with them. It fails and dies out, and, once wasted and gone, there is nothing to replace it ; and thus death, moral and spiritual, steals over all ; they are ' *withered*,' this withering of theirs being not seldom evident to the cyes of all.

' *And men gather them ;* ' or better, ' *And they gather them*,' bring them together into one bundle of death,[1] leaving who the gatherers are in the awful obscurity which rests upon it in the original. Some words of Isaiah, when the boughs thereof are withered, they shall be broken off ; the women come, and set them on fire (xxvii. 11), constitute an interesting parallel. The ga- therers are the angels, the ministers of the divine anger, to whom the final execution of the divine judgments is everywhere committed (Matt. xiii. 41, 49 ; xxii. 13 ; xxiv. 31 ; Luke xix. 24 ; Rev. xix. 14). ' *And cast them into the fire, and they are burned ;* ' or, in its simplicity more terrible still, ' *and they burn* ' (cf. Ezek. xv. 4). But all which is

---

[1] Συνάγουσι: cf. συλλέξουσι, Matt. xiii. 41 ; and Isai. xxiv. 2.

here expressed or implied, of 'the fire' (Matt. iii. 10),
'the flame' (Luke xvi. 24), 'the flaming fire' (2 Thess.
i. 8), 'the furnace of fire' (Matt. xiii. 42, 50), 'the gehenna
of fire' (Matt. v. 22; Mark ix. 43), 'the lake of fire' (Rev.
xx. 15; xxi. 8), 'the everlasting fire' (Matt. xxv. 41;
Jude 7), with all the secrets of anguish which words
like these, if there be any truth in words, *must* involve,
demands rather to be trembled at than needs to be
expounded.

We pause here. It is true that echoes and reminis-
cences of this allegory still recur through the chapter,
very distinctly in the next three or four verses, where
exhortations are clothed in imagery which it offers, promises linked with a fulfilling by disciples, of all which the
fact of being branches in Him implies, means by which
these shall abide in his love declared. But these remi-
niscences are ever growing weaker and weaker; the vine
and the vine-branches more and more fade out of sight;
so that after this verse there is nothing which of necessity
links itself on to this allegory; or which would not be
perfectly intelligible without any reference to it, and supposing that Christ had never uttered it. Here, therefore,
is the fittest place to conclude.

15. *THE PENITENT MALEFACTOR*

Luke xxiii. 39–43.

WE might beforehand have anticipated that, were the history of the penitent malefactor recorded in one Gospel only, it would be in the Gospel of St. Luke ; which is above all the Gospel of pardon and grace, and among the Gospels the correlative of the Pauline Epistles among the Epistles. St. Luke, the companion of St. Paul, lays, more than any other Evangelist, the groundwork upon which the latter builds ; teaching historically that which St. Paul teaches dogmatically, namely, that where sin abounded, grace did much more abound (vii. 47 ; xv. ; xix. 10).[1] We have in the history before us a very notable example of that wondrous law of selection, according to which, out of the inexhaustible treasure-house of our Lord's sayings and doings upon earth, each Evangelist severally appropriates that which agrees best with his special purpose and aim. Such a law of selection we may continually recognize, so soon as the eye is once opened to look for and expect it.

We read in the verses which immediately precede this wondrous story, of the wild flood of blasphemy and scorn and hate which foamed and raged so fiercely round the foot of the cross ; how his soul that hung on that cross was pierced and stabbed with taunts and reproaches, with

---

[1] See Holtzmann, *Die Synoptischen Evangelien*, Leipzig, 1863, p. 391, sqq.

words of malignity and hate, sharper and keener far than the nails which had torn his hands and his feet, or the spear which should penetrate his side. We read how heathen and Jew, as in a frightful rivalry, vied with one another, which should heap most of outrage upon the Christ of God; nor among the last was it the populace only; but the very chiefs of the Jewish nation, throwing off not merely all dignity, but all decency and decorum, and in the fierce delight of gratified hatred not caring to maintain even the religious hypocrisies which should have hindered them from openly rejoicing in the sufferings of another, were first and foremost in this crucifying afresh of the Son of God (Heb. vi. 6). And then, as to crown all, St. Matthew (xxvii. 44) and St. Mark (xv. 32) relate that two fellow-sufferers with our Lord, two who, fulfilling the prophecy made long before (Isai. liii. 9, 12), were crucified with Him, fell in with and took up the taunts of the crowd, reviled Him, mocked his pretensions, bade Him, if He were indeed the Christ, to save Himself and them—a fearful example, whether one only, or, for a while at least, both bore themselves thus, that the Greek proverb which ascribes to sufferings such a teaching power,[1] comes not always true. There are those whose hearts their own sufferings and the just punishments of God do not soften, but only harden and exasperate the more; so that they may howl upon their bed, nay, writhe upon their cross, and yet not repent them of their evil, but only go forward, adding new sin to their old, fierce, impenitent, and defiant to the last (Jer. v. 3; Rev. ix. 20, 21; xvi. 9, 11, 21; 2 Chron. xxviii. 22).[2]

---

[1] Παθήματα, μαθήματα, or in Latin, Nocumenta, documenta.

[2] The effects of crucifixion were very various on those who endured it.

St. Luke, indeed, tells us that not both, but that ' *one of the malefactors which were hanged railed on Him, saying, If Thou be Christ, save Thyself and us.*' A question presents itself here, Does the statement of the earlier Evangelists, and the necessity of harmonizing the several relations, require us to assume that he, who later in the day became a penitent, joined at first in these blasphemous ravings of his fellow-malefactor and of the multitude, and only after a while separated his lot from theirs, being convinced and converted by all the wondrous evidences of a divine grace and love which shone out in the suffering Lord? To this, which of course enhances the marvel of his conversion, making it still more sudden and miraculous, many interpreters in all ages have considered themselves bound by the statements of the preceding Evangelists; as counting that only by such an assumption is it possible to reconcile St. Luke's account with theirs. Thus Chrysostom,[1] Theophylact, Leo the Great.[2] Ambrose is more doubtful.[3] Augustine, on the contrary, is strong that one only blasphemed,[4] urging as a parallel case the words of Heb. xi. 33, 37, ' *they* stopped the mouths of lions,' when, in fact, it was but one, namely Daniel, who did so ; ' *they* were sawn asunder ;' when, in

While the Christian martyrs would praise God from their cross, or exhort the beholders to embrace that faith for the sake of which they were willing to endure even that worst, some would spit on the bystanders (Seneca, *De Vitâ Beatâ*, 19), or reveal hidden iniquities of their former life, or utter curses against their enemies (Josephus, *B. J.* iv. 6. 1), or blaspheme their judge, to render which last impossible it was not unfrequent to gag them; Cicero mentions a slave whose tongue was cut out before crucifixion for fear of inconvenient revelations which he might make from his cross (*Pro Cluent.* 66 ; cf. Justin, *Hist.* xxii. 7).

[1] See Suicer, *Thes.* s. v. λῃστής.
[2] Usque ad crucem reus, fit Christi repente confessor.
[3] Fortasse et iste prius conviciatus est.
[4] *De Cons. Evang.* iii. 16.

all likelihood, the allusion is but to one, namely to Isaiah. His parallel cases do not seem to me very convincing, yet, on the whole, I must decidedly incline to the conclusion at which he has arrived. The internal evidence in its favour is strong. The rebuke with which the penitent malefactor rebukes his fellow is very little like that of one, who has just been partaker in the sin which he condemns. His deliberate remonstrance, with no word of reference to himself, '*Dost not thou fear God, seeing thou art in the same condemnation?*' sounds not at all like the remonstrance of one,—would have fitted ill, in that shape at least, to the lips of one,—who had just before been joining in the blasphemies, which all of a sudden he condemns.[1]

Up to the moment when his fellow malefactor joined in the railings of the multitude, he, we may suppose, had listened in silence; the work of grace which had begun in him sometime since, in his prison perhaps, going rapidly forward; for all around him and about him was such as would rapidly ripen a man for heaven, or for hell. The other it ripened for hell, him for heaven. He had heard all—in silence, though with deep horror of soul; but now he can keep silence no longer. There is a time to speak (Eccles. iii. 7), as well as a time to keep silence, and now for him that time has arrived. In that '*Save Thyself and us*,' in that plural '*us*,' the other is seeking to draw him into the same blasphemy with himself, is presenting this as the common taunt of them both. Need is therefore that he should speak, that he should separate himself off by a clear and distinct avowal

---

[1] Cajetan: Hæc namque verba sonant non pœnitentem convicii proprii, sed increpantem alterius, quod simul cum aliis insultet Jesu.

from the other's sin, and not, by any longer holding his peace, become partaker of it.   The English Version here, '*Dost not thou fear God?*' is doubly at fault, missing the emphasis twice.   Read rather, '*Neither dost thou fear God?*'   'It is nothing so strange,' he would say, 'that these secure sinners, whom justice has not yet overtaken, for whom God's judgments are as yet far out of sight, should dare thus to open their mouths against the Holy One of God; but thou, upon thy cross, with such teaching as that might give thee, with such evidence as that affords that God is not mocked, that men eat at last the fruit of their doings, dost thou venture upon the same; "*neither dost thou fear God*,[1] *seeing*," as he goes on to say, "*thou art in the same condemnation?*"'   Two reasons are here alleged, though they may seem at first sight but one, why he should have refused to become partaker of the sin of those mockers; the first, which already lay in that question we have just dealt with, that he was in condemnation, that judgment had overtaken him; the second, that Jesus was a fellow-sufferer; community of suffering might have well inspired forbearance and pity of the one for the other.

And then, lest this word should seem to imply that they all shared in a common cross because they had shared in a common or like crime, he separates and distinguishes between Christ's cross and theirs.   The condemnation indeed is common to all; but not so the

---

[1] Maldonatus: Non dubito quin bonus ille et fidelis latro perversum illum latronem cum Judæis voluerit comparare, quæ comparatio in illâ dictione *nec* obscure delitescit; quasi dicat, Non solum illi qui pœnâ carent, sed nec tu, qui in eâdem pœnâ es, Deum times?   Corn. à Lapide: Esto, Scribæ et Judæi liberi et validi non timeant Deum, ideoque subsannent Christum; tu tamen, qui in cruce torqueris et ad mortem tendis, deberes timere Deum.

guilt; ' *and we indeed justly ; for we receive the due reward
of our deeds ; but this man hath done nothing amiss;* so
far from having committed enormous crimes, as we have,
there is no smallest fault or error in Him ; '[1]—another
reason why he should be spared these outrages and
insults. If these are for any, they are for the wicked, for
those who have wrought evil, not for those who are innocent and holy.[2]

Let us, before proceeding further, endeavour to realize
to ourselves what manner of persons these ' *malefactors*'
probably were, how they had deserved this name, and
by the course of what crimes they had reached a Roman
cross, as the end of their conversation, as the due reward
of their deeds. To understand this will, I am persuaded,
help us not a little to understand how one of those crucified with Jesus should, even in the hour of his own worst
suffering, have turned to the Lord with scorn and defiance,
the other with penitence and prayer. Both these facts
may, through such an enquiry, become more intelligible
to us. ' *Malefactors*' is the name by which St. Luke calls
them ; ' *thieves*' (according to our Version) the two earlier
Evangelists ; from whom, and from the blending of whose
record with his, we have learned to speak of ' the penitent
thief.' Our Translators would have done much better to
maintain the distinction which the Scripture maintains
between him, the ' robber,' or violent spoiler (see Matt.

---

[1] Maldonatus : οὐδὲν ἄτοπον, nihil quod virum bonum non deceat ; quibus
verbis indicare voluit non solum nullum magnum scelus, sed nullum etiam
vel levissimum peccatum in Christo esse. Yet ἄτοπος is too often used in
Hellenistic Greek as entirely equivalent to πονηρός (it is joined with it,
2 Thess. iii. 2), to allow us very confidently to press this.

[2] Maldonatus: Cum in eâdem quâ Christus pœnâ verseris, et, quod plus
est, tu quidem merito, ille vero immerito, tamen neque pœnæ societas, nec
ejus te movet innocentia, ut ejus misereare.

xxi. 13 ; xxvi. 55 ; Luke x. 30 ; John xviii. 40 ; 2 Cor.
xi. 26), and the 'thief,' or secret purloiner (Matt. vi.
19; John xii. 6; 1 Thess. v. 2; Rev. iii. 3; xvi. 15).
Many passages have suffered in our Version from the
neglect of this distinction, but none so seriously as that
with which we now have to do.[1]

These two were not ' thieves,' as we have learned to
call them, but robbers.   Having vindicated this title for
them, we may further enquire what at this time the name
probably implied, and whether more than lies on the surface of the word.   It will help us to answer this question
aright, if we put side by side the application of the title
of ' robber ' to Barabbas (John xviii. 40), and the other
notices of him which the Gospels supply, and then seek
to read all in the light which contemporary history affords.
Barabbas, this 'robber' according to St. John, was, we
are told, ' a notable prisoner' (Matt. xxvii. 16); ' which
lay bound with them that had made insurrection with
him, who had committed murder in the insurrection'
(Mark xv. 7) ; 'who for a certain sedition made in the
city, and for murder, was cast into prison ' (Luke xxiii.
19); plainly a ringleader in one of those fierce and
fanatic outbreaks against the Roman domination, which
on a large scale or a small so fast succeeded one another
in the latter days of the Jewish commonwealth.   This at
once explains how it was possible for the Chief Priests
with their religious pretensions to shew the interest on
his behalf which they did (Matt. xxvii. 20; Mark xv. 11),
explains no less the enthusiasm with which the Jewish
populace demanded his liberation (Luke xxiii. 18).   He

---

[1] On the distinction between λῃστής and κλέπτης see my *Synonyms of the
New Testament*, § 44.

was the popular hero, who had sought to realize his own
and their idea of the kingdom of God by violence and
blood ; who had actually *been* that which they wanted
the Lord to be, and which, because He refused to be,
they were now so eager to destroy Him.   He had wrought,
we may well believe, in that false Messias spirit, which
was filling with wild and insane hopes the whole nation,
and rapidly hurrying it on to that final conflict with the
Roman power, in which as a nation it should be for ever
broken in pieces.   There is every likelihood that the two
malefactors crucified with Jesus belonged to the band of
Barabbas.   For good or for evil they knew something
about the Christ, and that He was One who could deliver
his own ; the taunt uttered by the one embodies their
conviction of this, no less than the prayer of the other.
Barabbas, as we have seen, had been cast into prison
' with them that had made insurrection with him.'   Two
of the chief of these Pilate may have been very well
pleased to send to execution on this occasion.   It is
abundantly plain from John xix. 15, 19-22, that he was
willing in the bitterness of his spirit to retort in any way
on those who had driven him to what his conscience
told him was a hideous injustice, to the condemnation
(for this much he could see) of a perfectly innocent
man.   As he evidently sought in that title over the cross
to do an extreme displeasure to the Jews, so he may have
intended the same in this : ' If you compel me against
my better mind to send this man to the cross, I will
send, to keep him company, two of the servants of your
Messiah.'

Such seems to me a more probable explanation—I
speak but of the human explanation—of these malefactors

sharing in the cross of Christ, than to suppose that the additional indignity of being thus ' numbered with the transgressors' was devised for Him by the Pharisees. Doubtless they were quite capable of such a malignity, and insults of exactly this character have not seldom been heaped on high-souled sufferers in the concluding scene of their lives. Thus in the French Revolution, when some noble royalist was sent to the guillotine, it was constantly managed to mix up his execution with that of forgers, highwaymen, murderers, or the like ; to the end that their shame and disgrace might redound upon him ; and this last drop of bitterness not be wanting in his cup of pain. It is not that the Pharisees would have been behind the worst in modern times in any such subtle inventions of hate ; but the ordering of malefactors to execution lay in other hands than theirs ; and there is nothing to make us think that Pilate would devise any additional insult for Him whom he would have certainly set free, if the conscience of innumerable acts of violence and rapine and wrong, whereof the Jews might accuse him to Cæsar, had not made him the coward that he was. It was the Pharisees whom he desired, so far as he dared, to wound.

Whether, indeed, Barabbas had actually played the part of a false Christ, and set himself up as the true, we have no means of knowing. It is certainly far from unlikely. Keeping in mind the significance of names in Scripture, we can hardly fail to recognize a fearful mockery in his name, Barabbas (' Son of the Father ') ; as though in the very name he bore, not to speak of the work which he wrought, he should be the devil's counterfeit and caricature of the true Holy One of God.

This suggestion would acquire increased probability, if it could certainly be affirmed that he was not merely named Barabbas, but Jesus Barabbas, the lying counterpart, even to his human name, of the true Saviour of men. So, as is well known, three cursive manuscripts, at Matt. xxvii. 17, even to this day read, and two of the older Versions, the Armenian and the Syriac. It is clear too that this was the prevailing reading in the time of Origen; who, speaking of *many* copies in which Barabbas was *not* called also Jesus, implies that, many as they were, they were still the minority.[1] In support of this remarkable reading, which De Wette, Fritzsche, Meyer, Ewald, Rinck[2] approve, but Lachmann, Tischendorf in his later editions though in the earlier he admitted it into the text, Alford, Tregelles[3] reject, it may be urged, that while we can scarcely conceive anyone daring to introduce the sacred name of Jesus, to give it to Barabbas, of even a thought of the kind suggesting itself to the mind of any, we can very well understand that many transcribers should have been shocked to find it there; and marring the text, which they impertinently sought to mend, have ventured to omit it. Vestiges, moreover, of the existence of such a reading survive in the text as it now stands; the words, 'which is called Christ,' twice introduced after the human name of our blessed Lord on the occasions when Barabbas is brought into opposition to Him (Matt. xxvii. 17, 22), and nowhere else, seem to be employed by Pilate out of a necessity to distinguish between him and another who

---

[1] In multis exemplaribus non continetur quod Barabbas etiam Jesus dicebatur, et forsitan recte, ut ne nomen Jesus conveniat alicui iniquorum.

[2] *Lucub. Crit.* p. 285. Keim, *Jesu von 'Nazara*, vol. iii. p. 375, hangs in doubt, but inclines to accept this reading.

[3] *On the Printed Text of the Greek Testament*, p. 194.

bore the name of Jesus as well. It is at first strangely startling to think that this identity of name could possibly have existed ; and yet He who bore every other scorn and shame, why should He not have also borne this ?

All which has just been said being kept in remembrance, it will surprise us less, that so many elements of nobleness should display themselves in strength in one of these malefactors, than if we regarded him merely as a criminal of that meaner stamp whom we designate as a thief, or even as a robber, in our ordinary use of that word. His had been no petty larcenies ; as little, in all likelihood, had he meant at the beginning to have his living by violence and wrong. Those whom the Romans with a certain amount of truth called ' robbers,' were oftentimes wild and stormy zealots, maintaining in arms a last and hopeless protest against that yoke of the stranger, which God had imposed on his people for the chastisement of their sins, and which therefore it behoved them meekly to accept. This may have been one of these, seeking at the outset of his career to work by the wrath of man what he counted the righteousness of God.[1] Presently a fugitive from Roman justice, compelled to take to the mountains, and to live there by rapine, he may have gradually learned less and less to discriminate between friend and foe, may have earned only too well the title under which he was at last to expiate his offences on a Roman cross.

His own confession implies as much (ver. 41). How easily, under such conditions, those who have begun with

---

[1] In the record by Josephus of the final agony of Jerusalem the ζηλωτής and the λῃστής become nearly, or indeed altogether, convertible terms ; thus see *B. J.* iv. passim. In the first French Revolution the noble Vendeans are constantly designated as ' les brigands de la Loire.'

quite another aim degenerate into banditti, how imperceptibly and yet how surely the outlaw melts into the brigand, the story of Dolcino's Apostolicals, as of the Camisards in the Cevennes, abundantly teaches us ;[1] while in the history of Jephthah we see how under more favourable circumstances this freebooter may rise into the chief and champion of his people (Judg. xi. 3, 11). He would do this the more easily, inasmuch as he would never by his lawless occupation have wholly forfeited his own respect or the respect of his fellow-countrymen ; David, indeed, himself for a while was little better than such a freebooter as this (1 Sam. xxii. 2). Least of all would he forfeit this at a time when the whole framework of social life was dislocated and disjointed as it was at this period in Judæa; and when the disorganization of society seemed half to justify acts which would have been wholly without justification at another time. It is easy to perceive how a class like this, while it would enlist some among the worst, would also gather some into its ranks who, though miserably perverted now, might under more favourable circumstances have stood forth among the noblest of their age and nation. It is not altogether unlikely that an apostle of the Lord, Simon Zelotes, had been, as his name would indicate, on the very verge of becoming one of these ; until in Christ he had found a more excellent way, had discovered that the truth, and the truth only, could make him free, or help him to make others free. But these worst and best, however they might accidentally be yoked together, and called by a common name, would yet only be waiting for some contact with the absolute

---

[1] Renan, *L'Antechrist*, p. 280 : Il faut vivre, et des corps francs ne peuvent guère vivre sans vexer la population : voilà pourquoi brigand et héros, en temps de crise nationale, sont presque synonymes.

truth, to reveal themselves in the essential differences of
their character, differences which up to that decisive
moment may have been concealed alike from others and
from themselves. So it fared with this malefactor and the
other. The decisive moment had now arrived. Heaven
and hell claimed each its own. Of these two, so long
yokefellows in evil, it was manifest at length that one had
in him that which was akin to and was drawn to the light;
the other, that which hated the light, repelled the light,
and was in return repelled by it into a yet deeper darkness of its own.[1]

Few as are the words which this penitent utters in his
brief address to his fellow-sinner, and then in his still
briefer to his Saviour, they yet are sufficient to reveal to
us a most authentic work of grace going forward within
him. He is, in the first place, deeply convinced of his
sin. There is no more certain sign of an effectual work of
the Holy Spirit of God than a readiness on the sinner's
part to accept and acquiesce in his punishment, whatever
that punishment may be, to put his mouth in the dust,
and to say, ' Thou art righteous, O God, that doest this ; '
' Wherefore doth a living man complain, a man for the
punishment of his sin ? ' (Lam. iii. 39 ; cf. Ezra ix. 6, 7 ;
Luke xv. 18, 19) ; while, on the other hand, there can
be no surer token of an impenitent and obdurate heart
than the refusal of the sinner to receive correction, to

---

[1] There are many apocryphal legends about these two robbers; which
may be found in Thilo, *Codex Apocryphus*, pp. 93, 143, 580. Their very
names are there given, but variously, Dimas, or Dysmas, and Gestas,
Titus and Dumachus ; this last possibly a corruption of Θεομάχος. In one of
these legends it is told how the converted robber more than thirty years
before had allowed the blessed Virgin and her Child to pass unharmed on
their flight to Egypt, against the desire of the other, who would have
despoiled the fugitives.

humble himself under the mighty hand of God (Isai. i.5 ; ix. 10; Jer. ii. 30 ; v. 3 ; Luke xv. 14, 15 ; Rev. ix. 21 ; xvi. 21). And this man even in that bitter cross saw nothing more than he had earned, ' *the due reward of his deeds.*' How profound the conviction, how unreserved upon his part is the confession, of sin !

And then how many other principal graces shew them-selves actively working in him [1]—all compressed, it is true, and this by the very necessities of the case, within the narrowest limits of time ; but in their intension making up for what in extension they have not and can-not have. Ignorant he may very well have been of that special precept in Moses' law, ' Thou shalt in any wise rebuke thy neighbour, and not suffer sin upon him ' (Lev. xix. 17) ; but love is the fulfilling of the law, and love will not suffer him to keep silence now. They two may in times past have been frequent partners in guilt, associates in many a deed of violence and wrong, strengthening one another in wickedness ; but now, himself a penitent, he would fain lead his fellow-sinner by the same blessed path of contrition, repentance, and faith, which he him-self is treading.

And then, further, what courage, what boldness speaks

---

[1] Thus Gregory the Great (*Moral.* xviii. 40): Libet mentis oculos ad illum latronem reducere, qui de fauce diaboli ascendit crucem, de cruce paradisum. Intueamur qualis ad patibulum venerit, et a patibulo qualis abscessit. . . . In corde fidelium tres summopere manere virtutes testatur Apostolus, dicens, Nunc autem manent fides, spes, caritas. Quas cunctas subitâ repletus gratiâ et accepit latro, et servavit in cruce. Fidem namque habuit, qui regnaturum Dominum credidit, quem secum pariter morientem vidit. Spem habuit, qui regni ejus aditum postulavit, dicens, Memento mei, Domine, dum veneris in regnum tuum. Caritatem quoque in mente suâ vivaciter tenuit, qui fratrem et collatronem pro simili scelere morientem, et de iniquitate suâ arguit, et ei vitam quam cognoverat, prædicavit, dicens, Neque tu times Deum, etc.

out in his confession of Christ, in his avowal, ' *This man hath done nothing amiss;*' and still more in his open turning to Him as the one Helper and Saviour. Some perhaps might be tempted to rejoin, that at such a moment this did not cost him much, that for him, hanging on that cross, and doomed before many hours there to expire, the motives which would operate on others, the fear of men's reproach, the desire of their applause, must all have alike lost their power. But this is altogether a mistake. We have only to call to mind how often men, above all those who know no higher support, have in such a dreadful hour sustained themselves to the last on the sympathies of the beholders; how bold bad men, mainly upheld by these, have gone down with no sign of weakness, but as with flying colours, to hell. So far from costing him nothing, it must have required a mighty effort upon his part to separate himself, as now no doubt he did, from all the sympathies of all who surrounded his cross, and thus openly to cast in his lot with the crucified Lord. Hitherto, as a victim of Roman justice, as one of the ' *robbers*' described just now, that is, as one of the latest champions of national freedom, a member probably of the band of Barabbas, and sharing in the popular interest which Barabbas excited, this man had been an object of sympathy and admiration to all the scorners and blasphemers of Calvary. Such he would have become still more, openly joining, as his companion did, in their insults and outrages against the Holy One of God. But to all this he prefers the reproach of Christ, which surely he did not escape, when he made that bold confession of his faith, '*Lord, remember me, when Thou comest into thy kingdom.*'

And if other graces signally manifest themselves in

him, yet, more than all other, what a wondrous faith utters itself in these words of his. To believe that He, whose only token of royalty was the crown of thorns that still clung to his bleeding brows, was a king, and had a kingdom,[1] that He, on whose own eyes the mists of death were already hanging, was indeed the Prince of life, wielding in those pierced hands, nailed so helplessly to the cross, the keys of death and of hell, that He could shut and none could open, could open and none could shut; that it would profit something in that mysterious world whither they both were hastening to be remembered by this crucified Man—that was a faith indeed. What was the faith of any other to his faith? Everything seemed to give the lie to Christ's pretensions. Disciples and apostles themselves had fallen away and fled. They had trusted once ' that it had been He which should have redeemed Israel ' (Luke xxiv. 21); but they had now renounced that hope; and, indeed, every other hope; and then, in the midst of this universal unbelief, one, all whose anterior life might seem to have unfitted him for this heroic act of faith, does homage, not indeed in outward act, for his limbs are nailed to the tree, but in heart and word, to Jesus as the King of Israel, as the Lord of the spirits of all flesh. Truly we may say of his faith that it was itself one of the miracles of the crucifixion ;[2]

---

[1] Bengel: Regem profitetur, talem, qui mortuus mortuo benefacere possit.

[2] Augustine often magnifies the faith which breaks forth thus unexpectedly in this man, as a bright sun from behind thickest clouds. Thus (*Serm.* 232): Magna fides; huic fidei quid addi possit, ignoro. Titubaverunt ipsi qui viderunt Christum mortuos suscitantem; credidit ille qui videbat secum in ligno pendentem. Quando illi titubaverunt, tunc ille credidit. Qualem fructum Christus de arido ligno percepit? . . . Non solum credebat resurrecturum, sed etiam regnaturum. Pendenti, crucifixo, cruento, hærenti, Cum veneris, inquit, in regnum tuum. Et illi, Nos sperabamus [Luc. xxiv. 21]. Ubi spem latro invenit, discipulus perdidit. Compare *Serm.* 285

that in his conversion we have one of those glimpses
of glory with which the Father is ever careful to light up
the deepest depths of the humiliation of the Son.

But it will be well worth while to look a little closer
and more in detail at his words. ' *Lord* ' need not in
itself be more than a general term of respectful address ;
it is oftentimes this, and nothing further ; thus Matt. xxv.
20, 24 ; John iv. 11 ; xii. 21 ; xx. 15, and elsewhere.
But it may have a much deeper, and a theological
meaning ; and such no doubt it has here. For without
assuming, which would indeed be absurd, that this un-
taught man meant by his ' *Lord* ' all which the Church
now understands by Jehovah or Lord, yet was there on
his part the recognition of a divine character in Christ.
His ' *Lord* ' of itself would not be sufficient to prove this,
but only as it is read in the light of what follows, ' *Remember me, when Thou comest into thy kingdom.*' For
that ' *Remember me* ' is no mere counterpart of Joseph's
petition to the chief butler of Pharaoh (Gen. xl. 14 ; cf.
Ecclus. xxxvii. 6), but is itself a prayer, even as the
prayers of the Jews constantly clothed themselves in this
same form (Nehem. xiii. 14, 22, 31, and often in the
Psalms ; for another kind of remembrance see Rev. xvi.
19). But seeing that it was now at length abundantly
evident that Christ's kingdom was not here, nor on this
side of the grave, it must have been plainly in the glory
of some kingdom to be revealed hereafter that he desired,
through Christ's remembrance of him, a part.

Leo the Great (*Serm.* 51) : Quæ istam fidem exhortatio persuasit ? quæ
doctrina imbuit ? quis prædicator accendit ? Non viderat prius acta miracula ; cessaverat tunc languentium curatio, cæcorum illuminatio, vivificatio
mortuorum ; ea ipsa quæ mox erant gerenda non aderant ; et tamen Dominum
confitetur et Regem, quem videt supplicii sui esse consortem.

The words themselves of his prayer should not stand exactly as in the English Version they do. Our Translators have on various occasions failed to mark the distinction between the prepositions equivalent in the Greek to our ' into ' and 'in ; ' [1] seldom however incurring thereby so grave a loss as here. It is not, ' *when Thou comest into thy kingdom,*' as though Christ's kingdom could even in thought be contemplated as apart from Himself ; but, ' *when Thou comest in thy kingdom,*'—the words are correctly rendered at Matt. xvi. 28—' when Thou shalt appear as a king with all thy royalties around Thee and about Thee, the angels, ten thousand times ten thousand, with Thee, and Thyself the centre of all ' (Dan. vii. 10 ; Zech. xiv. 5 ; Matt. xxiv. 31 ; xxv. 31 ; 2 Thess. i. 7 ; Jude 14 ; Rev. xix. 14). Christ does not and cannot come *into* his kingdom ; He comes *in* it and with it, brings his kingdom with Him, and where He is, there is his kingdom as well.[2] He who could utter this petition had taken in what Pilate could not take in, that this Man was a King, and that He would one day return to establish his kingdom upon earth.[3]

---

[1] Thus εἰς has not its proper meaning, Rom. v. 5 ; nor ἐν, Rom. ii. 5 ; v. 21. On this, which is a fault common to many Versions of the New Testament, see Winer, *Gramm.* § liv. 4, 5, 6.

[2] Maldonatus forsakes his Vulgate, which, anticipating the error of our Version and of so many other, has here, in regnum tuum ; but he : ἐν τῇ βασιλείᾳ σου, in regno tuo. Itaque non est sensus, Cum veneris ad regnandum, sed, Cum veneris, jam regnans ; cum veneris, non ad acquirendum regnum, sed regno jam acquisito, quemadmodum venturus ad judicium est.

[3] In the *Evangelium Nicodemi* (pars 2ᵃ, c. 10) the petition put into the mouth of this penitent, though substantially the same, is formally different. It is as follows : Κύριε, ὅτε [ὅταν ?] βασιλεύσεις, μή μου ἐπιλάθῃ. As that apocryphal gospel dates probably as early as the second century, it is just possible that the difference here may, as Tischendorf (*Evangelia Apocrypha*, p. lxix.) suggests, represent another tradition of the words (verba latronis ita discedunt a Lucæ textu, ut ex aliâ veterrimâ traditione fluxisse videantur) ; but far more probably we have here nothing more than a

The reply of our Lord is a glorious example of what we may not unfitly call the prodigalities of the kingdom of heaven, of the answers to prayer, infinitely larger and more liberal than the suppliant in the boldest ventures of faith had dared to suggest. In two points the granting of this suppliant's petition immeasurably transcends the petition itself. All which he had been bold to ask, was that he might be remembered of the Lord. But one may remember the absent, may do them good at a distance, and keeping them at distance still. This to have done would have fulfilled the measure of all which he had desired. But for him, the first-fruits of the cross, the first who should set his seal to that word of the prophecy, ' I, if I be lifted up, will draw all men unto Me,' for him Christ has better than remembrance in store; far better than this—' *thou shalt be with Me.*'

And not this only; he shall be with Him on that very day.[1] Christ's ' *to-day*,' besides containing an announcement of his own departure out of this world within the limits of that day, contains also a pledge and promise for this poor pardoned sinner, that he too should find speedy release from all his agonies — a release indeed far speedier than according to common probabilities he might have looked for. Crucifixion, with all its sufferings, was so little mortal, that persons taken down from

not perfectly accurate reminiscence of the words as they stand in St. Luke.

[1] This is often urged by Augustine; thus *Serm.* 232: Quid ei dixerit Dominus audiamus: Amen, dico tibi, hodie mecum eris in Paradiso. Tu differs te; ego agnosco te; . . . invasisti in regnum cælorum; vim fecisti, credidisti, rapuisti. Non te differo; tantæ fidei hodie reddo quod debeo. Compare *Serm.* 327. 2. Instead of the rich and pregnant brevity of that prayer and this answer to that prayer, the *Narratio Josephi* (Tischendorf, *Evangelia Apocrypha*, p. 442) puts a speech of twenty lines into the mouth of the penitent, and one somewhat longer into that of our Lord.

their cross have been known to recover. Josephus tells us that at the siege of Jerusalem he recognized three of his friends among the multitude of those whom 'The Delight of the human race' had caused to be affixed to their crosses. Having begged and obtained their lives, he caused them to be duly cared for, and one of them recovered. In the lingering torture of this punishment the seats of life were so little assailed, that it was by no means uncommon for criminals to expire at length of mere hunger on their cross; while, besides the breaking of the legs, by which the death of these two was hastened, there were various other methods for accelerating, when this was thought desirable, the fatal close. They were sometimes suffocated by the smoke of fires lighted below, or were torn in pieces by wild beasts. But for him within a few brief hours, before that day had ended, it should be well. He should be at rest, and more than this—in Paradise and joy. The coming of Christ in his kingdom might very well be a remote contingency, as we know in fact that it was. In all likelihood this petitioner more or less looked onward to it as such. But it is no boon in some far off future which the Lord will bestow upon him; that very day he shall taste the sweetness of it: ' *To-day shalt thou be with Me in Paradise.*'[1]

We must not, however, dismiss without further notice a word on which so much has been written, a promise the form of which in times past has perplexed not a few. As many, indeed, as assume ' *Paradise* ' to be equivalent to heaven, and, in fact, identical with the kingdom of

---

[1] The promise of these words can hardly fail to remind us of another ' Thou shalt be with me,' Samuel's to Saul (1 Sam. xxviii. 19); that also in Sheol, in the world of spirits; but that announcement how unlike to this; as full of fear and terror as this is of hope and joy.

glory, cannot fail to find a difficulty here, inasmuch as Christ Himself was not on that day in heaven, but in Hades ; and these suggest various ways of escaping from this perplexity; which, however, is of their own creating. A not unfrequent one is the separation of ' *to-day* ' from the words which follow, with the joining of it to those which precede : ' *Verily, I say unto thee to-day, thou shalt be with Me in Paradise.*'[1] Theophylact says of those who offer this explanation, that they ' do violence to the words ; '[2] a judgment in which most will concur.[3] By others, who in like manner make Paradise equivalent to heaven, or at least fail to see its identity with Hades, or rather with the more blessed half of Hades, it is said that however his human soul was that day in this latter place, yet, according to his divine nature everywhere present, He was in Paradise,—that is, as they understand it, in heaven (cf. John iii. 13).

This is the usual interpretation in the early Church,[4]

---

[1] In the *Evangelium Nicodemi*, 26, the words are actually transposed, and stand thus, σήμερον λέγω σοι, μετ᾽ ἐμοῦ κ.τ.λ.

[2] Ἐκβιάζονται τὸ ῥῆμα.

[3] The first I know who makes mention of this way of escape from a difficulty, which after all is imaginary, is Hesychius, a presbyter of Jerusalem, who probably wrote in the fifth century (*Quæst.* 47) : πῶς ἡ ὑπόσχεσις τοῦ Κυρίου πρὸς τὸν λῃστὴν πεπλήρωται, ὅτι σήμερον μετ᾽ ἐμοῦ ἔσῃ ἐν τῷ παραδείσῳ ; Μετὰ γὰρ τὸν σταυρὸν ὁ Χριστὸς εἰς "Αιδου ἐπὶ τῇ ἐλευθερίᾳ τῶν νεκρῶν παραγίνεται. ἔδει δὲ καὶ τὸν λῃστὴν [scil. παραγίνεσθαι εἰς "Αιδου], ὑπεύθυνον ὄντα τῷ νόμῳ τῆς φύσεως. He goes on to state, but does not approve of, this solution : τινὲς μὲν οὕτως ἀναγινώσκουσιν, 'Αμὴν λέγω σοι σήμερον· εἶτα ἐπιφέρουσιν, ὅτι μετ᾽ ἐμοῦ ἔσῃ ἐν τῷ παραδείσῳ.

[4] Thus Augustine (*Ep. ad Dardanum*, 187) ; and this, although he has excellently well prepared the way for the right explanation by the distinction which he draws between Paradise, the waiting place of happy spirits, and heaven, or the kingdom of glory (restat igitur ut in inferno intelligatur esse paradisus, ubi erat illo die futurus esse secundum humanam animam Christus). This, however, he suggests only to abandon it again, and to take refuge in the omnipresence of Christ, who according to his divine nature

and in the medieval,[1] and generally in the modern Roman Catholic.[2] But it is not universal. Severus, the great leader of the Monophysites, has seen his way perfectly here ;[3] the only drawback to his exposition of this passage being that he makes Paradise here absolutely, and, so to speak, locally, identical with the Garden of innocence of our first parents; the truth being that in the evolution of theology in the later Jewish schools that Garden had lent a name to the happy place where the souls of the faithful, released from the burden of the flesh, are waiting their perfect consummation and bliss; therefore called often in old German, 'Wartehimmel,' or waiting-heaven; and that it is of this Paradise our Lord is speaking.

was everywhere, and therefore that day in Paradise = heaven. For similar explanations of the Greek Fathers see Suicer, *Thes.* s. v. λῃστής.

[1] Anselm in one of his deeply pathetic *Orationes* (the 42nd) expresses himself thus: Et quid hoc est, o rex desiderabilis? Tu clavis affligeris, et paradisum promittis. Tu pendes in ligno, et latroni dicis, Hodie mecum eris in paradiso! Et, o desiderium animarum, ubi est paradisus, quia dicis latroni, Hodie mecum eris in paradiso? An paradisus tecum est, et ubi tu vis, paradisus est? An tu indubitanter paradisus es, quia tam confidenter promittis, Hodie mecum eris in paradiso? Credo, Domine, credo certe quod ubi tu vis, et ubi tu es, ibi paradisus est; et esse tecum, hoc est esse in paradiso. Compare Aquinas, *Sum. Theol.* 3ª, 52. 4.

[2] Corn. a Lapide: Certum enim est Christum cum latrone die illo quo obiit non ascendisse in cælum, sed descendisse ad limbum patrum; ibique eis visionem suæ divinitatis impertivisse, itaque eos beâsse; quare tunc Christus eorum sortes mutavit; fecit enim ut limbus esset paradisus, ut inferi essent superi, ut infernus esset cælum. Ubi enim est Christus, ibi est paradisus; ubi est visio Dei et beatitudo, ibi est cælum.

[3] Valuable fragments of his *Commentary on St. Luke* are preserved in Cramer's *Catena*. A few words of his on this matter I will quote: τὸ δὲ ἀληθὲς τῆς ἐξηγήσεως, τοῦτό ἐστι· τὰ ἐπηγγελμένα ἡμῖν ἀγαθὰ βασιλεία ἐστὶν οὐρανῶν, οὐχὶ ἡ εἰς τὸν παράδεισον εἴσοδος, ἢ ἡ ἐπάνοδος. ἀλλ' ἴσως ἐρεῖ τις ὡς ταὐτόν ἐστιν ἡ βασιλεία τῶν οὐρανῶν καὶ ὁ παράδεισος, δύο προσηγοριῶν οὐσῶν περὶ ἓν πρᾶγμα τὸ ὑποκείμενον. ἀλλ' ἡ τῶν ἱερῶν γραμμάτων διδασκαλία δείκνυσιν ὡς οὐ ταὐτὸν ἐστιν, ἀλλ' ἑκατέρου πολὺ τὸ διάφορον. Having vindicated the higher dignity of the βασιλεία τῶν οὐρανῶν, he proceeds: ἡ δὲ ἐργασία τοῦ παραδείσου βαναυσός τις οὐκ ἦν, ἀλλ' εἶχε λογικὴν εὐφροσύνην ἀναμεμιγμένην καὶ ἐννοιῶν θείων ἀπόλαυσιν. Ὥστε ὁ λῃστὴς τοῦ μὲν παραδείσου τετύχηκεν·

Jeremy Taylor[1] has traced excellently well the history of the word, and what upon his lips it signified now : ' Our blessed Saviour told the converted thief that he should "that day be with Him in Paradise." Now without peradventure He spake so as He was to be understood, meaning by " Paradise " that which the schools and pulpits of the Rabbies did usually speak of it. By " Paradise " till the time of Esdras it is certain the Jews only meant that blessed garden in which God once placed Adam and Eve ; but in the time of Esdras, and so downward, when they spake distinctly of things to happen after this life, and began to signify their new discoveries and modern philosophy by names, they called the state of souls expecting the resurrection of their bodies by the name of Gan Eden, the garden of Eden. . . . It is therefore more than probable that when the converted thief heard our blessed Saviour speak of Paradise, or Gan Eden, he who was a Jew and heard that on that day he should be there, understood the meaning to be that he should be there where all the good Jews did believe the souls of Abraham, Isaac, and Jacob to be placed.'

This is the only occasion during the days of his flesh on which (so far at least as our records reach), Paradise was made mention of by our Lord. Once too He mentions it in his glory (Rev. ii. 7), and once it is on the lips of his chief apostle (2 Cor. xii. 4). These are the only times that it occurs in the New Testament. Hanging on the

τὰ δὲ ἐν ἐλπίσι τῆς βασιλείας τῶν οὐρανῶν μετὰ τῶν ἀπ' αἰῶνος δικαίων οὐκ ἐκεμίσατο, τοῦ Θεοῦ περὶ ἡμῶν κρεῖττόν τι προβλεψαμένου, ἵνα μὴ χωρὶς ἡμῶν τελειωθῶσι.

[1] *A Funeral Sermon on Sir George Dalstone.* For much which is interesting on Paradise, and on the successive meanings attached to the word, see Thilo, *Codex Apocryphus*; and an article, *Ueber die biblische Vorstellung vom Paradiese* in Illgen's *Zeitschrift für die Histor. Theol.* vol. vi. p. 145.

accursed tree his thoughts may well have travelled back to another tree, even the tree of life, standing in the Paradise of God;[1] in that Paradise, which by all this travail and sore agony He was at this instant winning back for the children of men, quenching in his own blood that fiery flaming sword which, since the sin and sentence of Adam, had kept it against them; even as He was opening for them the gates of another Paradise, and, as a Stronger, wresting from the strong one the keys of death and of hell (Rev. i. 18).

I will bring this *Study* to a close with one or two practical observations. There is sometimes a tendency to regard the grace vouchsafed to this penitent as exceptional, as not to be brought within the ordinary laws of God's dealings with the children of men. We may sometimes hear it said, that as that moment when the Son of God hung upon the cross was a moment unlike every other in the moral and spiritual history of the world, so there were graces vouchsafed then, unlike those of any other moment, larger, freer, more marvellous; such as were proper to that time and no other; the gates of mercy being, so to speak, thrown open more widely than at other times; and that therefore no conclusions can be drawn from what then found place as to what will find place when events have returned to their more ordinary course. This is sometimes urged, and chiefly out of a desire to withdraw the temptation to a deferred and late repentance, which the acceptance of this penitent at the closing moment of his life might else seem to hold out to others. I confess that even the desire to avert such an abuse,

---

[1] Bengel: *In paradiso*; in quo feliciores arbores quam in Golgatha; cum immortalitate, Rev. ii. 7.

cannot persuade me to accept this explanation of the grace which he obtained. The laws of God's kingdom, the conditions under which grace may be obtained, are unchangeable. This man was accepted and forgiven exactly on the same grounds as those on which any other will find pardon and acceptance, because he repented, and believed, and obeyed. Time does not exist for God; and if only this repentance, faith, and obedience of his were genuine, whether they were spread over the forty or fifty years to which his life in the natural course of things might have been prolonged, or concentrated into the few hours upon the cross which he actually did survive, this made and could make no difference in God's sight. I have said, 'if only these were genuine,' which in the present instance we know that certainly they were; for this is the fatal danger of all repentance postponed to the last, and thus withdrawn from all trial and proof, that the man, little as he may guess this, may be deceiving himself; that in all likelihood his repentance is *not* genuine, is *not* sincere; that almost certainly it is not so, when it has been deferred on so mean a speculation as this, of giving to God the least and obtaining from Him the most, grinding the corn of life, and, according to the old proverb, giving the flour to the devil, and only the bran to God. It is by the pressing of this, the almost universal self-delusion of death-bed repentances, that we must rescue this Scripture from dangerous abuse, from proving a temptation and a snare, not by excepting the dealing of God with this man from the category of his usual dealings in the kingdom of his grace and power.

One word more. We have admired, and with abun

dant reason, the faith of the poor penitent, who could believe, even in such an hour as that was, in the royalties of Christ, that the title set in bitter mockery over his head, spake nothing more than the truth, that He *was* a king, and would yet come in his kingdom, and that it would be well with them who should then be remembered of Him. But let us not finally take leave of this history without reverently admiring also *his* faith to whom this prayer was addressed, his confidence, not to be shaken by all which was happening round Him, which was finding place within Him, in his divine Sonship; his, who could believe that, crucified through weakness, He was yet Lord over all, that all things had been delivered into his hands by his Father, that He could grant to this suppliant for his grace all which he asked, and much more than he asked; who dispensed as confidently his favours from that cross of shame as the kings of the earth dispense theirs from their thrones of glory; who in this promise claimed and avouched all worlds as his own. Not when the victory had been already won, and He had been declared to be the Son of God with power by the Resurrection from the dead (Rom. i. 4), did He say to the beloved apostle, ' I am He that liveth, and was dead; and, behold, I am alive for evermore, Amen; and have the keys of death and of hell ' (Rev. i. 18), with a calmer and more majestic confidence than to this poor suppliant man He declares in the hour of his own agony, ' *To-day shalt thou be with Me in Paradise.*' [1] Truly this is the Lord

---

[1] Augustine (*Serm.* 285): Ita factæ sunt tres cruces, tres caussæ. Unus latronum Christo insultabat; alter sua mala confessus Christi se misericordiæ commendabat. Crux Christi in medio non fuit supplicium, sed tribunal; de cruce quippe insultantem damnavit, credentem liberavit. Timete, insultantes; gaudete, credentes. Hoc faciet in claritate, quod fecit in humilitate.

of life; and then, when He thus spake, was gloriously fulfilled that which so many of the early Fathers thought they found written as a prophecy of the triumphs of the cross in the 96th Psalm, and which is equally true whether there fore-announced or not, Regnavit a ligno Deus.

16. *CHRIST AND THE TWO DISCIPLES ON THE WAY TO EMMAUS*

Mark xvi. 12, 13; Luke xxiv. 13-35.

WE have a slight hint of this beautiful little history, and indeed the history itself, but in barest outline, at Mark xvi. 12. He gives there very much such a summary abridgement of it as he gives of the Temptation elsewhere (i. 12, 13). For the breadth and fulness of detail, which render this one of the most interesting records of the Great Forty Days, we are altogether indebted to St. Luke.

The Resurrection had taken place already; but the disciples had refused to credit it. The Sun of Righteousness, which seemed to have set for ever, had again risen with healing on his wings; but the disciples, not without grave fault of their own, are walking on in darkness still, in a darkness which in some sort they have made for themselves. So it fares with these two, of whom we here read : ' *And behold, two of them went that same day to a village called Emmaus, which was from Jerusalem about threescore furlongs.*' The name of one of these favoured wayfarers we learn a little further on. It was Cleopas (ver. 18), who must not be identified with the Cleopas of John xix. 25.[1] Who the other might be we are not told.

---

[1] This Κλεόπας is short for Κλεόπατρος, while that (Κλωπᾶς) is an Aramaic name.

Apostle he certainly was not; and those who suggest
Bartholomew or James cannot reconcile this with the
fact that the two report the mysterious interview to the
Eleven (ver. 23), could not therefore themselves belong to
the Eleven.   Neither is it at all likely that the unnamed
disciple was St. Luke himself; for this, again, seems
scarcely reconcilable with the announcement of the Evangelist that the account which he gives in his Gospel was
delivered to him by those who were 'eyewitnesses,' as
well as 'ministers of the word' (i. 2); herein implicitly
affirming that such 'eyewitness' he had not himself been,
that he had not himself beheld, as these two beheld, the
risen Lord.   Jerome and others suppose that they may
both have been of the Seventy ; which is probable enough ;
but we cannot affirm it with any certainty.   The village
of Emmaus, north of Jerusalem, and mentioned by Josephus,[1] to which they were journeying, must not be confounded, as it has often been, with another Emmaus in
the plain of Judæa, and not ' *threescore furlongs*,' or something about seven miles, from Jerusalem, but not less
than twenty from the capital city.   All modern attempts
to discover the site of this village have been unsuccessful.

' *And they talked together of all these things which had
happened.   And it came to pass that, while they communed
together and reasoned, Jesus Himself drew near, and went
with them.   But their eyes were holden, that they should
not know Him* ' (cf. John xx. 14; xxi. 4).   While St.
Mark seems to lay the cause of the non-recognition of
the Lord on the part of his disciples to his changed appearance (' *after that He appeared in another form unto*

---

[1] *B. J.* vii. 6. 6. See on Emmaus, Keim, *Jesu von Nazara*, vol. iii.
p. 555.

two of them'), St. Luke finds it rather in their ' *holden eyes.*'[1] ' *And He said unto them, What manner of communications are these that ye have one to another, as ye walk, and are sad?*'[2] More than one word here implies that the two disciples were in earnest debate; not unduly striving nor contending; but still regarding from different points of view, and each urging upon the other his own interpretation of, that stupendous event, of which they had three days since been the witnesses. To them thus earnestly debating, and allowing this earnestness to shew itself in their outward gesture and mien, the Lord joined Himself, in guise the most unpretending, as a fellow-traveller on the same road with themselves; but at the same time as one himself interested in the matter which could interest them so strongly, and moved no less by the settled sadness of their countenances; and who out of no idle curiosity would fain learn, if this might be permitted, what it was that stirred and saddened them so much.

The two disciples, as I think we may gather from their reply, were not perfectly pleased to be accosted, and interrupted in their confidential discourse with one another,

---

[1] The two statements are excellently reconciled by St. Augustine (*Serm.* 239. 2) : Alia enim effigies visa est, retentis oculis non apertis.

[2] ' *And are sad*' is hardly an adequate rendering of καί ἰστε σκυθρωποί, though it might be difficult to improve it. Σκυθρωπός, expressing the downcast look of a settled grief, pain, or displeasure, and occurring in the New Testament only here and at Matt. vi. 16 (where Basil the Great exchanges it well with στυγνάζων), and in the Old at Gen. xl. 7; Dan. i. 10; Ecclus. xxv. 23, from σκυθρός (and that from σκύζομαι) and ὤψ, would be better expressed by ' dreary,' if only this had not little by little drifted away in meaning from the ' traurig,' with which it is identical, and which exactly represents the force of σκυθρωπός. For proof of this partial change in the meaning of ' dreary,' see in Richardson's *English Dictionary* the quotation from Gower; and another passage in Richard of Hampole's *Pricke of Conscience* :

'Now es a man light, now es he hevy,
Now es he blithe, now es he *drery*.'

by one who seemed to have no right to meddle with the sacredness of their sorrow. They cannot forbear expressing their surprise that such a question should have been put to them : '*And the one of them, whose name was Cleopas, answering said unto Him, Art thou only a stranger at Jerusalem, and hast not known the things which are come to pass there in these days?*' The English Version is not here perfectly satisfactory. It seems to attribute the questioner's ignorance of what must be the cause of their grief to his being '*a stranger*' or sojourner at Jerusalem. But, not to say that such an event as the rejection and crucifixion of one who claimed to be the Messiah must have been just as well known to the pilgrims at the feast as to the actual dwellers of Jerusalem, the words will not bear this meaning. They are not without a certain difficulty; but on the whole it will be best and simplest to render the first clause in the sentence thus, '*Dost thou sojourn alone at Jerusalem?*' 'Dwellest thou,' that is, 'in solitude there, apart from the busy concourse of men, and thus so withdrawn from acquaintance with all which is passing in the city, that no tidings have reached thee of the mighty and marvellous events which within the last few days have befallen?' The disciples, in the all-absorbing interest which these events have for them, take for granted that, if only known, they must have the same for every other; and they have, moreover, been so blown abroad, that nothing but an absolute isolation from all company with his fellow-men can have hindered their questioner from having knowledge of them.[1]

---

[1] Beza: Tu solus commoraris Hierosolymis? with a shifting of the emphasis from παροικεῖς to μόνος. All which could be urged against this rendering is that παροικεῖς thus fails to obtain its full force, and is too much

The Lord's answer, ' *What things?* ' is exactly adapted to draw from the disciples a further communication. Had He replied that He knew, this would naturally have prevented Cleopas from entering further into a matter already familiar to his interrogator; and, of course, He could not answer that He did not know. His question serves the purpose for which it was intended : ' *And they said unto Him, Concerning Jesus of Nazareth, which was a prophet mighty in deed and word before God and all the people* ' (cf. Acts vii. 22). From this answer of theirs it is evident that the mystery of Christ's divine nature was hidden from them as yet ; or if at any time they had caught glimpses of it, these now were completely obscured by the thick shadows which during the last days had closed around their Lord. Jesus was to them ' *a prophet,*' and, as we presently see, *the* prophet, He that ' *should have redeemed Israel,*' the Messiah therefore ; but the Jewish anticipations of a Messiah (and they had not lifted themselves above these), did not involve more than glorious human prerogatives. That Messiah should come, and that God should come, they expected both ; but that both promises should be fulfilled in one and the same person, that these two stars of hope, which had lighted Israel through long ages of gloom, should in the actual fulfilment blend and become a single star, this was a mystery hidden, we may say, or almost hidden, from prophets and kings, from those who most waited for the consolation of Israel.

They go on to complain of the reception which,

rendered as though it were κατοικεῖς : but the other explanations, such as are offered by Theophylact, Castalio (quoted by Beza), Meyer, and others, seem to me either absolutely untenable, or encumbered with far more serious difficulties than is this.

notwithstanding all these' glorious manifestations of his power both in word and work, He had found from the spiritual chiefs of the people : '*and how the Chief Priests and our rulers delivered Him to be condemned to death, and have crucified Him. But we trusted*' (they speak of it as a trust which they must now renounce, which indeed they *have* renounced), '*that it had been He which should have redeemed Israel.*'[1] To say, as some do, that this redemption which they looked for at the hands of the Messiah was merely a deliverance from the yoke of their worldly oppressors, is certainly a mistake. It may have been thus with many; but there were always those who understood that the deliverance must reach much deeper than this ; that to be a redemption worth the name, it must be a redemption from sin, from the bondage of unruly appetites and inordinate desires. It was indeed true that this deliverance would necessarily, in God's good providence, have drawn after it that other deliverance ; that if Israel had turned to God, and welcomed his Anointed, the yoke of its Roman lords would, in one way or another, have soon been broken from its neck ; for this bondage was but an echo of the other ; and thus the faithful in Israel may very possibly have blended, in all likelihood did blend, the two deliverances into one ; but still this outward redemption was not in their thoughts the beginning, still less was it the whole, of the redemption. In the prophecy of the father of the Baptist the

---

[1] Augustine (*Serm.* 235. § 2): Quando enim cum illis fuerat ante passionem, omnia prædixerat, passurum se fuisse, moriturum, tertio die resurrecturum ; omnia prædixerat; sed mors illius, illorum oblivio fuit. Sic perturbati sunt, quando eum viderunt in ligno pendentem, ut obliviscerentur docentem, non exspectarent resurgentem, nec tenerent promittentem. Nos, inquiunt, sperabamus quia ipse erat redemturus Israël. O discipuli, sperabatis? ergo jam non speratis.

two redemptions, from the yoke of evil and from the yoke of their foreign oppressors, are wonderfully blended together. He whom God shall raise up, a horn of salvation for his people, shall deliver them from their enemies; but this, that they may serve Him in righteousness and true holiness all the days of their life (Luke i. 68–79; cf. John viii. 31–36).

They go on: ' *And beside all this,*' in addition to that cruel death inflicted on Him by our rulers, and sufficiently explaining the sadness which thou hast noted in us, ' *to-day is the third day since these things were done.* We might have had some glimpses of hope up to this present time, seeing that while He was alive, He more than once uttered mysterious words not merely about his own death, words which we have found only too true, but also about a triumphant reversal of that doom of death, mysterious words about what should happen on the third day after his death; but this day has arrived, and is unmarked by any change.' How much unbelief is there here. The third day has come, but it has not gone; and how could they be sure that He had not already made good his words? indeed, there was much to render it likely that He had. Their own words which follow imply as much: ' *Yea, and certain women also of our company made us astonished, which were early at the sepulchre. And when they found not his body, they came, saying, that they had also seen a vision of angels, which said that He was alive*' (ver. 1–10; John xx. 1, 2). The hesitating, doubting disciples will not confidently affirm of this that it was a mere subjective imagination of these women; as little pledge themselves to its objective reality. They speak of it therefore as ' *a vision of angels,*' leaving this matter undecided. They go on to tell of the visit of Peter and John to the sepulchre; ' *and certain of them which were with us went to the sepulchre, and found it even so as the women had said.*' But, having thus stated all which gave them warrant for hope, they yet leave off with the mournful, desponding words—' *but Him they saw not*' (cf. ver. 12 ; John xx. 3–10).

They have poured out all their hearts before Him. It is now his turn to speak. He still, indeed, preserves his incognito; their eyes are holden as at the first, so that they still see in Him no more than the sympathizing stranger, who has joined himself to them in the way. Much, no doubt, they must have wondered when they found in Him a scribe instructed to the kingdom ; one who took the part of their former hopes against their present fears; one whose very rebukes, earnest as they were, must have been welcome; for it was their despair which He rebuked ; and just so far as they acknowledged those rebukes to be just, their despair must have given place to hope, their sorrow have been turned into joy. ' *And He said unto them, O fools, and slow of heart to believe all that the prophets have spoken.*' Some Scripture they had believed, as much as fell in with their pre-conceived notions, prejudices, and opinions ; which is so often the way with us all ; but not ' *all that the prophets had spoken.*' Man's word, and woman's word, and angels' words, they had paid more or less heed to all these ; but God's word, that word which liveth and abideth for ever, they had not built and established themselves on it. Of that word they had not enquired, nor sought to learn from it how it should fare with the Christ of God ; else they would have discovered that the very things over which they were mourning, as the defeat and discomfiture of all their high-raised expectations, had long ago, even from the beginning, been fore-announced and declared needful preliminaries to his entrance into his glory. They would there have learned that these sufferings and this death, so far from giving the lie to their Lord's pretensions as the Christ, were actually laid down in Scripture as things without the endurance of which the true signs of the Messiah would have been wanting in Him ; that only through the vestibule of death was it appointed for Him to pass into the palace of life : ' *Ought not Christ to have suffered these things, and to enter into his glory* ' (cf. Acts xvii. 2, 3) ? They hitherto had spoken of Christ in a roundabout manner, as ' *He that should have redeemed Israel*' (ver. 21) ; but the Lord at once employs this word which stood at the centre of all Jewish hopes. They err who conclude from these words that Christ had entered into his glory already ; He did not do this till his Ascension, and this which He is speaking now is not history, but doctrine. Did not the Scripture announce a suffering Messiah before a reigning and glorious One ?

' *And beginning at Moses and all the prophets, He expounded unto them in all the Scriptures the things concerning Himself*' (cf. ver. 44 ; John i. 45 ; Acts xxvi. 22, 23 ; 1 Pet. i. 11). What, we may reverently enquire, were the passages to which the great Prophet of the New Covenant mainly referred, as having in Himself been fulfilled ? And first, what prophecies of a suffering Messiah did He recognize and allow, claiming in the books of Moses for his own ? He began, as we can hardly doubt, with the *protevangelium*. The Seed of the woman, who should bruise the serpent's head, or, in other words, inflict on him a wound which should be deadly, was not Himself to escape unscathed altogether; this same serpent should bruise his heel (Gen. iii. 15). And then there were the types, claimed by the Lord in the days of his flesh, or by those who wrote concerning Him, as fulfilled in Him ; the brazen serpent (Num. xxi. 9 ; John iii. 14 ; Wisd. xvi. 6) ; the Paschal Lamb (Exod. xii. 46 ; John xix. 36) ; and as the types, so also the typical persons; Joseph, who from the lowest humiliation of the pit and the dungeon passed to the highest place of dignity and honour, even to the right hand of the throne; David, who suffered so much and so long from the persecutions of Saul—these, with many more. And when the august Interpreter of the things in Scripture concerning Himself reached the prophets, it can be little doubtful that the fifty-third chapter of Isaiah was the central prophecy which He expounded. Around this there would be grouped the great prophetical Psalms of the Crucifixion—the Psalms are not specially referred to here, but at ver. 44[1]—as eminently the twenty-second, claimed by the Lord upon his cross (Matt. xxvii. 46 ; cf. Mark xv. 24), and the fortieth, claimed in like manner for Him by his apostle (Heb. x. 5) ; then further Daniel ix. 26 ; and the book of the prophet Jonah ; while Zechariah would prove eminently rich in prophetic glimpses of all which had just on Calvary been fulfilled (xii. 10 ; xiii. 7). These disciples had assumed that Jesus of Nazareth could not be the Christ, *because* He had suffered these things ; the Lord shews them from

---

[1] On the threefold division of the books of the Old Covenant, the Law, the Prophets, and the Psalms, this last being sometimes designated as τὰ ἄλλα βιβλία or τὰ λοιπὰ τῶν βιβλίων, or τὰ γραφεῖα or τὰ ἁγιόγραφα, see Professor Lightfoot, *The First Epistle of Clement to the Corinthians*, § 28.

all Scripture that He could not be the Christ, *unless* He had suffered these things.

And now, while He was still engaged in opening to them the Scriptures, ' *they drew nigh unto the village, whither they went ; and He made as though He would have gone further ;* ' not, that is, pretended, but actually would have gone further, unless they had detained Him ; by thus offering to proceed, proving them, whether his words had taken any mighty hold upon them or not ; and whether there was any desire upon their part for further communion with Him (cf. Mark vi. 48). It was seen that there was so. Much they had heard, yet they evidently desired to hear still more. ' *But they constrained Him, saying, Abide with us ; for it is toward evening, and the day is far spent. And He went in to tarry with them* ' —to be their guest now, as two of their number at the outset of his ministry had been his (John i. 39).

' *And it came to pass, as He sat at meat with them, He took bread, and blessed it, and brake, and gave to them.* ' He, in some sort the guest, assumes at once the place of the host, and, as on other occasions (Matt. xiv. 19 ; xv. 36 ; xxvi. 26), the prerogatives of the householder or goodman of the house, to whom this blessing and giving of thanks of right belonged. ' *And their eyes were opened, and they knew Him ; and He vanished out of their sight.* ' He was known to them, as they themselves report to the Eleven, ' *in breaking of bread* ' (ver. 35). This might seem to imply that there was something in the act of breaking the bread by which they recognized at last with whom they had to do. Perhaps, as has been suggested, and as may be seen in some old pictures, the stigmata, the marks of the wounds in the hands, through this action of his became visible.   At the same time the words, ' *their eyes were opened,*' going before ' *they knew Him,*' and put evidently as the condition of their knowing, imply that it was not a mere natural conclusion which they drew from something which they saw Him do, but a supernatural enlightenment, a ceasing of the condition indicated at ver. 16, where it is said, ' *their eyes were holden.*'   But what was there, it may be asked, in this ' *breaking of bread*' by which they knew Him ?   Some answer that this was a celebration of the Holy Eucharist,[1] and that they recognized the form of consecrating words.   But, in the first place, certainly these two were not present at the Institution of the Holy Eucharist, for only apostles, which these are not, were there.   And then, in the second place, it is an entirely gratuitous assumption that this was an Eucharistic celebration.   Roman Catholics are fond of asserting that it was so, thus to find warrant and authority for reception under one kind, only bread being mentioned here. The blessing of the bread can of itself prove nothing.   It quite true that this is mentioned, and that it constituted an essential part of the Eucharistic celebration (Mark xiv. 22); but as at other times also He blessed the bread (Mark vi. 41), no argument can be drawn from hence ; and for us the absence of one of the constituent elements of this sacrament may well be decisive that no such sacrament was here.   The words can scarcely mean more than that at that solemn moment their Lord revealed to them who He was.   The manner of his disappearance, like that of all his comings and goings after the Resurrection, is

[1] Thus Augustine (*Serm.* 239): In panis fractione cognoscitur, quia ibi percipitur, ubi vita æterna percipitur.   For reasons against any such conclusion see Scudamore, *Notitia Eucharistica*, p. 10.

mysterious (John xx. 19, 26), and quite unlike anything which had found place before. His body, it is evident, was not any longer submitted to the same laws as those to which ours are submitted now, and to which his own had been hitherto submitted.

'*And they said one to another, Did not our heart burn within us, while He talked with us by the way, and while He opened to us the Scriptures?*' They wonder that this had not enabled them long since to guess who it was that had thus been speaking with them. The nearest parallel to this of the heart burning within them may be found in the words of the Psalmist, '*While I was musing, the fire burned; then spake I with my tongue*' (Ps. xxxix. 3; compare Jer. xx. 9). With such tidings to tell, they do not tarry any longer at Emmaus. '*They rose up the same hour, and returned to Jerusalem, and found the Eleven gathered together, and them that were with them.*' Yet if they imagined that they were the first to bring the glad tidings, in this they were disappointed—if disappointment it could be called; they did but contribute another stream to swell the great flood-tide of joy, which every moment was rising higher and higher. They found the Eleven, and them that were with them, able to answer good tidings with good; nay, as it would seem, preventing their good tidings with those which they had themselves to tell, with evidence coming in from one quarter and another, and now from the very chief among themselves, that the barriers of the grave had indeed been broken, that their Lord was in truth that Conqueror of death, that Prince of life, which in their unbelieving ears He had proclaimed Himself to be: '*The Lord is risen indeed, and hath appeared to Simon*' (cf. 1 Cor. xv. 5). And yet, anticipated though their tidings had been, every confirmation of a fact so marvellous, so far transcending all experience and all hope, must have been welcome ; welcome therefore their confirmation of it, as they threw their symbol into the common stock of hope ripening now into glorious certainty, as ' *they told what things were done in the way, and how He was known of them in breaking of bread.*' [1]

---

[1] This Scripture, besides its literal and historic meaning, may possibly have a symbolic meaning as well. Such Hugh of St. Victor has traced in it (*Miscel.* i. 100) : Jesus in viâ ambulantibus faciem suam abscondit, ostensurus eam in patriâ. Propterea in fine viæ cum discumbere cœpissent, fregit Jesus panem ut interiora ejus patescerent, et ibi eum agnoverunt, quia post vitæ hujus cursum in regno cælorum cum Abraham et Isaac et Jacob discumbentes, et super mensam ejus edentes et bibentes in æterno convivio, Jesu claritatem videbunt. Nunc autem interim in viâ peregrinus apparet, ut exilium nostrum agnoscamus, et quod alia est patria nostra. Et colloquendo corda ad amorem inflammat, sed oculos ad contemplationem adhuc non revelat. Qui ergo in viâ ex sermonibus Jesu ignem amoris corde concipiunt, in fine viæ claritatem ejus videbunt. Sunt itaque linguæ igneæ quæ veniunt ad nos ; et verba flammantia quotidie Christum nobis loquentem audimus ; quia spiritum Christi non habet, qui verba Christi audiendo non ardet. I will occupy a blank space with one quotation more from the same illustrious theologian, its right to a place here consisting in the commentary which it supplies to those words of the disciples, ' *Did not our hearts burn within us?*' though indeed I am more tempted to quote it as a magnificent specimen of what medieval Latin in the hands of a great master, who had some mighty truth to set forth, could accomplish (*In Eccles. Hom.* 1) : In meditatione quasi quædam lucta est ignorantiæ cum scientiâ, et lumen veritatis quodammodo in mediâ caligine erroris emicat ; velut ignis in ligno viridi, primo quidem difficile apprehendit, sed cum flatu vehementer excitatus fuerit, et acrius in subjectam materiam exardescere cœperit, tunc magnos quosdam fumosæ caliginis globos exurgere, et ipsam adhuc modicæ scintillationis flammam rarius interlucentem obvolvere videmus : donec tandem, paulatim crescente incendio, vapore omni exhausto et caligine disjectâ, splendor serenus appareat. Tunc victrix flamma in omnem crepitantis rogi congeriem discurrens, libere dominatur ; subjectamque materiam circumvolitans, ac molli attactu perstringens lambendo exurit ac penetrat : nec prius quiescit, quam interna penetrando succedens totum quodammodo traxerit in se, quod invenit præter se. Postquam autem incendio id quod exurendum est concrematum a suâ quodammodo naturâ totum in ignis similitudinem proprietatemque transierit, tunc omnis fragor decidit et strepitus sopitur, atque illa flammarum spicula e medio sublata tolluntur, sævusque ille et vorax ignis, cunctis sibi subjectis et amicâ quâdam similitudine concorporatis,

in altâ se pace silentioque componit; quia jam non invenit nec diversum aliquid præter se, nec adversum contra se. . . . Sic nimirum carnale cor, quasi lignum viride, et necdum ab humore carnalis concupiscentiæ exsiccatum, si quando aliquam divini timoris seu dilectionis scintillam conceperit, primum quidem pravis desideriis reluctantibus passionum et perturbationum fumus exoritur; deinde, roboratâ mente, cum flamma amoris et validius ardere et clarius splendere cœperit, mox omnis perturbationum caligo evanescit; et jam purâ mente animus ad contemplationem veritatis se diffundit. Novissime autem, postquam assiduâ veritatis contemplatione cor penetratum fuerit, et ad ipsum summæ veritatis fontem medullitus toto animæ affectu intraverit, tunc in idipsum dulcedinis quasi totum ignitum, et in ignem amoris conversum, ab omni strepitu et perturbatione pacatissimum requiescit.

twin brooks series BOOKS IN THE SERIES